LEADING AND MANAGING CHANGE IN THE AGE OF DISRUPTION AND ARTIFICIAL INTELLIGENCE

Praise for Leading and Managing Change in the Age of Disruption and Artificial Intelligence

With *Leading and Managing Change in the Age of Disruption and Artificial Intelligence* Mat Donald has provided us with a much-needed management primer for the new economy. He effectively updates much of traditional management logic for a world that is characterized by dramatic change. A must read!

Leonard Schlesinger, Baker Foundation Professor, Harvard Business School and President Emeritus, Babson College

We are beginning to understand change dynamics in fairly stable environments, but these principles break down in disruptive environments. Along comes Donald to provide the critical information needed to extend our understanding about how to effectively bring about change in disruptive environments, which are increasingly what organizations face in today's global society.

Eric B. Dent, Ph.D., Uncommon Friend Endowed Chair Professor, Florida Gulf Coast University

This is an impressive and well-written book that is both thought-proving and eminently practical. We live in an age of disruption and, whether you lead or study organisations, this book will help you to understand its implications and how to manage the challenges it poses.

Bernard Burnes, Chair of Organisational Change, Stirling Management School, University of Stirling

This book adapts organisational management and leadership to the modern age, where change is constant and affecting the way organisations operate. This book will be of benefit to anyone wanting to consider the future of organisational management and change.

Jens Mueller, Professor of Management Practice, Massey University

We are living in a VUCA world; volatile, uncertain, complex and ambiguous. A time in which we may see and feel a shift of paradigms. This book describes global transitions which are influencing our businesses worldwide. Mat Donald points out global issues such as EU destabilization, rebalancing world powers, financial trade barriers and the influence of technology. These changes cannot be managed in a traditional and linear 'cause and effect' manner. Leadership in the new age requires skills that are more holistic, dialogic and take a systems and design thinking approach where the left and right brains act together. This book is excellent for students, managers, leaders and management consultants who work, or are starting to work, in an international business environment and want to understand 'a world that is on the move'.

Jos Pieterse, Ph.D., Institute of Business Management, Education and Technology, Hogeschool Fontys

LEADING AND MANAGING CHANGE IN THE AGE OF DISRUPTION AND ARTIFICIAL INTELLIGENCE

BY

MATHEW DONALD

Bachelor of Economics (major Acctg), Macquarie University
Master of Project Management, The University of Adelaide
Ph.D., Business (Management, Leadership and Organisational
Change), Western Sydney University
Fellow of CPA Australia (FCPA)
Member of Australian Institute of Project Management (MAIPM)

United Kingdom – North America – Japan – India – Malaysia – China

Emerald Publishing Limited
Howard House, Wagon Lane, Bingley BD16 1WA, UK

First edition 2019

British Library Cataloguing in Publication Data
A catalogue record for this book is available from the British Library

ISBN: 978-1-78756-368-1 (Print)
ISBN: 978-1-78756-367-4 (Online)
ISBN: 978-1-78756-369-8 (Epub)

Printed and bound by CPI Group (UK) Ltd, Croydon, CR0 4YY

ISOQAR certified
Management System,
awarded to Emerald
for adherence to
Environmental
standard
ISO 14001:2004.

ISOQAR
REGISTERED
Certificate Number 1985
ISO 14001

INVESTOR IN PEOPLE

With thanks to my family that have supported and encouraged me to complete this journey, being that of my wife, Louanne, and my sister, Kathryn Donnelly. Special recognition to my beloved Grandmother, Beryl Castledine, remembered as one that encouraged my academic thirst for knowledge from the youngest of age.

Contents

List of Figures

List of Tables

Abbreviations

- Australian Securities Exchange (ASX)
- Australian Institute of Project Management (AIPM)
- Security Exchange Commission (SEC)
- Artificial Intelligence (AI)
- Business to Business (B2B)
- Business to Customer (B2C)
- Change Management Tool (CMT)
- Chief Information Officer (CIO)
- Compact Disk (CD)
- Confirmatory Factor Analysis (CFA)
- Corporate Social Responsibility (CSR)
- Disruption Event Monitoring Table (DEMT)
- Electronic Funds Transfers (EFT)
- Enterprise Resource Programmes (ERP)
- European Union (EU)
- Exploratory Factor Analysis (EFA)
- Global Financial Crisis (GFC)
- Global Positioning Systems (GPS)
- Group of Seven (G7)
- Human Resource Management (HRM)
- Information Technology (IT)
- Intellectual Property (IP)
- Just in Time (JIT)
- Key Performance Indicator (KPI)
- Kaiser-Meyer-Olkin Measure of Sampling (KMO)
- Leadership Qualities Assessment Table (LQAT)
- Net Present Value (NPV)
- New Age Function (NAF)
- New Age Stakeholder Assessment Table (NSAT)
- New Idea Generation (NIGF)
- Non-Government Organisations (NGO)
- North American Free Trade Agreement (NAFTA)
- North Atlantic Treaty Organization (NATO)

- Programmable Logic Controller (PLC)
- Project Management Office (PMO)
- Resistance to Change (RTC)
- Trans-Pacific Partnership (TPP)
- United States Dollars (USD)
- Universal Serial Bus (USB)

About the Author

The author, Dr. Mat Donald, has over 30 years of business experience, commencing in chartered accounting performing audit and company accounting, advisory work. Once leaving chartered accounting, the author's career moved into industry where he has worked in a number of large multinationals in Fast Moving Consumer Goods, Construction, Services, Electricity generation and Mining. He has held various senior management roles including Divisional Accounting Manager, Commercial Manager and Financial Controller in a variety of listed ASX and SEC organisations amongst others. Whilst well experienced in the multinational, the author also has experience in small privately owned organisations, thus providing unique insight into large and small organisations.

The breadth of the author's experience provides a unique insight into organisational operations that will be relevant to a wide variety of readers, irrespective of their functional background or experience level. The author completed a Bachelor of Economics (Major Accounting) at Macquarie University in Australia and has qualified as a Fellow of CPA Australia. The author has significant interest in improving organisations in both an operational and academic context. In 2010, the author has completed a Master of Project Management (Distinction Average) at The University of Adelaide, where he has since qualified as a Member of the Australian Institute of Project Management. In 2018, the author received a Ph.D. (Business) at Western Sydney University, researching leadership, management and organisational change.

Since completing the Ph.D. (Business), the author has emerged as an academic, qualifying to teach at three Australian Universities, including subjects of management, leadership, accounting, business strategy and international business. In 2018, the author taught Management with Charles Sturt University and in 2017 tutored in accounting at Macquarie University. The author has presented at IQPC conferences, more recently presenting conference papers to the Australian Institute of Project Management (Donald, 2014, 2016). The author is a regular contributor in LinkedIn online forums, also having an article published with *The Conversation* (Donald, 2018). The topics that the author regularly promotes are related to organisational change, Management, Leadership, discrimination and ageism, where he is regularly available for key note and other speaking opportunities.

The author's experience in organisational change has included mergers, acquisitions, computer implementations, process, large projects and business improvement. The Ph.D. research of the author included in-depth interviews with senior change managers that confirmed his held belief that change is generally still not delivered in an optimal way. There are many published guides and now elaborate qualifications towards change; yet, all too often, the change is either unsuccessful or damages staff relations in the rush to complete. It is clear to the author that a new age of change is ahead, where more thought and understanding is required on the topic.

Preface

Whilst there has been considerable change to organisations in the last 30 years, a new age of change is ahead. It is now evident that the resulting change will be faster, more complex and less predictable than in the past. The dynamic of organisational change will have implications for the way leaders build organisations, teams and business plans, as the change ahead will be assisted by globalisation. Managers will need to manage change in a time when the future is less predictable, speed is increasing and information is more available in large quantities. Whilst the artificial intelligence (AI) may replace many workers the roles, the reduction in staff ratios will likely pose new challenges to the traditional manager. As leadership and management are critical factors to organisational change success (Donald, 2014, 2016), the new age of disruption and the AI has the potential to disrupt organisational systems, structures and management practices.

This is a broad-based book for those in leadership and management roles of the future, where the issues ahead will be immediate and broad. The book is written in way that is relevant to managing and leading irrespective of one's technical or functional background. This book will be useful to those in a variety of management roles of many functions including medicine, operations, engineering, finance or many other backgrounds. Some industries may be more exposed to the AI than disruption, especially where the roles are repeatable, labour intensive or require precision and fast knowledge. Disruption is emerging from a number of broad sources that the manager of the future may need to consider in order to prevent chaos or failure in their organisations. This book provides modern insights into emerging issues and provides critical thinking about options and directions.

The breadth of this book will be useful for a wide range of professionals, be they experienced or not, wishing to understand how roles may change in the modern age ahead. The topics covered by this book will be useful for students studying management, leadership, change, economics, accounting, engineering, human resources and many others. Future and current organisational leadership and management will benefit from the appreciation and critique of modern events in this book, where critical thinking is included. Organisations will likely be impacted by disruption and the AI in the future, where preparation and appreciation of these phenomena are relevant to organisational survival irrespective of organisational type or size.

The change in the new age will require managers, leaders, professionals and students to appreciate that the challenges ahead will likely be varied, fast moving and difficult to solve. Organisations that fail to change at an appropriate speed in a suitable manner may be vulnerable to error or even failure. The industrial revolution of the nineteenth century saw whole industries evaporated in just a few decades, where change of the future may even be much faster. The forecast is not all negative, as opportunities will present for those able to identify and take advantage. Whilst some practices may need to change in the future there is still much of the past 70 years of research and knowledge on the topics that remain relevant.

Disruption events are explored in this book so as to expose and inform business owners, leaders, managers and entrepreneurs of future issues to consider. Changes of the new age may increase the type and speed over time, creating changes to organisational responsibilities of those in governing positions and on boards. A higher degree of oversight may be required as management will be required to be abreast of big data, information and change, where fast uninformed or ill thought decisions may likely diminish value and organisational success. It will be important for governance and boards to ensure that authority delegations are appropriate and clear, whilst ensuring that processes are not slow, bureaucratic of hinder prompt decision making. The controls in the new age will need to increase accountability, provide appropriate rewards for outcomes rather than promises.

This book commences with a discussion of disruption, which is far broader topic than merely new computers or technology. Chapter 3 explores how the AI is emerging and may lead to large scale loss of jobs, occupation and even whole industries. Those with leadership or management experience will find this book refreshing through its exploration of current organisational dilemmas. The book is useful for the experienced manager, business owner or the student wishing to understand current topics in organisational change, leadership and management. This book does not prescribe simple solutions for the new age as likely the future forward will include thought provoking critical thinking as the predominant tool for the future. The use of critical thinking will enable the practitioner and student to identify alternatives, evaluate and choose rational decisions. Solutions and directions of the future will likely be limited by fast-paced time constraints, varying reliability of information and limited resources. These restrictions to decision making will ensure that any one strategy is unlikely will be unique, optimisable, stable or be long lived.

This book is unique on the market as it provides the broad knowledge of leadership and management topics in the context of organisational change in the new age. Included herein are tools, tables and analysis that may assist the student and the experienced manager prepare organisations for the future. There is unlikely to be a clear path forward for any organisation as the change ahead is complex and fast, aided by the interconnectivity of globalisation and new communication forms. Organisations may require new skills and more focus on the external or political environment than ever before, where an introspective approach may not be sustainable in the new age.

Chapter 1

Introduction

> Organisational change: the future must be performed differently
> to the past.
> —Mathew Donald

This book is specifically written for those that seek modern information and knowledge regarding leadership and management in a modern organisational context, be they a student or an experienced manager. The speed, size and volatility of organisational change are increasing (Burnes, 2009; Burnes & Jackson, 2011), where increased scope, variety and speed of change have occurred with world events (Taylor & Cooper, 1988a). It is possible that the speed of organisational change is now so fast that people may not be able to cope (Bruckman, 2008; Toffler, 1970), where the interconnectedness of organisations may result in a change being impossible to avoid (Shah, 2010).

The new age of disruption and artificial intelligence (AI) will see a change emerging differently and faster than ever before; thus, this book is relevant to a wide variety of reader, be they involved in profit, non-profit or government sectors. The new age will cause organisations to reconsider organisational structures, processes, market analysis and decision making. This first chapter clarifies the new age scope, key definitions and why it is important, irrespective of the market or organisational type.

Disruption, in the context of this book, is broader than those normally presented in a learning text for management and leadership topics. Disruption dimensions are not unique (Golightly & Dadashi, 2017) being included here not as fortune telling, but more as examples and possibilities. Technology change is not merely disruption in the context of this book, where the topic may include geopolitical changes, financial markets and other global events. Globalisation has influenced corporations around the world (Choo, Halim, & Keng-Howe, 2010) by increasing the interconnectivity and interdependence of trade. A single organisation, even if dominant or global and irrespective of size or market, may not have sufficient direct influence or power to prevent change in the new age.

Leading and Managing Change in the Age of Disruption and Artificial Intelligence, 1–19
Copyright © 2019 by Emerald Publishing Limited
All rights of reproduction in any form reserved
doi:10.1108/978-1-78756-367-420191002

AI is already emerging, where its influence may also be unavoidable and it will likely have more effects than merely the replacing of humans with machines. The nature of AI is likely to be so significant that it may lead to adjustments in organisational structures, processes and staff relations will be amongst many. The emergent AI will require special attention in order for organisations to survive, where both management and leadership roles of the future may require additional skills in order to optimise any emerging organisational risks and opportunities.

The terms of management and leadership are often defined colloquially as interchangeable. This book recognises that the functions of leadership and management are distinctly separate, despite any overlapping elements. Recent research has indicated that organisational change may be linked to leadership and management (Donald, 2016, 2017). It is quite possible for organisational managers to be a poor leader, or for a leader to be a poor manager; yet, those implementing organisational change may be required to hold both skills.

Apart from the management and leadership practices, the new age will likely require alternate organisational systems and structures. In Chapter 6, the changing nature of the organisation is explored, rather than prescribed. Finally, Chapter 7 explores recent research on organisational change, potential solutions and change factor interactions, where these may have implications for organisational governance and responsibilities of the future to improve chances for success and avoid failure.

Critical thinking is encouraged in association with themes and solutions discussed in this book, as critical thinking may be essential skill for any future decision makers. Sound decision-making skills have been linked to critical thinking skills (Heisler, 2014). The new age of disruption and AI is one where the exact future cannot be predicted with any level of certainty. Whilst management skills may be prescribed and developed (Law, 2016), higher levels of skill may be required for those managing in this new age. The author encourages readers to consider, discuss and even critique ideas presented in this book. The very nature of disruption and AI may mean that topics in this book may evolve over time, where the deeper value of this book may lie in the thought provocation and critical thinking, rather than any specific predictions.

Managers may already hold skills of value creation, problem solving and option evaluation, yet these may be insufficient for this new age. Organisational change has been linked to employee engagement (Donald, 2017), thus management styles that are autocratic or lack inclusion may fail to change. It may be tempting for some to utilise past experience, industry norms or historical data in decision making, where the lack of critical thinking and thought may increase risk. Critical thinking skills will likely encourage fact verification, logic, collaboration, data analysis and scenario development.

The remainder of Chapter 1 explores and defined the terms of disruption and AI as there is little point in using the terms without appreciation of their meaning and scope. The reader is encouraged to critique the definitions by considering the what, how and why questions in an effort to understand the topics. Early exploration of the terms may later assist critical thinking, where alternatives and evaluation will be required. Finally, this Chapter 1 will discuss the importance of disruption and AI as key influencers of organisational behaviour in the future.

What is Disruption?

This section of Chapter 1 explores the term disruption, thus articulating why organisational governance, leaders and managers should formally consider disruption as a key topic of the new age. Organisational change is not a new phenomenon as change is already increasing in speed, size and volatility (Burnes, 2009; Burnes & Jackson, 2011). The change is not isolated or limited to a specific organisation, where major world events have resulted in increased scope, variety and speed of change (Taylor & Cooper, 1988b). It may even be that the pace of change may have increased to a speed where people may not be able to cope (Bruckman, 2008; Toffler, 1970), or that all business is so inextricably linked and involved in change that it may be unavoidable (Shah, 2010).

Organisations emerged from the twentieth century after great upheaval and societal change that included two World Wars, the Great Depression and a Cold War. The first half of the twentieth century included the emergence of significant new technology for the masses, including electricity generation, automation, motor vehicles, aeroplanes and refrigeration, amongst others. These new items changed organisational interactions, structures and work practices. The second half of the twentieth century delivered space travel, satellites, television, mobile phones and computers that consequentially led to changes in communications, travel, trade and even globalisation. By the year 2000, organisations were no longer structured, processed or traded in the same way as those in the year 1900, where the resulting globalisation emerged as an environment that was international and tempestuous (Scott, 2000).

Despite industrialisation and invention associated with the Industrial Revolution of the nineteenth century, a great amount of work was manual and time consuming at the beginning of the twentieth century, especially in the home. In the year 1900, household tasks were still very manual, such as hand washing clothes, travel by horse and no electric refrigeration. Organisations were relatively simple and smaller than of today being associated with strong or autocratic styles that is but one of the five potential structures (Henry Mintzberg, 1980). These early organisations were thought to be the part of systems, where equilibrium and optimisation were possible (Lewin, 1945). In the early part of the twentieth century, there change was evolving into unions, worker's rights, communism and fascism, women's rights and voting, and rapid and turbulent political changes, where significant changes in inequality emerged (Goldin & Katz, 2018). Organisations adapted to the twentieth century changes that assisted the acceleration of aviation, automotive and other new industries.

A key driver of change after World War II was that of consumerism, where these consumerist values may further change in the twenty-first century in the pursuit of contentment (Brown & Vergragt, 2016). Change has been described as being essential for organisations and the future of humankind (Benn, Dunphy, &

Grffiths, 2014;Burnes, 2011; Kanter, 2008; Sackmann, Eggenhofer-Rehart, & Friesl, 2009), where the pace has accelerated in the past 20 years. Organisational survival may even be dependent upon change (Burnes & Jackson, 2011; Company, 2008), where competitive advantage may be lost if the organisation does not change (Kotter, 1996). Organisational change sources are varied, derived from market forces as well as corporate rationalisation, operational efficiency or deregulation (Bennett & Durkin, 2000).

Disruption has emerged as a new type and pace of organisational change, where some have perceived it as merely a type of pure technology and three measures (Rosenstand, Gertsen, & Vesti, 2018). In recent times, the term 'disruption' has broadened beyond mere technology, where it is now associated with economic variation (Krug & Reinmoeller, 2003), supply randomness (Fahimnia, Jabbarzadeh, & Sabouhi, 2017), product innovation (Teece, 2017), as well as politics and distrust (Kallianos, 2018). There is great potential for disruption to evolve further in this world of globalisation (Bordo, 2017), where it will be aided by high interconnectivity.

The term disruption is now commonly used in media and has emerged into the research literature in the last few years, often linked exclusively to technology change. Disruption, when related to occupations, does not appear to have a fixed definition, appearing to relate generically to change more broadly (Nizzero, Cote, & Cramm, 2017). The disruption innovation term is defined more specifically as being a complete change that has potential to change the competition fundamentally (Lourdes, Victor, & Jesus, 2017). Disruption has also been linked to divergent globalisation experiences, with a potential to form anti-globalisation movements (Gustafsson & Skohg, 2017). Whilst globalisation has produced benefits across many countries, it may have reduced the identity of borders, thus altering risk and security (Wright, 2017).

Disruption may be totally unpredictable with little or no planning, or one that is predictable, where some level of mitigation planning is possible (Zhao & Tang, 2010). When disruption is in the unpredictable form, it will not be possible to predict the change in terms of its nature, time or place, thus creating issues for the governance boards, leaders and managers. The nature of the unpredictable disruption could be one of war, earthquake, flood, government policy, political instability or unforeseen product emergence or technology. This book adopts the wider definition of disruption, where it can be either predictable or unpredictable, where the Leader and Manager of the future will need to include disruption as an additional factor to include in their roles.

Organisations will likely already have plans around some of the more likely disruption factors. Predictable disruption factors may already be planned for, including those of safety, environmental, product quality and media incidents. Organisations of the new age will need to prepare beyond the most likely events, as the more remote disruptive events will circulate faster and be more transformational than previous types. For instance, historically a coffee shop may have prepared for unusual events like the coffee machine breaking down or an alternate supply, if their cakes are not supplied. The coffee shop of the future need to broaden their disruption preparations, including actions required should rapid and large-scale changes emerge. Organisations in a state of disruption maturity may even create calculation models to assess the robustness of plans in light of the potential risk ranges (Lusby, Larsen, & Bull, 2018).

Disruption was originally defined as being simply a technology change (Christensen & Bower, 1996), where, more recently, it has been defined with two dimensions that are distinguished by a differing scale and effect (Schuelke-Leech, 2017). The first of the two disruptive dimensions is limited to having organisation or market effects, whereas the second dimension is one characterised by its broader effects with impacts to the broader society, industries or government policy (Schuelke-Leech, 2017). In the first disruptive dimension, it may be possible for organisations to identify scenarios and build advanced reactive strategies with detailed mitigation actions. The unknown nature of the second disruptive dimension that has significantly more impact on society and industry; yet, this dimension will be significantly harder to predict and harder to develop advanced mitigation strategies. Organisations are likely to develop mitigation strategies, rather than avoidance or elimination, as no single organisation is likely to control disruption in the new age.

This new change of the twenty-first century is already variable, fast and less predictable combined with great shifts in politics and world power occurring. Those seeking to lead and manage organisations of the future will need to be cognisant of the past change as there may still be relevant comparisons and learnings from study of the Industrial Revolution or other changes in the twentieth century. As has been the case in the past, there will be winners and losers during this change ahead, where organisational success may depend on abilities to understand change, set strategy and implement. Organisations that move too slowly or choose the wrong direction may fail or lose value more quickly than in the past.

In the last 20 years, change has been swift, where even just the simple introduction of electronic email as a communication source has resulted in the loss of many thousands of secretarial positions worldwide. Job losses from the introduction of email came about as managers and employees adopted typing as a skill that once was for typing pools and secretaries. Postal services have recently become loss makers in many countries due to physical mail being replaced by electronic mail. Email was widely adopted once it was perceived as being a faster tool, involving self-editing being simpler than dictating or drafting memos, faster than facsimile. Despite secretarial positions holding faster typing speeds and faster dictation speeds, managers and staff embraced typing emails themselves. The change towards emails was far reaching, as it also resulted in reduction in tradespeople that once repaired facsimiles and typewriters and the elimination of typing supplies and ribbons. In just the last 20 or so years, millions of typewriters have been made redundant, sent to the scrap recyclers and waste stations. Opportunity presented itself as typing changed to email, where the Internet fostered new accessories, including routers, computers, printers and faster communication lines.

Each form of new technology can result in a far-reaching flow on effects, be that through an organisation, an industry, or a country and across the world.

When the Internet emerged, it was not clear that it would later be a platform for social media, payments systems, currency, information or even movies. The Internet has transformed lives around the world, where even the previously profitable print and television media industry was transformed with thousands of jobs lost in a few years. It is the hidden effects of technology that should be considered by those leading and managing organisations in the future, as each change in technology may have the potential to transform work places or eliminate organisations and whole industries.

Less than 15 years ago, investment in a video store may have yielded good profits as it invaded the movie theatre industry. Yet, the video shop industry has almost been eliminated in the last few years as movies moved onto the Internet, where the past video shop may now be close to worthless. In similar changes that have occurred with relative speed diskette and the compact disk (CD) manufacturers have been eliminated upon the introduction of the universal serial bus (USB). Today, most new computers and laptops do not even include ports for diskettes or CD. Of course, each of the changes in technology involved secondary effect reductions for those involved in related service, repairs and supply and transport industries. The emergence of modern rapid changes should be concerning to many, including employees, business owners, leaders and managers as rapid job losses and organisational redundancy may be characteristic extended unemployment and social dislocation. Politicians and economists may promote global trade and benefits; yet, there is high potential for social upheaval and dislocation that may result from increased unemployment in regions adversely affected by the changes.

Organisational change can be internally generated or from external forces (Williams, McWilliams, & Lawrence, 2016), where it may occur in a controlled or reactive way. Leaders and managers design and implement organisational change, where the change may be for market reasons, risks or opportunities or innovation or many other reasons. The external forces that may influence organisational change include those of the market, government changes, globalisation and even changes in world power. There will be a great diversity in the way organisations change, some preferring to use change managers, others may hire new staff or use consultants. Those designing and implementing change need to be conscious that most organisational change fails, where the failure rate may be as high as 70% (Burnes & Jackson, 2011; Senturia, Flees, & Maceda, 2008).

The dilemma of all Leaders and Managers is to choose the most appropriate options for business success, where some risk is likely associated with all options. In the new age of disruption and AI, changes may occur faster with less predictability than in the past, thus introducing more risk and uncertainty. Organisations acting in this new age may require a level of critical thinking and facts in order to make good decisions. Disruption definitions range from being limited and tightly defined, through to one that is broad, including world events, politics, power, technology, trends and organisational behaviours. For the purposes of this book, disruption is defined as change events that are sudden and fast paced and may impact organisations, industries or society.

Why is Disruption Important?

Disruption events have the potential to create new opportunities and risk in short time frames that may affect a wide variety of organisations. Those responsible for organisational value creation will need to be wary and cognisant of disruption, as underlying events may lie far outside the normal environment (Williams et al., 2016). Organisations that seek out and discover disruption early will more likely have time to build scenarios ready for its occurrence, where those that fail to identify a disruption may suffer losses in value or earnings. As disruption may occur with little or no probability, organisations may benefit if they are prepared for change and ready to react in a rational, logical and prompt ways.

As disruption will be difficult to predict, the changing environment and the commensurate change in organisational directions may result in strains and breaks in relationships with shareholders, financiers and employees. The sudden changes in organisational decision making will likely be difficult for many stakeholders that may prefer certainty and clarity. Disruption is likely to require changes to the speed or direction of organisational systems, their structures and processes. In the need for speed and change, compromise and change will be required to governance processes, consultation and normal communication. Any sudden changes in corporate direction may lead to loss in confidence in management as shareholders or financiers may prefer certainty and returns as expected. The market traditionally rewards organisations that can delivery on target or to plan, yet that principle will increasingly be more difficult to achieve in the new age.

Government policy that is not clear and predictable can affect organisational decision making and financial outcomes. If government policy is difficult to interpret, some organisations may choose to not invest at all. An example of government disruption is that of the US Carbon tax policy, where the United States signed the Paris agreement on carbon under President Obama's administration only to later remove itself under the President Trump (Tollefson, 2017). The electricity generation provider may now be confused on how to invest as the values to be invested are large, requiring payback periods of 25 years or more. One can only imagine the chaos and dysfunction if a government introduced a carbon tax without notice just days after an organisation committed funds towards a new coal fired power plant.

Organisational investment requires overview and approval of many stakeholders, including financiers, shareholders and staff, where any sudden government changes may create difficulties and embarrassment for management. Changes of the new age that emerge suddenly will likely require management to gain additional approvals from stakeholders, where the re-approval process may include consultations, explanations and analysis. If stakeholders, or the market, do not understand any sudden changes originating from government policy, they may withdraw their support and market value may diminish. To avoid losses associated with sudden change, organisations may need to proactively identify and treat any potential threats and opportunities from, or face value losses.

The choice for management or leadership is either to ignore disruption and take the risk, or to prepare and plan for events that may not yet be apparent. The risk associated in the choice to act or not will likely need to be communicated with stakeholders and governance bodies in particular; otherwise, trust in the organisation may diminish. Organisations of this new age will need to consider how best to communicate risk and disruption without losing support. Additionally, governance bodies may need to consider how the new age will affect their role and current systems. Further consideration of governance in the new age is discussed later at Chapter 7 of this book.

Decision making in the initial phases of new disruptions may appear confusing to various stakeholders, as they may be characterised with lack of information and lack of analysis. Those organisations with advanced disruption planning may be better able to share the preparations with stakeholders and be in a position to source funds at a lower premium, also more likely to attract leading candidates. It is also likely that the absence of disruption planning may increase employee stress or increase customer and supplier tensions due to the lack of prompt and clear reaction pathways.

Unlike past changes, disruption will not be identified merely from market industry bodies, customer feedback or employee information, as globalisation will now transmit change through alternate paths. Identification of disruption may arise from social media, the Internet, email, websites or messaging, where potential consequences of wars, protests, terrorist events or political change may flow around the world before any mainstream media has investigated the matter. The issue for the organisation is whether to rely upon early notification of disruption events and whether there is sufficient information to decide and react.

There are a number of immediate, probable and possible disruptive events occurring now that should be considered by leadership and management of today. Chapter 2 explores a range of probable and possible disruption events, where they are presented here as a means of discovery and consideration rather than being a prediction for the future. Readers of this book are encouraged to identify additional disruption, listing any effects and appropriate actions. It is the method of appreciation and critical thinking about disruption that will improve organisational preparedness, not necessarily the specificity of predictions.

There will be winners and losers in this process of disruption discovery, as some will be rewarded for success, whilst others who merely foretelling events without critical thinking paradigms may be accused of being wrong, harlequins or even subversive thereby limiting career success. It is important that those foretelling disruption supply risk analysis, a range of possibilities and a range of actions and plans. Those in disruptive planning and analysis roles will need to communicate what they are doing and why, they should not position themselves as being predictors of the future as disruption by nature may be hard to fully predict. It will be the preparedness for a wide range of events and consequences that will enable a modern organisation to be best positioned for the future.

Case Study 1.1: Kodak®

Kodak® was once the largest manufacturer and developer of film in the world, a dominant leader in its market globally. The digitised market emerged in a disruptive way from the late 1990s firstly in digitised photos then later substantially changed the market. Upon the introduction of cameras in phones, the digitisation moved far beyond the initial large disks, capturing photos for business for retrieval and storage. One may have expected the leader in photos to have led the change to digitisation revolution, to have invested and promoted the benefits for customers. History now shows that the organisation failed to appreciate the impact of digitisation, including the significance of phones with cameras included (Chapman, 2011). The corporate failure was not due to the speed or the nature of the change, and was not related to intellectual knowledge or patents. This corporate failure has been attributed to the way the organisation was structured and positioned, where it failed to respond more broadly to technology and change (Lucas & Goh, 2009).

Exercise
Find and consider the competitors that Kodak had in 1990 and how they reacted and faired after digitisation. Does any of those organisations survive in 2018? What alternate strategies and identification processes should Kodak have had in place to identify the digital and camera phone risk before they emerged? How would your alternatives improveD the position of Kodak?

Please consider the Kodak example by providing evidence of the size and dominance of this once global organisation. What do you consider are the three important lessons from this example that organisations of the future should consider when planning for future disruption.

Case Study 1.2: IBM®

IBM® was once a dominant computer company in the world in the 1970s and 1980s. Investigate what products and markets the organisation was dominant in during this period. Upon the rise and success of the Apple® Corporation and Microsoft®, IBM® was under market pressure. The organisation successfully changed and moved into certain alternate markets to survive.

Describe the change in organisational market and position that IBM® evolved into. Was this a disruption event? How could IBM have developed disruption strategies in the early 1980s to prevent the change in corporate direction and image?

The disruption term began with technology, where over time it has broadened to cover topics of political, economic and market change. Disruption will likely have significant impacts on trade, culture and organisational structures and processes, where it will likely transmit around the world fast, aided by globalisation and new forms of communication. Organisational leadership and management will likely discover that the sudden, fast-paced nature of disruption may radically change the way they react to change in the future.

What is Artificial Intelligence?

Whilst disruption may derive from a wide variety of sources, there is a particular emerging change named AI that will likely have implications to change trade, employment and many whole industries. The topic of AI has existed since the 1980s, where it was initially considered merely an expert database system (Kostas, Kostas, Emannuel, & John, 2003). In more recent times, computing power has increased to a level where the complicated calculations required for AI are now possible, economic and even likely. The rise in computing power of the last 10 years is evidenced by the proliferation of smartphones, social media and the underlying algorithms, where AI is now proposed as an algorithm rather than merely as a knowledge source (Dobrev, 2005). The modern definition of AI now envisages the definition as including ideas of intellect, games and speech (Singh & Jain, 2018).

AI occurs where computers join and provide function or information that is superior to the human capability (Fernandez, 2016), where it may even be required for organisational success through the innovative use of knowledge (Buckner & Shah, 1993). There may be so much metadata now that AI processing will be required to interpret it (Fernandez, 2016). Despite the new capabilities in computing, some may still argue that AI is merely calculations and code rather than being the same as understanding or the human element (Davis, 2005). Developers of technology are now working hard to develop AI that will emerge as independent working units that may come in forms of robots, drones and voice, amongst others. If and when AI emerges, it has the potential to transform and replace millions of human jobs and improve efficiency or even accuracy.

AI may have impacts akin to disruption, yet the two terms are based on different underlying change events, where the former may be slightly more predictable in terms of its implications than those from the latter. Whilst AI can be disruption, certainly not all disruption is AI. Disruption may not be related to technology at all, the attack in New York, USA, on September 11 was a disruption that was not technology related. Yet, despite September 11 not being a direct technology change, there were secondary technology effects as governments reacted that now include facial recognition, smarter passports and body scan technology. Pandemic disruption is not AI, where recently several types of Pandemic disruption occurred for short periods, including bird flu or avian flu (Pipper et al., 2007), or swine flu (Smith et al., 2009) and Ebola (Saéz et al., 2015), leaving technology to respond in a secondary way to now highlight passengers arriving or leaving with unusually high body temperatures at airports. Technology changes linked and subsequent to September 11 or to Pandemic disruption appear to be a secondary technology effect rather than AI in themselves.

> *Question 1.1.* Where and when did the bird flu epidemic occur? Why was it a disruptive event? What additional planning should an organisation do to prepare for another Pandemic disruption?

AI is a new change that is different to the past technology change as it will likely involve machines, robots, computers operating independently that may result in them replacing a large number of human jobs. AI will likely achieve the change in employment if it functions in a superior way, is more cost effective or achieves higher levels of customer service versus current operating models. Organisations are unlikely to adopt AI unless the benefits of adoption are perceived as superior to those currently in existence.

What AI Has to Do with Organisations of the Future?

Thirty years ago, it was thought that AI was unlikely to copy the human intelligence, where only small prototypes were envisaged in the field (Brooks, 1986). AI may have once been thought to be no more than a rise of the computing power since the 1980s, where the current increase in computer computational power, processor size and speed are likely to develop complex products that may accelerate change fundamentally. The new wave of computing power has the potential to evolve fast, where products designed with new platforms will likely be smarter than ever before.

New technology can evolve quickly and be widely adopted, for example, the last 20 years of mobile phone development. Whilst the changes in mobile phones are not necessarily AI, they did involve more sophisticated changes in technology. Mobile phones became a communication tool for business use from around the from the mid-1990s, where the mobile phone proliferated with increased connectivity and taken up by business as a productivity change, as then staff could be contacted outside of normal business hours. Whilst the mobile phone usage increased during the 1990s, it was the increased computing power of smartphones that enabled the use of email, camera and social media. In the last 10 years, this smartphone revolution has resulted in private consumers buying them across the globe, where many people would have a smartphone on them nearly 24 hours a day. The increased volume of consumers has resulted in whole new industries on the platform, including thousands of apps. Whilst many apps were transferred for nil cost to the consumer, many apps gather information on location and Internet history that is sold to third-party advertisers. Business models in the 1990s would not have supported development of product to be given out for nil price, yet in the new age apps are downloaded in the millions for free daily.

The modern computing capabilities combined with other new technology has emerged relatively fast and is already influencing modern life. Organisations interface with the wider environment and thus seek to influence or control already in the new age, where many organisations already have policies on Internet use, social media policies and mobile phone policies. The rise of the Internet since the 1990s has resulted in organisations spending vast sums to keep up with the advancements including new and upgraded computer networks, firewalls to prevent hacking, new banking systems and electronic funds transfers. The emerging pace and scale of change of the past 10 years has been significant compared to the previous 20 years, where the current emerging technology is likely to be significantly faster and transformational than any prior period.

Technology change has resulted in improved efficiency and connectivity of trade over the past 30 years where many transactional and administrative type roles have already been reduced or eliminated. Organisations have embarked on change and staff reductions where ever they perceived cost benefits or benefits to sales and financial returns. It would have been very hard in 1980 to tell customers that there is no phone service for sales; rather today, organisations regularly ask customers to go online, type details and order their own goods or services direct without human intervention. Whilst new technology may have historically replaced human work, the technology generally lacked an ability to think independently or able to process complex tasks. Going ahead, AI is likely to emerge may be able to think and create independently, able to do complex tasks beyond the human capability, where robots may also emerge quickly.

Any emergence of AI may create many opportunities, risks and change for organisations that will significantly affect both leadership and management of the future. Managers may in the future be regularly challenged between options that are risky if adopted early or later, characterised by the uncertainty of information, benefits and consequences. There may be additional risk if AI is adopted early or later, where early adoption may yield benefits (Williams et al., 2016), or late adopters may gain advantage by avoiding experimentation costs and redundancy. The modern organisation may already be having to choose between cloud versus in house servers, where both options have risk associated with security and connectivity, technical knowledge, firewalls and hardware choices. AI choices of the future may have more risk and consequence than those between cloud and in house servers.

AI is far more than merely faster and larger computations, as AI is likely to take on more practical applications, possible intelligent thought or even invention. Robots have not emerged as quickly as earlier thought, limited by computer processor sizes and speed, where the limitations may soon disappear. An example of new technology emerging fast and being more sophisticated, is that of the drone. Drones may have initially been associated with military uses; however, they are now widely available at low cost to the general consumer that can fly remotely, with cameras and global positioning system (GPS) capability. The cheaper parts manufacture, the improvements in communication and GPS may soon allow drones to carry goods for commercial purposes. The military use of drones already allows drones to fly to distant places with precision, albeit with a remote human driver function (e.g. the US weapons programmes in Afghanistan). Drones may soon emerge with AI characteristics, being able to automatically evade obstacles and fly driverless, or choose their own routes and auto scheduling. It is now possible to imagine other AI capabilities emerging soon including driverless cars, delivery services based on drones, cyber wars and capabilities. Organisations and markets may not be able to avoid AI change ahead as efficiency, cost benefit and customer adoption may be high.

Organisations in a capitalist system are under pressure to deliver expected financial returns to shareholders. In not-for-profit organisations, there are expectations about service delivery or other non-financial metrics to deliver. AI will likely be adopted by profit and not-for-profit organisations whenever AI is perceived as being superior in terms of costs, service, efficiency or returns, thus placing management under competitive or stakeholder pressure. Despite any loyalty to staff, management may not be able to decline a reduction of labour costs by 50% due to AI advancement. Likewise, a manager may be compelled to adopt AI if it results in significant competition or a market improvement in customer service, logistics or financial results.

AI, by its nature, will likely replace human staff and processes, where the decisions may no longer need to be taken by management, staff or any human. Any emergence of AI has clear ramifications for the organisation, leadership, management and employees. Those wishing to avoid the impacts of AI on the customer, competition and markets may find that the change is so significant that their organisation cannot survive whilst remaining constant. Of course, there will be additional risk in early adoption of the emergent AI, these will be discussed in Chapter 5 of this book. The choices in an AI emergent future will be to be an early adopter, a late adopter or remain with some niche market advantage, where each choice will have significant consequences for the organisation.

Question 1.2. Discuss why an organisation may choose to not take up a significant AI emergence. How could the management support a suboptimal decision to their stakeholders? What support may be required to convince stakeholders that avoiding AI change is the right decision? What are the implications or competitive effects may arise if this suboptimal decision is implemented?

In relation to this question, please consider a range of AI changes in various industries and stakeholder structures including mining, medical, mobile phone manufacturer.

Question 1.3. Consider what AI may do for a particular organisation or industry, detail what ways AI will or could affect business outcomes in either a positive or a negative way. Whilst this question is open and requires creative thinking, please find examples or identify trends that may support your reasons on why this AI will affect the industry or organisation identified.

AI will be explored further in Chapter 3. AI will likely affect organisational culture, systems and creativity, where failure to appreciate the impacts will potentially leave an organisation exposed. There are likely to be new forms of risk and opportunities as AI emerges, irrespective of organisational type or size. AI of the future will likely emerge into new forms beyond our current forecasts, as the new capabilities are already emerging with higher computing power and speeds, more sophisticated algorithms and interconnected programmes. Globalisation will assist AI transformation due to the interconnectivity of trade and organisational processes.

Organisational Survival in the New Age

Irrespective of organisational nature and size there is no guarantee of survival in the new age, despite any ongoing support of shareholders and stakeholders. Organisational survival is related to satisfactory financial performance or acceptable service delivery performance as measured by stakeholders. Performance is often measured through a variety of measures including finance, strategy, market position, cash flow or service delivery. Stakeholders are not satisfied with organisational performance have a range of options available including separation, sale or to close the organisation. Alternately, shareholders may seek to influence, mentor or even hire new management roles as a way of moving an organisation towards acceptable results.

Management generally is tasked with running the organisation, where the performance targets are usually set and agreed with stakeholders. In attempting to achieve the set targets, management organise structures, job roles and processes that they foresee are appropriate for the targets they aim for. Stakeholders are not always interested merely in financial measures as they may require ethical behaviour, legal and environmental compliance as well as connections with society values. Shareholders are not the only interested party in organisational performance, as trade creditors have legal rights if bills are not paid on time, be that through court orders, administration or even liquidation. Secured creditors, such as banks and financiers, often have more influence and control of the organisation, where indices, ratios and comparisons can be mandated and under can lead to the cancelling of credit, cessation of future debt, sales of secured assets or again even liquidation.

Trust is a key component of management (Donald, 2017), where the setting of goals may require consistent agreement between staff and management in order to succeed. Management support is not entirely based on historical or financial results, thus boards and stakeholders may choose to support an organisation despite poor results where they can understand. Goal achievement is often not sufficient for stakeholders, where variances are required to have logical reasons and unexplained variances or surprises are often not tolerated. Any future goals are unlikely to be supported by stakeholders, where management proposes plans with returns below stakeholder expectations or are below competitor achievements.

Management seek to control the goal achievement by building plans and systems to ensure that stakeholder expectations are achieved over time. Stakeholders will also require increases in organisational value beyond mere financial returns, where relationships, branding and reputation may be equally as important.

Failure to pay bills may cause concern for stakeholders, where their concern may be related to perceived value or reputational loss, rather just the cash flow issue. Management gains the confidence of stakeholders by creating and maintaining systems, structures, incentives, roles and responsibilities that go on to achieve the desired results. There are many management skills required in order to design and operate so many organisational levers, where the new age management requirements are discussed in Chapter 5 of this book.

In the new age, changes to market and organisation will likely be fast, sudden and hard to predict, where the change required is likely to be fundamental and transformational rather than incremental. The full extent of changes that may be required are discussed in Chapter 5 of this book, where new management skills will be considered that involve entrepreneurial opportunities, large data and analysis, heightened uncertainty and fast speed of change. The nature of the new age changes is likely to be broad, affecting all aspects of the organisation, including processes, structures and staffing combined with stakeholders, products and services.

This book explores the various types of AI and disruption in Chapters 2 and 3, which will be useful for the professional or academic wanting to prepare for this new age. As critical thinking will be important to management and leadership in the new age, this book considers a range of events and their potential risks and opportunities, without necessarily trying to be a predictor or prescriber of the future. Preparation for unlikely or uncertain events may be key in this new age of change, thus consideration of the future disruption and AI presented in this book may be a useful starting point for those in responsible positions of the future. The new age will present many direct and indirect changes that may co-exist in multiple layers, causing the organisation to no longer operate as it may have done in the past.

Question 1.4. Consider the new age of disruption and AI by reading research and articles on the topics. What organisational structures and processes do you believe will remain unchanged in the new age? Why? Write a report to brief your senior management on the topics as they are trying to assess the potential impact. Include options and critical thinking in your brief.

During the Industrial Revolution, workers were exploited, resulting in poor working conditions and child labour (Humphries, 2010) and the introduction of collective bargaining by workers in union structures (Wyman, 1989). In the second half of the twentieth century, society and organisations embraced consumerism (Durning, 1991), where rapid innovations emerged and trade expanded across borders into a globalised trade environment (Deardorff & Stern, 2002). Globalisation is a recent change that has resulted in interconnectivity of trade and communication, where the world economy is now intertwined and fast.

The pace of organisational and societal change has also increased with time, thus whilst the Ford motor company of the early twentieth century was new and focussed on efficiency with an autocratic structure (Jacobson, 1977), it would be an unlikely to operate in that way today. As with the Ford example, it is unlikely that the structure or functions of Microsoft or Apple today will exist in those forms in 20 years from now. An organisation may be innovative and modern at a point in time, yet to survive in the new age continual change may be required for sustainable longevity.

Despite the increase in organisational change, most organisational change continues to fail (Candido & Santos, 2015; Decker, Durand, Mayfield, McCormack, & Skinner, 2012; Kotter, 1995), despite the large amount spent on the change programmes and associated governance. The new age of disruption and AI will likely place more pressure on those implementing organisational change. Success in an environment of continual change may require innovation, creativity and changes in skills.

Question 1.5. What in your opinion (supported by facts and journal articles) were the key factors that led to the formation of unions and collective bargaining? Why has the influence and memberships of unions fallen away in the past 30 years? Are there any learnings from your answers relevant to the modern organisation in the new age of disruption and AI? How might employees in the new age have differing requirements to those in previous ages? What plans should organisations have ready for the employee?

Hint – Use and read references included in Chapter 5 of this book to get you started in finding research journals related to this question.

The scope of awareness for change in the new age will likely be wider than ever before, as remaining insular and devoid of change may be impossible. The new age will likely see change permeate across whole countries, markets and into unrelated industries with fast speed, where globalisation is a likely conduit. The advances in technology, communication and social media the organisation will have vast sums of information available (otherwise regularly named as Big Data), where not all data will be of equal quality and reliability. In order to use the Big Data, substantial quantitative analysis, new mathematical modelling and superior decision-making skills may be required. Conservative leadership and management that are slow or overly procrastinate, are likely to hold their organisation back in the future ahead by substantially limiting the accuracy and success of decisions.

Decision makers that are risk averse may perceive their future as stressful and risky as there will be high amounts of information, where the information may not be able to be verified prior to decisions being made. Although risk takers may not necessarily be the alternate choice in the future as making decisions without adequate information will likely introduce significant new risk. The new age may require additional entrepreneurial and innovative skills that are discussed later in this book, where other new skills required may include information gatherers, data verification and analysis, governance and uncertainty identification.

The hierarchies and structures of the organisations may be insufficient for this new age as often these are too inflexible or slow to change even in the current environment, where proposals and governance may be slow to get approved.

The speed and agility required in this new age may require organisations to attract skills of resilience, flexibility and adaption. Pure technical skills that were highly prized in past eras will likely need to be complimented with new skills of adaptability, analysis and critical thinking. Employment hiring practices and tests will need to change so that skills beyond the technical are sought and valued. There may be little benefit in the new age to hire technically proficient engineers, medical workers, operators or managers if they crave stability and formality, or if they do not like accountability. Employees of the future will likely add more value to an organisation if they are fact based, analytical, flexible and accountable.

Organisations may already prepare strategic plans, budgets, reviewing variances and market trends that may seem structured, mathematical with appropriate review and governance. Despite holding processes, some organisations failed during the global financial crisis (Allen & Faff, 2012), in the Asian Crisis (Marshall, 1998) and the Dot Com crisis (Faulkender, Kadyrzhanova, Prabhala, & Senbet, 2010). Some large organisations may already spend up to half a year developing plans, reviewing and gaining approvals to proceed, without any real guarantees of performance . In the new age, the current planning and control processes may be too slow or too inflexible for the organisation to adequately cope with AI and disruption . The small organisation may have simpler less defined systems to assist with agility and organic growth, yet the small may lack skills and resources required for data capture, analysis and governance.

Organisational investment in systems, structures and resources built in past eras may be inappropriate for this new age. Conservative, slow and considered investment in capital, technology and systems may be far too slow and bureaucratic for the new age, where new AI may emerge and be adopted quickly by customers and competitors alike. Investment returns may need to be higher or payback periods shorter in order to operate in an Age that is characterised with shorter redundancy timeframes where shorter lifespans of capital, technology and processes may occur. Investment returns and hurdle rates may be significantly lifted if the higher risk and uncertainty is not mitigated in the future.

Question 1.6. Imagine that your market is taking up a new technology that is better, cheaper and faster to implement than your organisations current technology. How would you communicate and convince your stakeholders that the new age requires a sudden different direction to the one you have recently communicated? Include details of your approach to banks, shareholders, employees and suppliers. How would you ensure that your new message is not perceived as reactive or un-coordinated?

As with governance, management structures, strategy and processes of the future will likely be significantly different to those of the past. Future emerging disruption or AI may require early and fast changes in structure, or staffing numbers, capital or financing. The suddenness of this substantial change may require changes to authorities and delegations, yet some form of review and accountability will likely be required to stay in place. Some form of governance and review may be more important than ever before as decision making without review or risk appreciation may expose the organisation to heightened failure risk. Implications for the organisation of these new age events in terms of leadership, management and organisation are discussed at Chapters 4–7 of this book.

Recap and Thinking Extension

Based on your reading of this Chapter 1, it is encouraged that you should be able to explain, with critical thinking towards the following topics:

- What are the dimensions of disruption? Consider current academic articles in your response, compare and discuss any key differences found.
- Do leadership and management functions overlap? If so, how? Consider academic articles in your response. Discuss any articles that may appear to be different in the interpretation of either term.
- Is management separable from leadership? After reviewing a range of academic articles discuss how and why?

Assignment and Consideration

- Nominate an organisation or industry and explain why disruption planning may be useful. Explain the issues that may be encountered where the exact nature of the disruption may currently be unknown.
- Discuss the organisational effects (structure, culture, process, etc.) that may alter when an organisation prepares for disruption.

Hint – Review current literature and topical books before answering the aforementioned questions.

Summary

This chapter has defined the emerging terms of disruption and AI, where it has been explained as to how both of these signify and relate to a new age. Globalisation has fostered interconnectivity in trade and markets, where globalisation may assist and encourage disruption and AI. Organisations have changed significantly in the last 20 years as a result globalisation and technology. Today, most organisations, irrespective of size and nature, have websites, financially transact over the Internet and have social media presence. The new age will likely be characterised by sudden and fast transformational waves of change that may be impossible to avoid.

Disruption is not merely a non-regular natural event like a volcano or earthquake, nor is it merely a simple new technology change. Terror events in one part of the world can quickly inspire or create fear in others living far away, where other events, such as uprisings, protests and market events, are also likely to be transmitted instantly around the world. Once events are shown on social media or online, the recipient is able to immediately perceive and respond without verifying the information with mainstream services. New Age information may flow without any filtering or verification by traditional media or government, where organisations will increasingly have to decipher between the untrue, fraudulent and fake news.

Chapters 2 and 3 of this book review disruption and AI in detail, exploring current and potential emerging events in the context of the organisation. Chapters 4–6 explore how organisations will likely be affected by these new age changes, so critically assessing skills, processes and actions that may be required of leadership and management in the future. Chapter 7 concludes by exploring recent research on organisational change and recommends some tools for future students, leadership and management. As exact nature and timing of disruption or AI may be difficult to predict, the reader of this book is encouraged to look for additional evidence and critically assess concepts and ideas presented herein. The new age is characterised by a substantial, fast-paced change, thus a complete review and adjustment of the organisational systems may be required in order to survive.

Chapter 2

Organisational Impacts from Disruption

Prepare for change: avoiding it is no longer possible.
—Mathew Donald

Avoidance of disruption may be unavoidable for organisations of the future as globalisation will enable disruption to ripple around the world in rapid time, be that through market connectivity, Internet or social media. Whilst not all world change will automatically affect all organisations, the speed and uncontrolled nature of information in the new age will enable disruption to be more widespread than in the past. It is possible that disruption is read and passed on without any deep and meaningful assessment of the accuracy of the information or its consequence. The rumble in social media from market change, political change or other disruption may be more akin to a herd charging without direction, or may even include an element of groupthink (Williams, McWilliams, & Lawrence, 2016), where emotions may exceed logic in the consequences imagined. Early reaction to disruption may be risky due to lack of verifiable information and critical thinking, yet the alternative of late adoption may be equally as risky if competitors adopt early and are successful.

The various forms of disruption are considered in this chapter, which may have primary and secondary effects for consideration, where the secondary more indirect effects may require deeper critical thinking than the primary event. This chapter is not positioned as a predictor or fortune teller of the future, rather it includes disruptions that are worthy of consideration, critical thinking and preparation in order to yield benefits or reduce risk. The primary direct effects of change in the new age may be easier to identify than the secondary effects; for instance, a regional war may result in immediate travel restrictions, supply shortages and labour resource issues. A regional war may have secondary effects that emerge much later, including famine, lack of hygiene, lack of education or medical supply shortages.

Early identification of disruption will not necessarily guarantee organisational survival or success, as data, analysis and strategy are required to position

Leading and Managing Change in the Age of Disruption and Artificial Intelligence, 21–56
Copyright © 2019 by Emerald Publishing Limited
All rights of reproduction in any form reserved
doi:10.1108/978-1-78756-367-420191003

satisfactory responses. It is unlikely that enough information will be presented on time for an organisation to optimise a response, rather a range of possibilities with risk, uncertainty and opportunity are likely to emerge. Organisations that fail to adequately assess options in the new age may well make decisions that are risky or inadequate.

The disruption events discussed in this chapter are presented to be thought provoking for consideration, rather than a complete guide to the future. Many issues may present when disruption emerges fast, where this book seeks to consider various disruptions in the context data, analysis and strategy that may be required to appropriately prepare for such change. Some of the disruption discussed in this chapter may at first appear to be political or geo-power struggles that are too remote to the organisation. In this globalised world, change effects may be considerable and worthy of critical thinking in order to understand and set options forward. Organisations can no longer sit back and be separate from world disruptions events, where late actors may reduce their ability to be an influencer or leader of change.

Question 2.1. Why should organisations consider secondary indirect disruption effects? How will an organisation identify secondary indirect disruption effects? What should be considered in order to plan for disruption and react in suitable time? Explain.

Question 2.2. Please name at least three matters that an organisation should identify or consider when a disruption event occurs (e.g. strategy, employee retention, cash flow, pricing or costs, supply).

Question 2.3. Describe how a single disruption may lead to loss of organisational value. Are there any examples disruption causing such a loss in value? How might an organisation prevent or reduce lost value from disruption?

Hint – Provide answers with examples and consider alternatives in your answers.

In the past, organisations may have scanned their direct and indirect environment to identify changes and organisational direction (Williams et al., 2016), where the direct environment scanning may have been far more frequent than the indirect. Disruption assessment will likely involve creative thinking, in-depth analysis, scenarios and assessment prior to choosing any direction and acting. Simple annual assessment of strategy, direction and action will not likely fully appreciate the broader scope of change resulting from disruption. Critical thinking on disruption is considered further in chapters 5 to 7 of this book; however, it is fair to say that it should be performed with an independent mind, seeking alternatives and ranking with logic. As disruption may include elements of politics, power and technology or ideology, the independence of thinking may be important. DISRUPTions may overlap, work in combination or be opposing, where the analysis and conclusions may cause considerable dissention.

Organisations that consider the past 20 years as being particularly difficult and fast may well need to reconsider how fast the organisation may need to operate, analyse and respond in the future with disruption. Some may argue that the following events are unlikely to emerge as disruption, or that they are too broad for leadership or management students, yet many of these examples are already affecting organisational decisions and thus should be debated or critiqued. Ignoring disruption may already be impossible and thus Chapters 5 and 6 of this book explore leadership and management changes that may be required to prepare for the future. The reader of the following sections should approach each topic with an open mind, ignoring personal preferences and politics, whilst applying critical thinking and a thirst for more data. It is hoped that readers are awakened after reading about the following disruptions, where the reader is encouraged to consider the resulting risks and opportunities.

Global Political Change

In 2008, the global financial crisis (GFC) emerged as a new disruption, which is today continuing to affect financial systems and models (Elder, 2014). The GFC has resulted in debt crises for a number of countries resulting in government fiscal policy changes (Lane, 2012), social and monetary changes (De la Porte & Heins, 2016), political and competitive power changes (Ozturk & Sozdemir, 2015). Several disruptions have emerged since the GFC. These have been characterised by high and rapid unemployment (Drydakis, 2015), political system changes and significant retrospection (Lyrintzis, 2011), value changes and the emergence of popularism (Inglehart & Norris, 2016).

New age changes are of such significance and pace that organisational management and leadership will likely need to seek out and be aware of potential consequences well before they emerge. Owing to size and resource constraints, only a few organisations may have considered all of the changes discussed in this Chapter 2. Organisations may find the following disruptions difficult to understand in an organisational context, or be challenged by the resources and skills required. Stakeholders of future organisations may demand that management and leadership positions be abreast of various future disruptions, where irrespective of organisational type, disruption ignorance may not be tolerated.

UK and Brexit

Up until fairly recently, it was commonly thought that the European Union (EU) was likely to continue to expand, where it was likely that the EU might soon include Turkey, Albania or Iceland (Dixon & Fullerton, 2014). The UK joined the EU in 1973 (Dhingra, Ottaviano, Sampson, & Reenen, 2016) without joining the Euro currency in 1999 (Risse, Engelmann-Martin, Knope, & Roscher, 1999), preferring to be as an independent floating currency. In recent times, since the GFC, a number of European countries have taken on high levels of sovereign debt (Beirne & Fratzscher, 2013), where some EU members have considered leaving the Union. Remaining in the EU has the potential to involve reduced wages for an extended period of years (Meltzer, 2011) or other austerity measures. Whilst leaving the EU or the Euro is possible for member nations, the current complexity and interdependence between EU members, thus, may make leaving difficult to consider. The UK has remained on its own independent currency, where the valuation of the currency is dependent upon the UK banking policies and government debt rather than the debt of other EU countries.

In recent years, UK citizens came to question the benefits EU membership including those of cost, identity, politics and income (Vasilopoulou, 2016). Over time, the UK political system recognised the citizens' views and decided to allow a vote to cease EU membership, the vote process was termed by Mr Peter Wilding as 'Brexit' (Winning, 2016). Despite wanting to remain in the EU, UK Prime Minister David Cameron allowed the vote on Brexit to be open. The Brexit vote was characterised by many of the middle class, less educated voting to leave the EU, where subsequently some have questioned the fundamentals of the EU establishment (Hobolt, 2016). In the aftermath of the Brexit vote, Prime Minister Cameron resigned and was replaced by Prime Minister Theresa May, who also had wished previously to remain in the EU.

Brexit not only resulted in a change in Prime Minister for the UK, but also resulted in the Brexit protagonist of Mr Boris Johnson, going to the Foreign Minister role rather than the Prime Minister role or the chief negotiator for Brexit. Late in 2018, when the Brexit deal was released, Mr Johnson and a number of other front benchers resigned their positions, opposing the proposed deal. The Brexit vote to leave the EU was a surprise to many in the media. The varying and unexpected nature of Brexit places it as one example of disruption in the new age that has affected organisations in the UK and globally due to its uncertain future. In late 2018, the parliamentary vote on the Brexit deal, negotiated by Prime Minister May, was withdrawn before a vote, where it is unclear at January 2019 whether the Brexit will be smooth per a deal with the EU or it will be a hard Brexit.

It is unclear if the UK will be the only country to leave the EU into the future, as several other EU countries have also considered their EU membership status, including Italy (Baker, 2018) and Greece (Gold, 2012), whilst Spain has considered recapitalising its banks as an alternate strategy (Archick, 2014). Political change has occurred across a number of European countries in the post-GFC environment, where the union may not be certain into the future. Further uncertainty occurred as prior to Brexit, when Scotland only voted marginally to remain with UK (Mullen, 2014). Depending upon where Brexit ends up, Scotland may subsequently return to a vote on remaining in the UK or to re-join the EU.

At the end of the year 2018, the UK, Northern Ireland and Irish Republic borders remain a contentious issue in the UK and the EU. Significant risk and uncertainty exist for any organisations wishing to trade or be based in the region as the border controls, tariffs and trade relations are not clear for the UK, Scotland or Irish borders in the longer term. The lack of clarity around immigration may make it difficult for UK employers to attract overseas talent, or EU citizens may prefer to leave the UK and work in other regions of the EU.

There is clearly great uncertainty, possibly for years to come around operating or trading in the UK or Europe. Organisations historically prefer certainty around decisions, where the current uncertainty around immigration, currency, payments and trade post-Brexit may inhibit investment, or at least cause delay in decisions.

Small organisations located in other regions to the UK or EU may first consider the issues of Brexit as irrelevant to their operations. Smaller organisations may also lack skills and resources to analyse Brexit and surrounding issues and thus may ignore and not monitor Brexit-related developments. Risk and opportunities may arise in the aftermath of Brexit, be it a soft Brexit, or perhaps especially if it is a hard Brexit. The hard Brexit possibility may leave the UK vulnerable and short of resources to feed its citizens or supply its industries, delays across the EU borders may be unbearable and expensive, organisations may choose to meet and be placed in the EU rather than incur issues with staff and immigration. In the globalised nature of world trade, ramifications of a hard Brexit or if other countries leave the EU will be fast and considerable. A hard Brexit may leave the UK cut off from EU through tariffs and border checks; yet, the UK may be open to trade in new and revitalised markets of the United States, Canada, South America or Australia.

In a few short years, Brexit has developed from a remote possibility to now one that is imminent, one that still has great uncertainty to play out in the coming years, where the risks or benefits of Brexit may not be clear for some time to come. Even an election in 2017, which was aimed at increasing a mandate during Brexit, failed to achieve its goals, resulting in smaller margin in parliament. The reduction in power and authority of the UK parliament has only increased the instability of the Brexit negotiations, where further disruption may emerge once the exit arrangements have settled.

Even if an organisation wanted to locate in the post-Brexit UK, it currently could not be clear on export trading terms or delays between the UK and the EU. Whilst an organisation may believe the UK has bright prospects for future investment that may not be the case if the split is a hard Brexit and a recession of sorts arises. Organisations that currently supply parts to the EU may decide to exit markets if costs of transport from the UK rise too high. The region of UK and EU is significant in world trade, where the lack of clarity and agreement around Brexit will be troubling for many.

Question 2.4. An organisation is intending to invest $100 million into a new car plant, producing electric vehicles. Write a report explaining the EU environment and Brexit. Do you recommend investing in the region given the uncertainty post-Brexit? What opportunities may arise post-Brexit?

In 2018, Catalonia commenced actions to leave Spain, resulting in political change and tension in that country, where there is still no clear resolution to the matter. Brexit forms of disruption may continue to emerge over time, where there is potential for alliances to change and new trade blocks to form. It is clear that the world order is in change, where tariffs and trade relations may be subject to disruption, characterised by fast changes to costs and access to markets. Leadership and management should no longer continue to expect markets to have free access or remain stable. In the new age currencies, immigration and even staff mobilisation may be subject to change without notice. The changes involved in a Brexit style change may radically change costs and benefits for organisations and increase uncertainty beyond what investors are willing to bear.

Trump

In late 2018, it is apparent disruption occurred when President Trump won the US presidential election, the nature of this disruption is well beyond any surprise about him winning the election. The widespread use of social media and fast policy changes by US President Trump have created new forms of disruption, at times occurring daily. This book does not aim to provide commentary or political views about the change of the US president, rather the discussion here is to highlight that organisations are affected by this new form of disruption. The United States has historically been a world leader in foreign policy, trade, in the United Nations and global defence since the 1940s; therefore, any disruption by the United States has the potential to affect many other countries, organisations and governments. In the new age, organisations around the world are affected directly and indirectly by the fast and unpredictable Trump disruption actions and social media statements.

Trump disruption may be characterised as little policy consultation and lack of collaboration, where President Trump does not have a traditional party-political background. The President has a background in business, property and media, where his own power may have been more important than politics to his elevation. Trump disruption is also associated with sudden and ongoing staff changes, trade wars, global tension and US government shutdowns amongst many other changes as compared to previous administrations. Change around President Trump has been so unpredictable that senior media commentators and even close colleagues may be unable to predict imminent directions. Previous administrations of varying parties may have taken years to achieve changes to government policy, involving negotiation through committees and trade-offs or compromise. At the end of 2018, many international institutions, organisations and governments are still in confusion as to how to influence or work with the current US administration.

President Trump appears to work within his own network of advisors, friends and family or those he perceives of like mind. Trump disruption arises when President Trump makes fast decisions that are announced publicly on social media, often occurring without consultation with advisors or providing background briefings. An example of the pace and confusion that may be associated with this new Trump disruption occurred when President Trump announced a meeting with the leader of North Korea, without seemingly the knowledge of the US Secretary of State at the time, Rex Tillerson (Schwartz, 2018). The new presidential style is one of unilateral direct announcements to the media or on social media, where organisation and other governments may be unaware of the new direction.

This style of Trump disruption may cause some to perceive these behaviours as unstable or risky, where longstanding international alliances and agreements may be changed quickly without consultation or predictability.

In March 2018, President Trump announced a US import tariff on steel and aluminium (Madhani, 2018), where this Trump disruption would had widespread direct and indirect effects on other countries and many organisations. Whilst President Trump's electoral policies indicated that steel tariffs were likely, the lack of policy openness still caused surprise when the tariff was announced. The tariff on steel resulted in a number of close trading partners immediately lobbying for an exemption to the tariffs, including that of Canada, Mexico and Australia. Europe was not granted the exemption from the tariff and thus was placed at a disadvantage compared to those countries, which were granted exemptions. This fast-changing tariff has advantaged some organisations over others around the world, where it is unclear if the tariffs may be reversed at some point in the future.

The steel tariffs may be viewed merely from a United States or China perspective, yet there are likely to be wider global effects from the tariff changes on steel. If China decides to continue steel production at the constant volumes and sell into global markets outside of the United States, steel prices outside of the United States may fall. Alternately, if China sells their steel volumes to the EU without additional tariffs, a number of German steel producers may be adversely affected as they may have to accept lower margins or reduce production volumes. It is therefore possible that a US trade tariff on steel could have an adverse impact on steel or car manufacturers in Europe, despite a US intent to harm China.

The aforementioned tariff example discussed how a simple Trump disruption can have effects that flow around the world, where further secondary effects can occur as a result of retaliation. Retaliation from China over the US tariffs occurred swiftly in 2018 (Li, Zhang, & Hart, 2018), where there is now high potential for a full-scale trade war that is not necessarily limited to China and the United States. Yet, the tariffs imposed in 2018 are likely to be should President Trump achieve a satisfactory deal at any point in the future.

Trump disruptions are characterised by fast policy change, no consultation with further risk of negotiated deals. If an organisation tried to secure steel, setting a price and being clear on the supply would be quite difficult to determine when Trump disruption occurs. Organisations that set a price based prior to a tariff may find they are adversely affected when a government changes its policy without notice. In order to react to tariffs organisations may need to adjust volumes, prices or even repudiate agreements; therefore, organisational reactions may further increase instability to trade. Trump disruption, like a trade war, may affect all steel production and related products globally. Global manufacturing is one industry that is quite dependent upon steel and aluminium, where investments required are often large; therefore, sudden changes in costs may be quite problematic for organisations.

Despite economic theory showing that trade wars have negative growth effects, Trump disruption in the form of tariffs and unilateralism continues at the end of 2018. It may be very difficult for organisations or even industry lobby groups to influence the direction of the current US administration. Where organisations lack power and influence, they will likely find themselves as a disruption recipient rather than as a leader of the change. Trump disruption, which may lack policy development and consultation, may be perceived as high sovereign risk in some organisations, where new investment may disappear in some regions.

Financiers and other stakeholders may choose to withhold funds and defer decisions in a Trump disruption. Reactions to US presidential announcements on social media will likely be swift, as readers of social media can read and pass on the information quickly or may choose to react without necessarily verifying information or considering alternatives. Trump announcements that are read and interpreted may lead to fast and significant shifts in financial markets, currency and organisational decision making. Markets may reverse their initial responses as additional information emerges or once information is clarified and understood later.

Trump disruption is likely to continue through his first term, where changes may occur in waves potentially overriding and confusing each other. Markets have remained relatively buoyant despite the Trump led trade war in 2018, yet the future stability of the system is not guaranteed (Ciuriak, 2018) in this new age. Trump disruption events in 2018 have been significant, where even North American Free Trade Agreement (NAFTA) was initially repudiated and later amended (Zhou, Baylis, Coppess, & Xie, 2018). The NAFTA was originally based on theory of open trade, mutual economic benefit, whereas that has now been modified by unilateralism and Trump disruption. It is still not clear how organisations will react to Trump disruption, where uncertainty around commodity and product prices, supply and markets exist. Markets may fall, investments and finance may be put on hold whilst organisations wait for clarity around US government policy or tariffs. As there is little stability in policy in this new age, many organisations, markets and individuals may have to operate on rumour or social media bursts, rather than confirmed facts.

Whilst Trump disruption has increased tension with China, the relationship with Russia is another relationship that may appear confusing and difficult to explain. If the Trump campaign is ever shown to have colluded with Russia, some in the administration may be trialled or even the US President could be removed. The removal of President Trump or a loss at the next election could see many of the directions reversed quickly. Organisations may find that setting direction or large investments are impossible to secure when uncertainty presents, as stakeholders often prefer stability and certainty.

In the two years after being elected, President Trump has openly demeaned and complained about North Korean nuclear arms, Iran deals and Chinese trade. Whilst the various Trump disruptions may merely be rhetoric aimed at his internal constituents, they do add significant uncertainty to the world in the way they are delivered. Organisations spend vast sums of money and time in developing investment decisions, convincing stakeholders and financiers of investment reliability; therefore, sudden changes in US policy may adversely affect organisations in the re-work associated with re-approvals and changes.

The interconnectivity of globalised trade in this new age is highlighted when one considers situations where a part is manufactured or developed in Australia, the final product manufactured in China and sold to the United States. A range of countries and organisations may be affected when tariffs are applied in the United States on China imports. Other examples of globalisation are a call centre located in China or India that may service many other countries. Trade restrictions by the United States or China are not limited to one another, rather many other countries and organisations are affected, be that produced goods or services.

The Trans-Pacific Partnership (TPP) trade deal was signed in 2016 (Laursen & Roederer-Rynning, 2017) being in the year prior to the Trump administration, where free-trade and benefits were planned for the members. When the deal was signed, many organisations may have commenced planning for the changes and opportunities; yet soon after the US election, Trump disruption occurred when the United States withdrew from the agreement in 2017 (Griffith, Steinberg, & Zysman, 2017). The TPP may still form without the United States, where a future US administration may reverse the Trump disruption or any US involvement in the TPP may be scrapped forever; this is characteristic disruption that future organisations will have to work through. Uncertainty characterises the Trump disruption, where organisations may perceive rapid and substantial changes are too risky to invest in.

Question 2.5. What effects may arise since now the United States has withdrawn from the TPP? How should members prepare for the potential impacts? Consider the implications from a country and individual organisational perspective. Further explain any risks and opportunities from the TPP that you envisage . How might organisations approach the issue of the TPP where there is potential for the United States to join the TPP later? What might happen should the United States decide to form a rival group to the TPP?

Further, US tensions with China exist currently in the South China Sea and the Spratly Islands around sovereignty and access, potentially affecting sea routes, trade and organisational connectivity (Buszynski, 2012). Whilst the tension has not as yet emerged as a Trump disruption there is great potential for it to do so, where any restriction to free shipping in the region may impact global trade. It has been reported as far back as 2010 that China may be erecting barriers to prevent free sea travel in the region (Kaplan, 2010), where tensions may increase as US ships test and sail in the region. There is great tension in the North Pacific including food tension between Japan's Fukushima prefecture that has sold fish to Hong Kong and North Korean missiles fired over Japan. Tension does not automatically result in wars or trade restrictions, yet the regional tension does present as risk and uncertainty for organisations wanting to base or trade in this region. Organisations should consider this region as a potential disruption that may emerge, where disruption planning around increased trading costs, slower sea lanes or supply risks may be already necessary.

Trump disruption may continue for the remaining length of the current administration, as his style is unlikely to change. Organisations based anywhere in the world may be affected by the nature of this disruption, the effects of Trump disruption may be advantage US manufacturers or disadvantage organisations based in China, where the secondary effects may occur all around the world with varying benefits or risks. The primary effects of this disruption may be direct and sudden, where the secondary effects may require analysis and understanding. Organisations can no longer expect that political directions will be signalled, logical or well developed as the current US administration does not appear to operate that way. Investment in likely Trump disruption arenas of trade, South China Sea, Middle East and Europe may all be difficult as the path forward is unclear. Organisations may not easily insulate themselves against these emerging events, where constant monitoring and cognition may be required in order to adapt to Trump disruption.

This section on the Trump disruption indicates that there is significant policy risk in operating in the United States, or operating in rival or related industries or countries. The disruption associated with President Trump and the United States is so significant that an organisation of today will be impacted upon suddenly, transformationally and irrevocably than ever in the past. The changing direction of US policy will likely require organisations to read presidential social media posts, news headlines and changes in United States administration staff whilst gathering data on the matters, analysing and planning for a variety of options. Organisations may not have had so many changes in the global arena to monitor in the past, hence their current systems and structures may not yet be appropriate. Chapters 5 to 7 of this book discuss and explore potential organisational responses required in this new age.

Germany, France and European Community (EU)

In the years since the fall of the Soviet Union age, the EU has accepted members from the east, where the boundary now extends as far as Estonia, Poland and Hungary. In recent years, Ukraine considered joining the EU, where Russia has recently annexed Crimea and opposed the widening of the North Atlantic Treaty Organization alliance (Mearsheimer, 2014). Despite the tensions over Crimea and Ukraine and associated trade restrictions, Europe has continued to trade with Russia, despite some restrictions. At the end of 2018, tensions between the EU and Russia remain that may affect organisational trade in the region, where potential for escalation remains.

European disruption is not limited to relations between the EU and Russia or the UK. Other European disruption has occurred including several German car manufacturers producing diesel cars that had false emission reading tests (Oldenkamp, van Zelm, & Huijbregts, 2016). A number of court cases are now likely to emerge in relation to this diesel scandal that may require rectification costs and fines. This diesel disruption is significant as sales of German cars with false diesel emission readings occurred around the world, not limited to the EU region, where the scandal has already resulted in lost reputation and trust in those organisations, lost value and removal of several senior executives. Failed management and governance oversight may be a significant contributor to this diesel disruption.

The diesel disruption is not yet resolved at the end of 2018 as whilst the issue involved vehicles illegally emitting pollution levels way above the EU standards (Leake, 2015), there is now discussion of these devalued vehicles being sold in Eastern Europe illegally (Macho, 2018), thus forming a secondary effect. Whilst some Eastern European countries may have purchased the illegally emitting vehicles at cheap prices, the vehicles are still polluting illegally, where further tension may emerge if the Eastern European countries seek compensation and fines. Diesel disruption emerged without notice and destroyed value in many of the offending organisations and involved the loss of trust in regulators. It is clear that diesel disruption has secondary effects that are yet to fully emerge, where further tensions and market distortions are possible.

As discussed in Section 'Trump' of this book, the Trump disruption over steel tariffs may adversely impact German steel manufacturers. Following this argument, the impact of the trade changes in steel may affect or cause restructuring of car, plane and other steel dependent industries in the EU and other regions. At the end of 2018, it is still unclear to what extent the EU will be engaged in any trade war between the United States and China. Organisations that fail to appreciate the risk, or fail to analyse and build plans with options, may incur losses or fail to identify associated opportunities.

In 2015, a deal was signed with Iran that attempted to limit conflict and nuclear tension in the Middle East (*Economist*, 2018), where the flow on effects is still difficult to predict. This deal involved disruption as there was political disagreement in the United States, where it is now unclear what the future US policy will be on the matter (Economist, 2018). The Iran deal had potential to have increased trade and opportunity, combined with improved relations with the EU, Russia, China or the United States. In another Trump disruption, the United States recently reneged on the Iran agreement (Kelley, 2018), whereas the UK and EU remain committed to the deal. This disruption will now likely cause concern for organisations wishing to trade with Iran, whilst Iran has funds from oil sales to buy commodities there may be too much risk of US sanctions for many to take up the new arrangements. Sanctions against individuals or organisations supplying Iran may result in limitations or restricted access into the United States, where the secondary effects of this new disruption are currently unknown.

Question 2.6. Countries within the EU or UK have the potential to increase volume and create opportunities by trading with Iran. Name organisations or industries that may benefit from trade with Iran. Explain how those organisations could take the opportunities, whilst mitigating any risks of trade with Iran. How might risks of sanctions from the United States may be treated when negotiating trade deals with Iran?

The EU region that may have prospered and been relatively stable since World War II is now changing as the UK leaves with Brexit, countries consider joining whilst it increases trade with China and battles with trade wars and tariffs of the United States. Many countries of the EU have had ongoing austerity due to high sovereign debt levels and there are a few countries pondering about remaining. Europe has also accepted many asylum seekers from the Middle East that is related to political tensions in a number of member countries. At the end of 2018, France is undergoing ongoing protests about reforms led by President Macron. The future of the European region, its allies and influence are more difficult to understand and project than anywhere in the past 70 years. Organisations trading in the EU region have more to now consider than merely prices and product, where the risk and direction of trade between the EU, the United States and Middle East is uncertain. Opportunities will present alongside of the new EU risks, where organisations may have to closely analyse the changes ahead before investing in the region.

China, Russia and North Korea

No official peace treaty was signed at the end of the Korean war whereas, in recent times, there have been many talks and yet tension remains in the region. Some may argue that Russia is seeking power in the negotiations for peace in North Korea (Joo & Lee, 2018), yet others may argue that North Korea is the most difficult relation for the United States (Cha & Kang, 2018). China may be the most influential country in the North Korean region and thus has a part to play in any peace negotiations. It is not clear if any agreement with North Korea will be reached; however, the region is full of tension that may impact trade, shipping and relations with organisations around the world. It is important for leadership and management of the future to consider disruption of a geopolitical nature in this new age, as changes may arise quickly with great global interconnectivity. Whilst Russia, China and North Korea have varying relationships that influence in the world, it is clear that there is increased tension in trade, borders and influence with various countries of the region and elsewhere.

In 2017, the estranged brother of the North Korean leader was assassinated in Malaysia (Wong & Hutzler, 2017), where the relations with this isolated state are poor and a new Cold War may have emerged. Further evidence of a new Cold War emerging occurred in March 2018 when an ex-Russian military double agent was assassinated in Salisbury, UK, by Russian operatives (Mark, 2018). Whilst Russia or North Korea may denounce and repudiate involvement in such assassinations, there is emerging evidence of tension between the East and West. The countries of China, Russia and North Korea appear to still be in some loose sort of alliance, separate to the Western regions of North America, Europe and parts of the Pacific. In recognition of their alliances, the United States has attempted in 2017 and 2018 to leverage China and Russia to assist and influence the North Korean situation.

Whilst tension and relations between East and West may exhibit like a new Cold War, Trump disruption occurred when President Trump surprised the world by holding a prompt face-to-face meeting with the President of North Korea. The rhetoric of both presidents earlier in 2018 may have caused many to believe a face-to-face meeting was unlikely in the near future, yet by June 2018 both presidents signed a document agreeing to work towards denuclearisation of the Korean peninsula (H. Park, 2018). Whilst this agreement may present as a positive sign, it is still unclear if tensions will eventually cease or if new trade opportunities exist. At the end of 2018, there is great uncertainty as to whether large opportunities to trade with North Korea may emerge out of the isolation, or whether the region may continue on with tension and risk of war.

Despite potential benefits of increased trade with China, a risk of trade wars increases the uncertainty and instability of trade and market value across the world. Trade tensions are not limited to China or North Korea, as other restrictions also exist with trade to Russia (Schneider & Weber, 2018). Tensions and tariffs may come and go, where the timing and types of negotiated deals are quite uncertain. As China exports many everyday items, including cars, shoes, clothing and electronics, avoiding trade with China may be almost impossible. The interconnectivity of trade in globalisation allows effects of trade tensions to flow around the world quickly.

Disruption events such as tariffs, trade wars and restriction on travel to South China Sea will have fast and far-reaching implications. If ships are not allowed to travel in the South China Sea, there will be slower transport and higher costs involved in shipping to various parts of North and South East Asia or the Pacific. Owing to the relative ease of trade in globalisation, many organisations may have reduced inventory levels and optimised based on dependable sea routes. Restrictions to trade or slower trade routes may result in shortages occurring quickly. Australia, for instance, may have become so interdependent of oil imports that by 2030 all oil may be imported (Patel, 2018). The Australian government has recently commenced analysis of the oil minimum stockholdings (Macdonald-Smith, 2018), as sea lane restrictions could result in Australia having no fuel inside of a month at current inventory levels. Sea trade restrictions in the South China Sea may never occur; yet, in this world of trade globalisation, interconnectedness and independencies any changes to delivery schedules can have serious consequences so many need to be considered by organisations.

In April 2018, China imposed 15% and 25% tariffs on imports from the United States in reaction to the previously mentioned tariffs applied by the United States. Whilst the United States imposed tariffs on many countries, China imposed its tariff just on US goods. Owing to the way China has imposed its tariffs, there will likely be comparative advantage to exporters not based in the United States. China has a growing economy and an evolving middle class to feed, thus cutting off supply or arbitrarily increasing the cost of imports may inhibit growth in China. The changes initiated by the United States against China may provide competitors an opportunity to supply goods previously imported from the United States.

Chinese citizens now holiday abroad, creating opportunity for organisations that promote safe and interesting places to visit, it is unclear if trade wars will impact this emerging opportunity. President Macron visited China in January 2018, indicating that many EU countries may seek relationships with China whereas this change is occurring whilst the United States introduces tariffs and trade wars. Uncertainty and changes in geopolitical relationships is a complex topic for organisations of the new age that can no longer be ignored, as primary and secondary effects may occur suddenly.

A new form of influence and trade is emerging with a train line being built from China to Europe via the Middle East and Russia (Moss, 2017). This transport connection appears to be a way that China can increase its influence and trade with many countries, where it is possible that increased trade may result in decreased prices or increased volumes, benefiting all organisations trading across the new line. The emergent disruptions that are likely to occur in Asia may eventually alter costs, trade balances, insurance costs and even container volumes around the world. Changes in the Asian geopolitical or trade environment may be unavoidable, where the potential effects could be large and flow in either positive or negative directions. Despite the negative effects, there are potential high positive effects if EU organisations choose to send goods to China. China may well seek to buy bulbs from Denmark, or wine from France, food from Russia and fuel from Iran; therefore, there may be clear benefits in improving trade routes to Europe. Strategically, a train line will be of advantage to China and for those willing to buy or sell goods using it. An organisation of the new age should consider the events of Asia as important to its success.

> *Question 2.7.* Name five ways a small organisation in a Western or Eastern country may find opportunity or advantage from the expanding influence of China. Detail what risks may arise from such trade and how the small organisation may need to build contingency against the risk and uncertainty.

Russia has increased its international influence in the past fifteen years or so to a level that it has not had since the end of the Cold War. Expansion of the Russian area of influence includes the annexation of Crimea, support for the proxy war in Eastern Ukraine, and increased relationship with Syria, Turkey, Iran and the Middle East more broadly. These changes in relationship and influence allow the Russians to continue to holiday in the Middle East, assure oil supply and provide military influence. Whilst there are sanctions on Russia, Western organisations may be unwilling to build new trade relationships with Russia, yet should the sanctions be removed great trade opportunity could emerge.

Various disruptions are likely to emerge in the East, be that originating in Russia, China or North Korea, where the effects may be positive or negative to global trade and individual organisations. Relations between the East and the West are variable at the end of 2018, where Trump disruption may complicate trade with EU or UK. Alliances are variable and changing where the Cold War boundaries are likely to be blurred as EU countries seek to build trade with China and others. In this new age, it is clear that Russia and China seek increased influence and power, where the reactions and relations with the United States and Europe may well determine the nature of any emerging disruption.

Middle East: Iran, Iraq, Syria and Turkey

The Middle East has seen significant conflict in the last 100 years. The Arab uprising of 2010 resulted in several regimes falling and alliances changing, where there are now calls for rethinking and new insights (Pace & Cavatorta, 2012). The wars in Syria and Yemen may be proxy wars between Saudi Arabia and Iran (Ryan, 2012; Salisbury, 2015) that further complicates the nature of warfare and potential resolutions. This book is not confirming a proxy war or making comment on the events in the region, rather this book is tabling that the region is unstable, where disruption is likely to emerge as alliances shift and if peace is not reached. The region is characterised with significant oil deposits, important trade routes and conflict, where many factors in the region could change quickly and are likely to be influenced by the super powers of the United States, China and Russia.

Geopolitical changes in influence may cause the Middle East to change quickly without notice, where there may be significant secondary effects on global trade, currencies or oil markets. Change in various Middle Eastern countries may be difficult to understand due to a lack of verifiable data due to travel restrictions and media controls. Information may only appear on social media that may be fake news or bias, yet organisations may have to interpret and monitor this information to make decisions. Ignoring the region and its potential for organisational impact is no longer possible, where the Arab uprising has now shown that social media can accelerate change and influence places far away.

The two oil shocks of the 1970s (Blanchard & Gali, 2007) indicated how early Middle Eastern disruption could affect world markets, region continues to have a potential to affect world oil prices, trade and inflation. Organisations operating in transport, oil, gas, mining or power generation may not trade in the Middle East, yet can be significantly affected by changes in that region through global prices of oil. Monitoring changes in geopolitics, government changes, war and prices of the Middle East may be more important than many organisations may consider today, where in the new age some form of cognition and analysis may be important.

Iran may seek to now engage with the world, improve trade and reverse the impacts of the past sanctions, where it will also require capital and investment, yet the potential trade may be inhibited as the United States has reimposed sanctions (Motevalli & Talev, 2018). The internal tensions shown by recent internal Iranian protests (Henderson, Pleitgen, & Demirjian, 2017) may confuse organisations about who they should bargain with in Iran should they wish to trade. An organisation that engages with Iran may yield great benefits, or could suffer sanctions from the United States, or lose trade entirely should political change occur in Iran quickly. The uncertain effects that may arise from trade with Iran may be too difficult for many organisations. Organisations of the new age may engage political advisors and agents, risk assessors and government advisors if they were to trade with Iran in the future as the uncertainty and downside risk could present quickly without notice.

Question 2.8. If your organisation is based in the EU, UK or the United States and sanctions are about to be placed on trade in a country that you buy from in the Middle East, how might you change your contract with your supplier on a short notice? What risks may be associated with changes in contracts due to sanctions or geopolitical changes? Write a report to your organisational senior management on the risks or opportunities associated with trading in the region.

The Middle East has many confusing and turbulent relationships that may confuse or inhibit investments. In 2015, Turkey shot down a military plane flying over Syria (Gibbons-Neff, 2015), yet in September 2017 (Service, 2017) and again in April 2018 (Atlas, 2018) Turkey announced that it will buy military hardware from Russia. Turkey has also moved troops into Syria against the Kurdish fighters to assist the Russian efforts (Kofman & Rojansky, 2018), yet it previously had purchased a lot of military equipment from the United States. The recent changes in Turkey's alliance with Russia have created a form of disruption, where Turkey previously had sought to join the EU (B. Park, 2018); therefore, relations with the EU and the United States may be strained. These changing relations with Turkish allies may affect those organisations seeking to use Turkey as a safe entry point into the Middle East.

The Middle East has never been an easy place for organisations to trade in, where many organisations have perceived it too risky and uncertain to engage with. Recent wars and internal conflicts combined with shifts in powerful alliances may see this region as remaining problematic to many organisations despite any potential for opportunity. The flow of information and interconnectivity of the region will continue to affect organisations in distant places in the new age, as social media reports of chlorine attacks in Syria can lead to immediate United States firing of missiles into Syria (Henriksen, 2018). The pace of disruption is now more apparent, as events can be reported faster, without filtration through social media, assisted by the widespread proliferation of phones with cameras. Tension in the Middle East shall likely remain an area of interest for organisations around the world as it has the interest of super powers and is interconnected to trade.

Trade and Defensiveness

As may be seen from the previous discussion, there is great change in the world emerging be that political, power based or alliances, where Trump, Brexit and others may be part of greater movement. Increasing change and uncertainty has the potential for tensions, sanctions or trade wars between the United States, China, Europe or Russia, where the traditional Cold War alliances may no longer prevail. Organisations in this new age will need to be cognisant of the potential for supply shortages, rapid cost increases or trade restrictions that may appear with little notice. Potential disruptions may have effects impacting on investment decisions, credit and financial results for a wide range of organisations. Whilst there are risks for organisations in this new age, there will certainly be opportunities for those willing to engage and take risk, invest or build relations whilst monitoring closely any changing tides.

Various trade restrictions, tariffs and sanctions may influence trade, relations, volumes and prices where governments may be called upon to intervene where negative effects emerge. The interventions from various governments may have flow on effects in relation to monetary policy, fiscal policy and interest rates on a financial front. Government reaction to negative trade restrictions or trade wars may lead to additional secondary effects including new pacts and alliances. Organisations trading in a geopolitically changing environment may experience less stability and predictability than encountered in the past. New skills may be required of organisations in the new age that are discussed at Chapters 4–7 of this book.

Financial Market Change

Financial market disruption may be linked to many of the trade and political disruptions discussed until now. In this new age, disruption will be transmitted without filters over social media, blogs and the Internet, where financial market analysts and investors may immediately react to new information without necessarily seeking verification or independent commentary or analysis. Unfiltered information may result in incorrect reactions or overreactions as the information may be fake, erroneous, heavily manipulated or unverifiable. Financial market change can be a source of disruption in its own right, or it may be a secondary effect from another disruption source. Market disruption effects may ripple far beyond those of the market itself, where banking, government policy, prices, international trade or even wages could be affected.

The new age, with its higher risk profile, may result in organisations experiencing additional difficulties in accessing bank, finance or credit. Restrictions in credit or other finances may restrict organisational development or secondary effects of financial market corrections. Should credit be restricted due to ongoing risk, alternate funding sources including government may be required as lenders may be averse to lending in uncertainty. Organisations that may have once ignored government political changes, or previously ignored wars far away, or have ignored geopolitical instability may no longer be able to operate in such an insular way. Information flow in the new age may be so fast via social media and the Internet that reaction may be required before organisations understand a change. Organisations may need to become politically aware and active, may be required to have information sources beyond the traditional as a defensive mechanism, as a way to avoid being last to know of impending disruption. The nature of fake and unsubstantiated information may require organisations to seek information verification or employ analytical services, where acting without verification may be perilous.

Restrictions to credit may restrict the growth of organisations and small countries in the new age. Countries like China and Japan already provide funds for emerging Asian countries (Er, 2018) that may assist in their growth, or some may argue the real goal is to improve the influence and power of the lenders. When credit is difficult to attract, rejection of funding from larger powers may be difficult as other sources may not be available. Countries and organisations may need to consider tensions and alliances if they accept funding from powerful powers, as failure to do so may affect future relationships or increase insecurity. Organisations may be required to hire experts, analysts and political advisers in order to assess options before signing new funding agreements. A simple lease granted in Australia over its Port in Darwin to a Chinese organisation (Chen, Fei, Lee, & Tao, 2018) created controversy as it had not consulted with its US ally. There are now many examples across the world where geopolitical power is generated from funding be that in Africa (Henderson, Appelbaum, Ho, & Mohan, 2013), Asia (Goh, 2016) or Latin America (Kotschwar, 2014) to name a few regions. Organisations wishing to avoid unintended influence may find the information and analysis required as prohibitively expensive, time consuming and beyond their means completely.

The geopolitical changes discussed in this chapter may continue to emerge and create uncertainty, where the disruption so formed may restrict capital funds available and create difficult choices for organisations of this new age. Organisations that are not politically informed or are conservative or are risk averse may choose to not engage or invest when capital is provided with influence and power. Other organisations may be more innovative and opportunistic, taking on new investment from geopolitical powerful countries and negotiating through any relationship tensions. The new influence sought by lenders may require organisations to adjust their governance and analysis resources in order to appropriately assess new situations.

Predicting market responses is quite difficult, especially when combined with significant changes in geopolitical alliances. In the new age, market positions can move very quickly as the market is connected to large computers and traders on line; therefore, new issues or results can transfer fast over social media and the Internet without very much filtering or analysis. The stability of markets is hard to predict as the US tariff announcements in June 2018 had little market impact, yet market losses in October 2018 may relate to the tariff introduction. President Trump's communication style may now be having less market influence, where markets appeared to be unresponsive when the United States would not agree to sign the Group of Seven communique in June 2018 (France24, 2018).

The unpredictability of disruption may increase market volatility, or social media may be so unstable and unreliable that the markets settle and largely ignore unconfirmed reports. It is difficult to predict the effect of disruption on markets in the future as the phenomenon is still relatively new. If markets choose to ignore early indications of any new disruption, some form of information verification and analysis will occur eventually that may emerge as a market correction, be that in a positive or negative direction. Avoidance of new age disruption may be impossible, where there will likely be significant challenges to operating in fast speed, where information be unverifiable.

Monetary Change and GFC: Prices and Market

In 2008, there was an excess of debt and high asset prices across the world that impacted organisations, individuals and countries, being known as the GFC. The GFC was clearly the most significant global financial event since the Great Depression. The excess borrowing had over a number of years caused asset prices to rise, where individual and country indebtedness reached levels that left some without the ability to pay. The excess lending was so large in 2008 that it resulted in a combined market disruption, where asset and market prices fell so suddenly that fiscal and monetary controls were released and interest rates fell sharply, reduced to zero in some countries. Many organisations were forced into bankruptcy globally as a result of the GFC where high debt levels could not be repaid at a short notice. Whilst GFC origins may be debated (M. Bordo, 2018) the long term effects of the GFC are clear, where sovereign debt has emerged as a secondary effect of the GFC, including the countries of Greece, Spain, Italy and Portugal (Buchanan, 2010). Whilst austerity has emerged as a tool for countries with high debt, the issue remains at the end of 2018 that may continue to evolve into the future.

The GFC was a significantly large disruption that caused great concern to organisations, investors and individual workers. The GFC stress arose from the rapid pace of change, the large numbers of organisational failure and the size of job losses globally. In the days immediately post the GFC, information and understanding were lacking, where many had no view of the size of the crisis, or its origins and effects, thus creating chaos in markets and finance systems. It would have been very difficult for any organisation to have predicted the GFC, its size and the secondary effects of lowering interest rates to zero for extended periods. Even fewer organisations would have been able to predict before the GFC the potential for austerity in some EU countries or pension changes in Greece. The lack of clarity and ability to predict consequences of GFC style disruption should be of concern to the organisational investor today, where the awareness of such global matters may still be deficient in organisations.

Whilst market have always fluctuated, it is the interconnectedness of the globalisation that has introduced the concept of market disruption. In the past, investors did not have mobile phones, smartphones, social media and constant Internet access. Past times allowed investors to wait and consult mainstream newspapers, read analyst reports and consider before deciding to buy or sell. In the new age, investors receive information on social media and email, prior to reading reports in mainstream newspapers or online publishers and before analysts have written reports. It is the spontaneity of market reaction to disruption without verification that opens markets to potential fake news and potential over reactions or incorrect valuation. Management and organisational governance bodies may have to seriously consider market disruption risk and ways to avoid error or overreaction without necessarily restricting innovation and good decision making.

Cryptocurrencies and Emerging Currencies

A number of cryptocurrencies have emerged recently in the market (Zhang, Wang, Li, & Shen, 2018), where the new currency systems are characterised with encryption and open sourced data (Bizcommunity.com, 2017). The blockchain system requires cross verification as transactions occur, where the system is less vulnerable to attack (Viola, 2018). Blockchain emerged with cryptocurrencies, where the technology has potential to improve a number of transactional systems that may require high levels of verification, including those of election systems, banking and insurance (Dai & Vasarhelyi, 2017).

Despite emerging some time ago, the cryptocurrency and blockchain technology has had only limited reach, where some have used these currencies to avoid government restrictions, where they have been characterised by wide fluctuations in conversion rates (Sier, 2016). The new cryptocurrencies are open to money laundering, where they are monitored for tax evasion by some governments (Hughes, 2018b). Taxation of cryptocurrency gains is still being debated (Hooi, 2014; Hughes, 2018a; Kably, 2017), where the uncertainty may have inhibited the acceptance of the new currencies. Organisations may still globally prefer to trade in United States Dollars (USD) or the Euro, yet there is now potential to trade in cryptocurrencies and the currencies of China and India as alternates.

The variation of exchange with cryptocurrencies may be but one of the issues causing concern for potential users of the cryptocurrencies on offer (Stone, 2017). Despite the security of blockchain included with these emerging currencies, there have been a number of cryptocurrency thefts reported (Maillet, 2018; Martin, Eun-Young, & Russolillo, 2017; Peters, 2018), thus may be another concern for potential users. Cryptocurrencies may also be limited due to the large calculations required, or may be due to the currently slow calculations (Morris, 2018), or due to the relatively high use of electricity in the computations (Noack, 2018). New signs of technologies are emerging to improve cryptocurrencies (Morris, 2018), although it is not clear whether these currencies will ever be reliable, efficient and able to compete with regular forms of currency. The verification and security of these new currencies may have appeal, yet the difficulties with the current cryptocurrencies may inhibit adoption of the new currencies.

Organisations may ignore cryptocurrencies for now as they may not have the skills to assess the risks and opportunities, despite concepts that physical currencies may soon be redundant, to be replaced by digitised currencies (Kobie, 2017). Organisations that do not investigate the new currencies and their potential may be surprised and unprepared should they be widely adopted in the future. Regular banking institutions have not as yet adopted cryptocurrencies, yet their market power may be radically altered if customers ever widely adopt the new currencies. Organisations may already be advantaged if they awaken to the potential of Crypto disruption emerging in a fast and transformational way.

Currency Risk

Currencies have for some time been allowed to float, fluctuate by many countries for over 30 years. Currency disruption may emerge from sudden changes in traditional markets of debt, productivity and trade, or it may emerge from less predictable sources including market confidence, political instability, social media or even war. Organisations may prefer to trade in USD or the Euro, where they have choices now of cryptocurrency, China and Indian currencies. At the end of 2018, the emerging currency of China is still a state-controlled currency, where the currency could be perceived positively due to its short-term controlled stability, or it may be perceived with caution. An organisation trading with China may prefer to avoid the exchange controls of China and trade in traditional currencies that are market driven.

Currency disruption may influence trade and investment relations around the world, as any significant change in the USD exchange rate may affect global trade, despite the alternate currencies including Euro, China or India or crypto-currency. Currency disruption somewhere in the future is very likely, where the source of the disruption may be difficult to predict or time. One example of future currency disruption may coincide when a Brexit deal is sorted, where the currency effect may be impossible to predict with any accuracy. These types of currency disruptions create dilemmas for organisations, where there may be heightened risk should any large transactions be in progress at the time of any major currency adjustment.

The currency disruption concept is different to normal market fluctuations, where potential changes may be transformational, where the change size and pace may be so significant as to threaten organisational survival. As was discussed earlier in this book, there are many likely disruption forms including geopolitical changes, trade wars and other tensions, where secondary currency effects may arise from any disruption. Sudden instability across currency markets may have significant influence on market competition, as one organisation may be hedged and another unhedged when currencies fluctuate that may result in large variations. Whilst risk may be managed through hedges or even futures markets, many smaller organisations may not be in a position to understand or use such tools.

Question 2.9. Write a report to your organisation explaining currency disruption. Explain in the report what may need to be monitored in order to be an early identifier of currency disruption. How might a small organisation protect against the uncertainty of currency? What risks may emerge if an organisation hedges specific transactions against currency risk?

The world has experienced in the last 10 years how the GFC resulted in fast and sudden change around the world. Currency disruption may emerge as a result of many other disruption forms that have emerged since the GFC or are likely to persist in the new age. There is now heightened uncertainty related to various geopolitical tensions and Trump disruption, where world order, predictability and consensus are less likely to occur in the future. The new age, characterised by a 24-hour media cycle, social media and fake news, may enable currencies and other markets to move fast, with more volatility. Organisations will likely need to monitor various world tensions and disruption in order to identify risk and uncertainty, where verification and analysis skills may be key to success in the new age.

Climate Change

Climate change policies and risk registers may already exist for many organisations, regardless of any political view relating to its reality. Many governments have commenced implementing climate policies, greenhouse subsidies and implementing new related taxes. Organisations operate regardless of any policy uncertainty, taxation uncertainty, electricity generation policy changes or generations subsidies. Government policies may be subject to change without notice, where the organisation will be expected by stakeholders to continue to generate financial and other returns to expectations. The unexpected nature of global trade is indicated by the 2015 United Nations Paris Agreement (Paris Agreement) that was signed originally by the Obama administration and hailed as a success (Brauers & Richter, 2016). Yet, the deal was later reneged by the Trump administration just two years later (Gies, 2017). Organisations in the United States received two opposite policies on climate change in a short period, where the change in policy may significantly reduce investment in alternate technologies for years ahead.

Climate change disruption does not originate in a policy or the absence of policy, rather the disruption relates to the lack of certainty and rapid changes to policy, causing confusion and risk. The United States may not be the only country that has potential for sudden climate policy directional change, as it may occur wherever consensus of policy is not achieved across a political divide. A lack of public policy consensus on climate change may affect a wide variety of industries including fossil fuels, transport, mining, electricity generation, wind and solar industries. If the Paris Agreement is not widespread and binding with certainty, organisations may fail to attract renewable support or investment.

The Paris Agreement is likely to continue in place for most of the remaining world, despite the United States' withdrawal from the agreement. Organisations that may have been planning to base renewable manufacturing in the United States, based on their market potential and economies of scale, may already have cancelled such plans. A small number of organisations may choose to take a longer-term view and risk being based in the United States anyway, despite the uncertainty and trade wars emerging. Benefits of the Paris Agreement may have diminished once the United States reneged on the deal as lower economies of scale and lower returns may result without the United States' inclusion.

US banks and shareholders may now be more inclined to invest in fossil fuels than the years prior to its withdrawal from the Paris Agreement, yet there is a risk that a future or even the current US administration may return to the agreement. Climate change disruption will likely affect global trade and investment due to the sovereign risk and uncertainty of US policy, where the United States may no longer be an investment destination for those seeking to produce renewables. Should climate change policies remain uncertain investment in renewables and fossil fuels may result, where failure to invest may in the long-term result in energy shortages in the future. This climate change disruption will likely create divergence, risk and opportunity, where some organisations will be innovative and take risk, whilst the risk averse may wait for more stable policies to emerge.

Resource Management

Despite policy uncertainty on climate change, organisations regularly make decisions related to vehicles and choice of fuel type including those of gas, diesel, hydrogen or electric. The short-term choice of fuel type may vary between the short and long term; thus, whilst hydrogen vehicles are still in development and expensive in the short term, they could be a very cheap alternative in the longer term if they were widely adopted. A number of countries are already announcing policies to remove all petrol and diesel vehicles over varying time frames, including that of Norway by 2025 (Kass, 2018). It may also appear confusing that California continues to propose new legislation to restrict car emissions, whilst the US administration has removed itself from the Paris Agreement on climate change (Spector, 2017). Organisations, irrespective of size, country or nature, will need to be cognisant of climate disruption, where changes to policy may occur frequently and in opposite directions.

Organisations may choose to ignore climate disruption and wait, thus avoiding the early adoption costs until as late as possible, hence avoiding development costs and potential redundancies. The late identification of climate disruption may advantage an organisations competitor, if they market changes to customers and achieve benefits. Early climate disruption recognition may yield high development costs in the short term, yet they may gain advantage in the longer term through lower costs and more knowledge of the technology. There are great choices to be made in terms of climate policy including those of early or late adoption, where risk may attach to either alternative, and ignorance may be the highest.

In countries without a carbon tax, such as the United States or Australia, it may be difficult for an organisation to decide on how to respond to climate change. These dilemmas are faced by organisations all around the world today, where future changes in policy may impact future returns in both the short and long term. Countries that can find political certainty in climate policies and taxes may find that organisations may be attracted to the more stable region, not because of ideology, rather due to stability and stakeholder perceptions.

The future of carbon certificates, taxes and trading thereof is also uncertain, thus increasing the risks and complexity associated with climate disruption. Currently, carbon certificates are not tradable globally, thus restricting organisational choices. Governments may arbitrarily change the way carbon taxes are imposed in the future, or may change the certificate regimes, or even change the tax rates so creating further uncertainty. Electricity, car manufacturing and mining require large capital investment, where the current lack of certainty regarding climate policies may restrict capital flows.

Despite the positive environment post the Paris Agreement on climate change there would still appear to be high likelihood for continued climate disruption in to the future. Some organisations may choose to limit risk and incur the early adoption costs, whilst other may do the opposite. Organisational stakeholders, financiers and governors may need to clarify the climate policies, thus their management can continue to operate despite the government political dilemmas. Failure to openly determine a climate policy and associated risk at the organisational level may be perceived as unconscionable conduct in the future as climate change is clearly in the political sphere today for organisations to respond to.

Property and Staff

Climate disruption is not limited to taxes and government policy as it has great potential to affect property prices globally quite suddenly. Now, and into the future, there is the potential for new government restrictions on properties near the sea, or for investors to refrain from seaside investments. Some may believe that sea rises are likely or imminent, where over time that view may result in decreased seaside land price premiums that were previously associated. It is even possible that seaside locations could become worthless should physical evidence of sea rises emerge. The timing and size of property price changes may well be affected by the perception of when the sea rises are likely to occur.

Despite the lack of seaside property prices changes to date, there is real potential for substantial change once the likelihood is reasonably high. Organisations may ignore potential property price changes related to climate disruption, yet the risk remains irrespective of any political or scientific view about its reality. Organisations are in the process of responding to carbon taxes and renewable subsidies, thus at this stage many have not considered property price secondary effects. Failure to consider and discuss property related disruption to climate change may at some point lead to reduced stakeholder trust in management and leadership.

Staffing preferences may change as climate change emerges, where staff may not be willing to locate near the seaside or if they are adversely affected by carbon taxes and increased travel costs staff may be less willing to travel or drive to work. The possibilities discussed here are not predictions, rather they are considerations that organisations today may need to consider even if they are considered remote, irrational or improbable by some. It is worth noting that societal changes can affect organisational directions, as society no longer accepts child labour that was common just over 100 years ago. Organisations should consider staff and property secondary effects from climate change, if they are to attract and retain staff, or choose property locations, that are appropriate for the future.

Power Alternatives and Associated Costs

China has strongly supported wind, solar and now electric cars, where the support is already affecting investments and decisions on climate change. Even though the nickel market has underperformed (Ris, Trannoy, & Wasmer, 2017) a turnaround for the metal based on vehicle battery support and innovation in China (Facada, 2018) is possible. The large support for renewables and a cleaner world, especially by China and Europe, will likely influence mining decisions globally and affect prices and volumes of associated raw materials. Batteries are just one product that may grow with climate change directions, where other materials like iron ore, steel and coal may also be affected if wind farms increase in volume.

Raw material and commodity prices and volumes are dependent upon global government policies, where sudden changes in policy may influence sudden change in prices or trade. The United States, as a large economy, has enough size and impact to dramatically increase or decrease prices and volumes of key

materials based on their policies in the renewable sector. An organisation investing in mining, renewables or associated industries will need to contemplate how
global political changes may affect the volume or prices of associated inputs. One
might expect prices of solar equipment to fall, if large economies all embraced it;
yet, it is currently unclear how committed countries may be to the Paris Agreement. Where there is divergence in power, politics and policy between China,
Europe and the United States the path forward is unclear, where organisations
may need to seriously consider current and future impacts.

Technological Change

Technology is moving and changing faster than at any time previous; the changes
now being experienced are quite fundamental and therefore are affecting a
wide range of users and consumers. Organisations today may need to consider
technology disruption as either a threat or opportunity in the new age, where
avoidance may be impossible. The introduction of vast mobile phone networks,
clouds, Bluetooth, optical fibre, hardware changes and computer interconnectivity has increased the complexity of the information technology (IT) systems
to a point where some have created the Chief Information Office (CIO). Organisations will be likely be affected by technology disruption on a regular basis
in the new age, where ongoing assessment of the possibilities will be required.
It may be that the pace of change is beyond what a person may be able to keep
up with (Burrows, 2018). Technology change is a broad topic, where artificial
intelligence (AI) is seen as the area that will most likely have transformational
impacts on organisations in the new age, thus AI is specifically covered in Chapter 3 of this book.

Scams

Beyond the ongoing and rapid technology change, organisations are exposed to
additional risk through the emergence of scams. Scams, due to additional interconnectivity globally, are much more likely and easier to deploy than before the
Internet and globalisation. Scams now regularly target individuals, organisations
and government, where the intentions may include fraud, to hinder or annoy or
use the recipient's data or identity. Organisations increasingly need more protec-
tion than merely firewalls, passwords or physical security as the risks associated
with scams are complex and may even lie internally. Staff may inadvertently or
deliberately introduce scam risk to an organisation as they may have Internet
access and can be tempted to accept emails or downloads from outside of the
organisation. The increase in volume of business-to-business (B2B) relationships
between customers and suppliers has also increased the potential for scams. Technology disruption may occur quickly and in hidden ways, where the party affected
may lie outside of the initial targeted organisation.

    Small organisations are particularly vulnerable to scams as they may lack the
resources and skills required to build robust preventative systems. Organisations
may need to rely on staff in their scam-avoidance strategy so ensure that staff

are appropriately trained to identify risks as they emerge, where larger organisations may have more resources in this regard. Training alone, like that of IT and firewalls, will be insufficient to prevent scams from hurting the organisation, where broader means may be required to prevent or even react to scam issues as they arise.

Smartphones and Technology

Individuals have embraced technology to a point where it is now common place for staff to hold multiple mobile phones and computers that allow them to work outside normal working hours or even at home. The smartphones now have Internet capability, banking connectivity and are able to reach inside many of the organisations systems, where this additional traffic increases exposure and risk to the organisation. The technology risk is not just one of access and volume, as there is an additional physical control risk as staff travel into airports, taxis and motels with their interconnected organisational assets. Further risks arise as staff use phones and computers over open connection systems offered for free by café's, airport lounges or other communal areas. The smartphone and new technology have no doubt changed the way staff work, where the additional risks of the connectivity may not be fully appreciated by all organisations.

Organisations that are large may expect their CIO to identify and manage new technology risk, yet the small-to-medium-sized organisation may not have that luxury, employing less skilled or outsourced alternatives to assist. For many organisations, new technology may have accelerated due to competition, customer or cost, yet appropriate risk assessment and due diligence of the development may be slow and complex. In the rush to compete and take up new technology issues and risks of increased transaction volumes, integration complexity and physical risks may not be fully appreciated prior to implementation.

Organisations may have embraced Facebook, created profiles and advertised in that forum in recent years, where many may have not considered the topic of privacy. It may have been concerning and surprising to organisations and individuals alike that Facebook had on sold private information, where government regulation and consideration may also have been lacking (Lazcano, Avedillo, & Del Real, 2018). Disruption may arise, in a technology context, when new technology adoption occurs ahead of due risk consideration or ahead of appropriate controls development.

Case Study 2.1

An organisation has recently rolled out smartphones and electronic forms that have been integrated into main organisational computer. There are now over 100 technicians with the new technology over a few months. The organisation had only one IT manager, who was already responsible for B2B, Enterprise Resource Programme and 15 sites that were connected on an intranet and landline telephones. The organisation is small, with around 150 employees.

During this technology change, there have been no changes to the quantity IT people in the organisation, nor was there any formal review of processes before it was introduced. To assist in the additional workload, a senior staff member outside of the IT area assisted in building up the new smartphones and forms, as the deadlines were tight and a customer was expecting the change on time.

Case Study Question

Was this increase in speed and size of IT and smartphone rollout appropriate for this organisation? What risks should have been identified before this change occurred? How should risks have been identified? What actions would you put in place to reduce risk and reduce disruption effects for this organisation?

This section indicates that technology may continue to evolve at a fast pace, where the increase in speed may be related to its ease of use, flexibility and reduced time. The competitive pressure to implement new technology may be so fast that risk assessment and governance may be overlooked. The future organisation may be left with a dilemma as to how it can adopt technology change fast, satisfy customers and stakeholders, yet avoid risk and uncertainty.

Technological Integration and Ease

As already discussed, technology is advancing at a rapid pace in both hardware and software, where increased functionality and technology speed are a result. The required interconnectivity of technology in the new age may often result in integration issues, resulting from the interconnectedness required with internal or external parties including government, customer or even supplier. An improved organisational interconnectedness may result in market advantage or cost reduction versus competitors. Integration risk and complexity occur as organisations interconnect, upgrade or attempt to retrofit technology. Organisations in the new age may have great future challenges in technology, where choices between risk and capability may be required in order to operate. The complexity presented through systems integration may result in increased risk of data loss, data copying or theft. It is possible that organisational IT staff may need to be more concerned with systems defences, risk management and strategy than merely worrying about wires and code.

Organisational Change in Global Organisations

The nature of multisite, multicountry organisations has been significantly assisted by new technology, be that the Internet, social media or email. Organisational change is now more transformational and faster than ever, aided by globalisation and the increased interconnectedness of trade, systems and communication. There are now significant differences in organisational operations as compared to the 1990s, where email and the Internet now fundamentally support many organisational processes. The globalised organisational environment was not formed through strategy by a single organisation, rather it emerged over time, out of various elements including governmental trade openness and support, tariff reduction.

Communication

Organisational communication has dramatically changed in the last 20 years, where up until the mid-1990s most managers would not have typed any internal or external communication. Secretaries once did all organisational typing and supported the flow of documents internally and externally via facsimile (or telex and telegram before that time) and physical mail. The emergence of intranet, Internet and emails eliminated secretarial positions and typing pools in a short period of time. The new email tool was perceived as being so easy to use that even many senior managers took on the typing emails. The transformation to emails as a key organisational communication tool occurred as it was perceived as more efficient, private and faster than the previous secretarial system of hand writing or shorthand, typing then amending and sending by facsimile. Over just 20 or so years, a majority of organisations have transformed in communication, where almost no old type writers or secretarial positions remain as they once were and email or other communication forms are extensively used.

Organisational communication with staff, customers and suppliers today extends to websites, social media and other forms of technology, being far beyond the email form. These new forms of communication require information to be continually relevant, current and informative. New roles and structures have emerged in response to the new communication forms where organisations may now employ web designers, communication experts and others to ensure that the communication is valid, controlled and up-to-date. Failure to achieve relevant and valid information in communication channels may expose new risks that have the potential for reputational, customer and value loss or financial loss.

Communication disruption may when sudden new forms of communication arise and affect organisational processes and structures in a short amount of time. New social media forms may also cause disruption as information or comment posted with haste could almost immediately lead to organisational reputational damage or damage to product brands. In the new forms of communication, a simple click or comment from a smartphone has potential to influence customers or stakeholders around the world, without any verification or filtering. Organisations that do not monitor or control their social media content may be particularly exposed if negative comments are allowed to flow without knowledge. Organisations in this new age must include communication forms and risks into their planning or risk-averse reactions and loss of value.

Question 2.10. Discuss the way that communication disruption may likely change the internal operations of an organisation? How often should an organisation review social media feedback? What should the response be when negative influence appears on social media about an organisation or its products and services?

Communication disruption is not limited to information direct to or from an organisation, as other information exists on the Internet, email and social media. Fake news occurs on the Internet when information is of an unknown or unreliable origin, which may include partial or no truth and the source lacks independent verification. Fake news has also been described as being deliberately deceptive and appearing in forms that are akin to news stories created by mainstream organisations (Gelfert, 2018). The concept of news being false or misleading is not new, being in existence for nearly 100 years (Schapals, Bruns, & McNair, 2018), where the new pace and ease of transmission is completely different than the past.

The new age forms of communication and news have eroded the mainstream newspaper business models (Phillips, 2018). Millions of consumers may have once perceived the mainstream newspapers as a reliable source of truth, yet the mainstream printed form is no longer the main source of information for the masses. Fake news has more recently been used as an attack and defensive term in politics (Farkas & Schou, 2018), where it may assist in improving power in authoritarianism (McNair, Bruns, & Schapals, 2018), where a number already regularly use fake news to support their authoritarian positions (Lees, 2018).

Mainstream independent, reliable sources of information are falling in a time when fake news and the number of independent unverified sources are rising. The unreliability of information creates troubling times for organisations as they may have only limited resources and skills to create and identify information from their own sources. News events can be sourced in unfiltered ways without government controls or professional review, increasing uncertainty for organisations to form opinion and make informed decisions. The old mainstream media that supported credible and reliable news no longer supports business models of the past. US President Trump also now prefers social media over the mainstream media. It is quite a dilemma for society that the role of journalist may be diminishing at the same time organisations may be lacking verifiable information for decision making.

Those with verified information may have advantageous positions and rising power over those without such a verification. The new technologies and social media consistently emerge as sources of disruption, including recent events of the Arab and Egyptian uprising (Brym, Godbout, Hoffbauer, Menard, & Zhang, 2014), the recent false announcement of UK Prince Philip dying (Hallemann, 2018) or Russian influence over US elections (Rutland, 2017). The Arab uprising was clearly assisted by social media that enabled fast spread of new ideas, protests and group rebellion. Whilst aiding change in the world like the Arab uprising, there is still now great potential for false or fake news to influence and cause trouble in the world.

As a result of the face pace of communication with social media and globalisation, organisations will need to monitor communication and information, and assess and analyse the data whilst verifying authenticity. The organisational processes required in this new age are likely to be different to those of the past, as they will likely gather information from various online unverified sources, having to verify and clarify before analysing and acting. Failure to build appropriate processes for this new age may leave the organisation exposed, by either not reacting or reacting too fast to possible fake news. The organisation that assesses information incorrectly may impair the organisation reputationally, financially or structurally. Verification of new information may take time and resources, where long delays may leave an organisation exposed should competitors be in a position to verify and act faster.

> *Question 2.11.* How should an organisation monitor, verify and assess indirect information about technology, political or market changes? What processes may be required for the organisation to assess and dissect information between real and fake news?

Cross-cultural Mixes

In the greater interconnectivity of globalisation additional challenges to organisations have emerged in relation to cross communication between cultures, countries, religions and time zones. In this new age, organisations are increasingly diverse, where it is now very common place for multinational organisations to have employee, customer and suppliers across multiple countries with significant variations in religion, customs and language. These differences are so common that it is now very normal for staff to be asked about their food preferences before meetings are booked, or common to travel regularly for business.

Organisational staff in this new age are more likely to be mindful of language, gender, hierarchal or other differences than ever before. It may be common for staff to encounter differences in values say between western-based staff and eastern-based staff with say confusionist beliefs. Cultural value differences may occur regularly in multinational organisations of the new age, where it is possible that the direct and open style of western culture may be considered disrespectful in other cultures. Silence in the West may be seen to be weak or lacking contribution, whilst the same behaviour in the East may be one of respect and agreement. This is not to say that differences are causing concern in organisations today, rather organisations working cross country or cross culturally may need to invest in training on these differences to ensure appreciation and avoid issues.

Cohesion and Integration

Cohesion and integration of staff across international lines will not be automatic nor easy in many cases; therefore, organisations may need to specifically invest in cross-cultural cohesion programmes and train staff. Organisations that have outsourced to offshore service centres may wish to train both parties about issues that may result from differences in time, language and cultural values. Outsourcing may be considered as mere cost savings by some, where the broader impacts on customer, suppliers and even government relations may need deeper consideration. Failure to appreciate the impacts of the offshore outsourcing and failure to build appropriate actions may result in organisational reductions in reputation or financial outcomes.

Communication disruption is a very important topic for the organisation of the new age to consider, where fast and transformational effects on reputation and performance could occur. An assessment of communication channels and the various risks associated may be a requirement for organisations that seeking to survive in the new age. Dedicating sufficient time and resource into communication and cross-culture cohesion may be important to prevent losses and poor decision making.

Wiki and Impacts on Organisational Control

Prior to the emergence of the Internet, email and social media, organisations may have been reasonably protected against potential widespread mass data theft, protected entirely by physical controls. The physical controls of the past may have made it impossible for mass data leaks to competitors, yet the physical controls are no longer sufficient to protect an organisation, where large-scale data leak or theft is now possible despite any physical controls. There have been several well-publicised data and vulnerability leaks (Fuchs & Trottier, 2017), where large data breaches can occur through a simple email or the sharing of files on a USB. Recent data leaks include those of government data (Mazzetti & Schmidt, 2013), science data (Brumfiel, 2011) and information data (Eidam, 2015), where a number of leaks may have been derived through actions of employees or due to lacking security controls (Nathan & Smith, 2016). There is now great complexity for the IT manager of the new age to consider.

The IT manager and organisations will likely need to monitor and avoid data breaches that may occur from disgruntled or careless employees, scams or competitors. Other changes may occur through increased protections of firewalls, passwords and access controls, where these increased controls may also increase complexity. Organisations of this new age will likely need to constantly monitor and control the IT environment in an attempt to avoid data disruption and exploitation. In evaluating over control in the organisation, there will be a point where consideration of risk versus the cost of control may be exceeded, thus should be monitored and analysed regularly. Avoidance of data disruption may be impossible, where some form of risk management approach may minimise potential effects.

> *Question 2.12.* You have just been appointed as the CEO of a large organisation and you have little IT knowledge. Write a detailed report on your risk mitigation approach to data disruption. Explain how you will convince your board, shareholders and financiers that it is appropriate. How might your customers influence your organisational policies against data disruption?

Knowledge Mobility

Data disruption may not always be covert or aimed at harming an organisation. Staff may seek to show their value when they start in new organisations and thus may acquire intellectual property (IP) that they bring to their new employer, legally or illegally acquired. Staff or suppliers may copy various data and decision models, forms and processes that are later transferred to their future employers. Individuals taking IP from one employer to another may do so innocently or it may be simply aimed at promoting their careers, where some may also seek to harm previous employers. Irrespective of motivation, the copying of forms or processes by staff has potential to damage the originating organisation. To address the heightened risk of inadvertent or unknown IP transfers, the organisation may consider increased uses of copyright or trademark protections and audits. An alternate strategy to reduce IP theft may be to encourage employee loyalty, employment longevity or rewards.

Organisational knowledge may be considered an asset or value to an organisation, thus losing staff may reduce organisational value. Whilst physical controls over hard disks, plug in disks and email may reduce the access to systems, they are unlikely to be totally effective. Tactics that improve staff morale and longevity may reduce data loss or increase the likelihood of discovery.

Each staff member has knowledge and information about organisational operations that may not need to be copied in order to create data disruption risk. A large organisation may be exposed to knowledge loss and mobility due to the complexity of systems and higher quantity of employees, whereas the small organisation may be exposed more through resource and technical constraints. Organisations may need to assess internal IP loss risk, or may require new governance systems to oversee, report and insist on mitigation. These risk strategies against data disruption should not be directed purely to the IT professional through hardware and software controls, organisations may need to consider that culture and employee engagement may be just as successful at addressing loss risk. Chapters 5–7 of this book propose several actions that may assist the organisation of the new age.

Employee Change

Organisations do not operate in isolation, nor are they always in a position to lead and manage change for their employees. Employee requirements are not homogenous, varying vastly between the age profiles, genders, demographics and country of origin. Organisational staff may not exclusively be interested in pay rates and conditions in this new age, as social and ethical performances of an organisation may now be very important. Employees may be interested in life-work balance, climate change, recycling, corporate citizenship and ethics, where these interests may not always align with organisational goals of profit, shareholders and competition. Organisations now regularly address the emerging interests of employees by creating environmental policies, charity support or local community support activities. Employees may be attracted to work for organisations that are perceived to act ethically or socially responsible, where a lack of appropriate policy and action may offend potential employees and customers. Competitive advantage may be achieved if staff are hired based on organisational policies towards ethics and society.

An organisation is very dependent on their staff for ethical behaviour, competition and creativity, where the combination may support organisational value. Staff of the future may not be willing to follow organisational direction without challenge, thus increasing issues for concern in attracting and retaining staff. Increased organisational controls and processes, without sufficient explanation, may be negatively interpreted by staff. Disassociated, disgruntled employees may cause concern for an organisation as lower satisfaction levels may lead to poor employee retention rates, poor relations or poor performances, where new actions and policies may be required. Staff of the new age may not wish to work in organisations that are autocratic, discriminatory or social irresponsible, creating issues for leadership and management of the future.

Knowledge and Skills Changes

The new age environment many involve fast paced change, automation, new technology, new structures and new processes, where new skills may be required in order to survive. It is likely that emerging AI, and other new technology, may result in roles being eliminated (Talley, 2018; Wilson, Daugherty, & Bianzino, 2017), where those with the highest skill levels may be the least impacted. New skills will likely be required in the new age (Gurchiek, 2017; Sousa & Rocha, 2019), where the pace of change and nature of the new technology may be influential. Employees will need to show their value to the organisation, be that through innovation (Sousa & Rocha, 2019) or other unique properties in order to survive.

Organisational success and value may intrinsically be tied to staff skill levels, where competitive advantage may be based upon these skills. In order to succeed, an organisation may likely need to attract the most skilled people, thus skills identification and training may be important. Organisations that include staff that have superior communication skills are likely to provide clearer information to staff. Organisations that lack the required communication skills to explain change adequately may confuse staff, incur higher turnover of staff and so lack the knowledge and creativity required in order to survive, which may result in poorer earnings, lower creativity or lack of staff engagement. As is discussed in Chapters 4–7 of this book, organisational success may be linked and dependent upon on leadership and management actions.

Attitude Changes and Generational Imbalances: X, Y and Millennials

In the near future, the baby boomer generation is likely to retire and be replaced by later generations (Dionida, 2016), where organisations may incur significant shifts in attitudes, skills and outlook as the other later generations fill the roles. The generations after the baby boomers may be divergent in their needs and even require generation specific leadership styles (Cox, 2016; Yu & Miller, 2005). The baby boomers were often loyal and without many complaints during their working lives, possibly influenced by their parents' endurance of the earlier Great Depression and World Wars I and II. The baby boomers are now at the end of their careers, being replaced by later generations that will have considerably different attitudes to work and leisure (Twenge, 2010). The latter generations, called Y and the Millennials, may not be willing to wait for the long term in order to run organisations.

The changing nature of generational ratios in organisations probably should not be portrayed as merely good or bad, as the changes are significant involving changes in power, attitudes and skills. It is already apparent that some organisational attitudes are emerging, where some already identify an emergence of ageism in recent years (Marchiondo, Gonzales, & Ran, 2016), where the millennials may be less interested in pay (Pickett, 2013) than in a perceived higher importance of equal rights, or policies on gender, sexuality, social and carbon. Employee disruption may emerge from differences in values, diversity or policies where the organisation may have to prepare and respond in a transformational way.

Employees of the future may have new requirements as the new technology will increase connectivity leading to demands to work from home, variable working hours or ad hoc leave without notice. Organisations that are unable or unwilling to embrace the flexibility required by employees may fail to attract or retain employees or performances may be sub-optimal. Developing new policies towards social change, equal pay, green policies and diversity may position an organisation more favourably in the eyes of both staff and customer. Technology evolution may influence future employee preferences to work from home, or in groups, working collaboratively rather than any autocratic or hierarchical structures of the past. Organisations using older communication methods, expecting loyalty or support may be disappointed if employees of the future reject their cultures, fleeing to more modern organisations.

Work-life Balance Changes

The younger millennial generation is less likely to automatically follow organisational directions, or may not want career, or power and status than earlier generations. This group of people is likely to be interested in flexibility, work-life balance and feel, being considerably different values to those of older generations. Previous generations may have valued their organisational type, or the career, where the career may have been linked to status of home, job longevity and loyalty. The intergenerational value differentiations may be stark, where tension, conflict and distrust are possible. The sort of differences likely to exist are that one generation may cherish employment stability, whilst another may value personal time, travel and play.

Tolerance may need to be promoted in organisations as the cross-generational working relationships may be more complex in this new age. Organisations of the future are more likely to encounter cross-generational, multicultural and multireligious differences, occurring more frequently in multinational organisations. The knowledge sharing, career development and mentoring requirements of employees will not easily be achieved unless an organisation acknowledges the diversity and varied requirements of employees.

In previous times, employers may not have approved staff taking a six-month extended holiday without notice, yet in the new age a millennial employee may require such flexibility. Employers may need to redesign and consider past processes and policies in order to be flexible and modern for millennial employees. Where flexibility is achieved to the satisfaction of staff, it is more likely that staff may increase their longevity, engagement and loyalty. Flexibility requirements are not restricted to the merely the young, as some approaching retirement may prefer to work into later life, whilst others may prefer part time work or career change. It may be that the older semi-retired employee can even be utilised to mentor others, perform short-term assignments or training that will assist knowledge retention and cohesion.

Inflexible organisations with fixed views on employment times, conditions and leave may not attract and retain employees as they may have done previously. Staff requirements are not likely to be homogenous, signified by variations between generations, culture and religions. Organisations will likely need to consider how to avoid internal tension arising from demographic variances. Of course, tensions caused by divergences between staff requirements will need to be monitored and explained as some staff may be confused if some but not all are allowed work part time, others casual or from home. The organisation that retains inflexible practices may fail to attract and retain younger employees or encourage older staff to retire early.

Question 2.13. A young marketing assistant approaches their employer, says they 'don't like this job any more' and resigns. The employer knows that the employee is very good at maths and computer skills and very well liked by the customers and colleagues. As the employer values loyalty and career, the employer says 'fine, I can see that you are not interested in this role', then asks for a resignation date.

How might the employer above responded differently to the marketing assistants comment about not liking the job? What benefits may have been achieved if the employer had been more open to career change or flexibility for the aforementioned marketing assistant?

Summary

Disruption forms are widespread as the world enters 2019 and beyond, changes in society will likely occur as a result. Globalisation has aided the interconnectivity in the world, where a change can flow suddenly with fast speed and organisations will likely have to respond at similar speed. The disruptions discussed earlier were included for those seeking a breadth of understanding of the issues management and leadership of organisations need to understand in order to operate. Whether management is from technical backgrounds of engineering, HR, nursing, accounting or operations, the disruption effects are likely to require appreciation of current events well outside of one's functional base. Likewise, a broad range of organisations are likely to be involved in disruption effects for many years to come including medicine, manufacturing, services and finance amongst many more.

Communication tools are now so common and capable that almost every world protest, world event, crises or accident will likely be spread immediately to an audience far from the originating event. The speed and uninterrupted, unedited and unverified nature of new age information has the potential to panic individuals, organisations and markets. The dissemination of information in the new age is no longer controlled by government or mainstream media as it once did, potentially proliferating even in countries that still restrict media, including that of Russia, China or Syria. Organisations, like citizens, are but side-players in this globalised world, where reaction and analysis of emerging events may be critical to success.

Chapter 2 has discussed many new age changes that either have occurred or may emerge. Globalisation has increased the pace of change and the inter-connectedness of organisations be that through trade, geopolitics, investment, communication or employee attitudes. The new age currently presents many challenges, where faster and higher quantities of change are likely into the future. The nature of disruption and its various forms introduce new threats and opportunities to the organisation as changes can occur and influence the organisation without notice. The nature of the emerging disruptions is one that organisational leadership and management will likely need to monitor and respond to. Whilst technology is likely to disrupt organisations into the future, it is AI that is the most technology disruption type that may transform society and organisations alike, thus discussed in Chapter 3.

Chapter 3

Organisational Implications of Artificial Intelligence

AI does not mean no humans; it will just change the way things work.
—Mathew Donald

Artificial intelligence (AI) may be transformational (Boyd & Holton, 2018), where the concept of automation and AI have been discussed in the literature since as early as the 1970s (Felsen, 1975). The amount of data available in repositories may have exceeded the human capability to process (Crombez & Dahms, 2015), where AI may now even be an essential element to operate them. Science fiction has imagined for over 50 years that AI may emerge to rival the human race (Benson, 2018); yet to date, that has not occurred. A more robust definition for the term AI may be required in the future should quality, ethics or other legal matters present as AI develops (Lehman-Wilzig, 1981). AI may also have elements of games, mimicking human thought and products for use by humans (Parnas, 2017). As AI emerges, there will be new product opportunities, whilst there is a societal risk of dislocation and widespread unemployment in its wake (Makridakis, 2017), where new skills may be required (Engelbrecht, 2017).

Smartphones today have vast computing power, connectivity to Internet and social media, with many including location and the global positioning systems (GPS) and other advanced technologies. These new technologies impact on individual and organisational communication, information and transactions amongst many others. Many new cars are already fitted with computers that control engines, many with smartphones or GPS capabilities and thus driving is already vastly different to that in 1980. As was discussed in Chapter 2, there are many changes emerging, where new AI and other technology may be positive in terms of economics and efficiency (Caruso, 2018), yet the change may also be associated with negative risks.

AI revolution may be more pronounced and transformational than the automation of the twentieth century, potentially involving more human impact than the industrial revolution of the nineteenth century. The earlier revolutions were

Leading and Managing Change in the Age of Disruption and Artificial Intelligence, 57–74
Copyright © 2019 by Emerald Publishing Limited
All rights of reproduction in any form reserved
doi:10.1108/978-1-78756-367-420191004

characterised by job losses, yet not all change effects were negative and new opportunities emerged (Dombrowski & Wagner, 2014). The industrial revolution was not limited to a few individual organisations as whole industries were affected and many were lost together, where past skills were lost. The industrial revolutions of the past changed organisational structures, processes and affected employee relations and thus the future new age may lead to similar societal and organisational changes. It is envisaged already that AI may affect library operations (Arlitsch & Newell, 2017), grain production (Patrício & Rieder, 2018) or even daily water forecasting (Seo, Kim, Kisi, & Singh, 2015) amongst many other changes. Organisational effectiveness and survival may be at stake given the potential for AI to transform the future, where organisations that identify, analyse and react promptly with a level of innovation may be those best to take advantage. This remainder of Chapter 3 considers how emerging AI may cause or influence organisational change.

AI and Human Interactions

AI may yield significant benefits to organisations that adopt the technology including time savings, complexity reductions, work elimination and efficiency, cost savings or ease. Whilst AI may, in the longer term, create new industries, it is in the short and medium term that it will likely reduce or eliminate human work (Needleman, 2017). Whilst some organisations may prefer to initially keep their job levels stable on ethical or moral grounds, it is likely once significant advantages present workplace stability may be impossible. Despite the potential for AI to eliminate a vast number of jobs, staff will likely remain in some form in areas that AI cannot to some extent organisations, where the new age issues may likely surround the interactions between AI and humans.

Driverless cars are but one emerging AI technology, where some are already be willing to pay premiums for the technology (Daziano, Sarrias, & Leard, 2017) and forecasts abound about significant consumer advantages once various technical issues are resolved (Olson, 2017). Some believe in the potential benefits of driverless vehicles and are already committing to large volumes of them (Gibbs, 2017), yet the benefits of driverless cars are still to be proved. Driverless vehicles could transform the taxi industry and eliminate thousands of drivers' work, or alternately the whole concept may prove too expensive or difficult and the change may never emerge. Recently, there was widespread publicity around an early reported death in a driverless car (Boudette, 2018) that may lead to investor re-evaluation of the technology in the future. As with other disruptions the future is unknown, where organisations will need to evaluate the future risk and opportunity of driverless cars.

Early forms of AI are already emerging, where voice recognition forms have already partially replaced call centre staff, where algorithms continue to emerge and attempt to improve the customer experience and replace humans. Social media is another space where emerging technology is attempting to improve the customer experience, although mere algorithms may not be the answer (Passariello, 2017). New smartphones readily synthesise the phone location with social media in an attempt to improve information, posts and various advertising for the user and new hardware has increased speed. Technology may soon be able to know enough about an individual's preferences, location and purchasing so that a smartphone may be able to suggest to the user places of interest, shops, restaurants and advertising (Gogolin & Gogolin, 2017). Smartphones and social media may be able shortly have sufficient understanding to rival what a close friend may be able to suggest. It is conceivable that as the smartphone is so connected and important that it may be on day miniaturised and even implanted.

Whilst the technology of today may not have as yet reached the full potential of AI, it is already impacting organisational structures, processes and employment (Subramanian, 2017). A number of organisations have already outsourced non-core activities (Kuzmina, 2016), including the IT function (Geis, 2010) and outsourced help desk services (Amcher, 2010). New governance protocols may be required to gain the benefits (Handley, 2017) of the outsourcing change. Outsourcing is often implemented due to perceptions and promises of increased efficiency that is associated with automated ticket tracking, smart email systems, key performance indicators (KPI) and other automated systems. Organisations may even attempt to achieve improved efficiency and effectiveness by outsourcing through activity-based models (Bals & Turkulainen, 2017).

The above discussion indicates that organisations are already embracing technology and some are outsourcing in a pursuit of reduced costs and other advantages. As the ratio of human resources reduces due to AI, some argue that human concerns around the changed relationships should be studied (Lemaignan, Warnier, Sisbot, Clodic, & Alami, 2017). It will be prudent for organisations to now commence identification of potential human issues should AI emerge in their organisation, as the process of change may be better analysed and planned for. AI, at the present time, has limited ability to monitor and improve related processes and thus, for now, process improvement will likely remain with staff or management to monitor, analyse and recommend improvements. Whilst AI is in its infancy, there will be requirements for the organisation to oversee and blend AI capability with their staff skills.

It is likely that early forms of AI that may replace humans in the workplace in areas that are perceived as simple, repetitive, transactional or predictable as those will require the least amount of AI advances and programming. As computing power expands, it is likely that AI will increase its potential to take on higher-level more complex roles in the future. As many programmes are already performing beyond the human capability (Strickland, 2017), it is possible to imagine that AI may, at some point, be able to think independently, autonomously create or even communicate in various forms. Alternately, it may be that AI lacks intelligence that is critical and thus could hurt society (Kraus, 2018). The nature of AI replacing staff roles and interfering with current human interactions should be of concern to organisations that are planning for AI. Staff required for the new age may need to be more analytical and comfortable working with less human interactions, where the new work types may be considerably different to the past.

The nature of organisations and work is already changing, where it is now possible to make a doctor appointment over the Internet or buy goods or services without any human interactions. Customers may already be engaging with these new forms of organisational experience on convenience grounds, where organisations may also be benefiting from the labour cost avoided. As with most changes of the new age, there will be divergence between customer preferences, where some may like less human involvement, whilst others may not have the education or technology to be so satisfied. This customer diversity will present as an opportunity to those organisations that are able to bridge emerging gaps by offering new solutions to the elderly, the disabled or the poor that may be inhibited and disadvantaged by the new technology.

Organisations that introduce AI may require employees with higher skills to use the emerging technology, where more complex computer skills, complex analytics or decision-making skill may be useful. The increase of logic and mathematical skills required in staff of the new age may create bias and lead to a lack of creativity in the staff retained and thus an organisation may have to reconsider and balance its skill requirements once AI emerges. Until AI is able to perform the higher end tasks, an organisation may likely still require skills of creativity, competition, analysis and marketing. Whilst having great computer and math skills may be useful to review and analyse AI data, staff may still be required to still understand and make appropriate decisions or add organisational value.

Workplace games have been associated with organisational change (Donald, 2017) as well as sense-giving (Drori & Ellis, 2011) and thus influencing further change in the new age may be more difficult once there are fewer staff employed. Organisational processes and culture may need to change in order to provide sufficient games, human interaction and sense-giving in the future for staff. Failure to appreciate the new age requirements, including the changed human to AI interactions, may result in declining organisational productivity. A lower ratio of humans within an organisation may also increase the relative importance of those employees remaining as it may be harder to replace the skills they hold. The labour market may also be affected by the new age changes as there may be an excess of skills in areas of high redundancy, and shortages in other areas required for the AI new age. AI may result in fewer employees overall, whilst the remaining employees within an organisation may have additional power to negotiate higher pay and more flexibility.

Corporate image may be affected in the new age where employee roles are being eliminated and replaced by AI and thus redundancies and changes may be best implemented in a socially and ethical way. Failure to retrain past employees or respond in a socially responsible manner may attract poor publicity, staff or union revolt, or suffer poor employee engagement. Training, flexibility and organisational culture may be a few key elements requiring change in the new age so as to avoid organisational value losses. It is clear that AI is emerging and likely to have serious impacts on organisational systems, structures and staff, where the remaining roles are likely to be more highly skilled. Organisations are likely to face challenges on the required skill sets required going forward, where the way those decision are decided, communicated and implemented may have consequences for the value and income in the future.

AI–AI Interactions or Communications

As AI emerges there will be reductions in staff numbers, yet the potential business-to-business (B2B) growth and the increased sophistication of AI over time that may eliminate whole industries or whole professions. B2B sharing of data and communications directly between computers began a number of years ago, where the extent of this exchange has increased substantially. New markets may emerge from B2B (Strasser, Weiner, & Albayrak, 2015) that may partially offset the reduced staff numbers required as B2B emerges. Despite the gloomy outlook for employment as AI emerges, it may be comforting to foresee that staff will likely be required to do the programming, maintenance and the improvements in AI for at least the short-to-medium term. These B2B relations also require communication protocols, checks and balances to ensure that there is accuracy and prompt information transmission and thus work in the area may increase in the short term.

B2B interactions are complex requiring the development of specific methodologies to manage the growth (Sierra, 2004). Although the B2B relationship may at first appear to be one of pure data interactions, the concept has now been linked to brand (Veloutsou & Taylor, 2012), where related value may emerge beyond the setup costs. There may be inequities in the B2B relationship as one organisation may have more power than another, where legal changes may be required to address the imbalance (Abdollah Dehdashti, 2018). Organisations operating in B2B may seek to change their focus from traditional concepts of customer, where new models of stakeholder or broader sustainability may be required (Sheth & Sinha, 2015). Laws have been slow to respond and market competition is high (Wise & Morrison, 2000), thus B2B may emerge ahead of legal boundaries.

Whilst it is likely that B2B will proliferate in the future, new and heightened risk will likely associate with this change (Paluch & Wünderlich, 2016). The perceived B2B risk may vary significantly between that of the provider and the customer (Paluch & Wünderlich, 2016), where the risk perception may even influence the way technology evolves. In an attempt to increase speed and use of the B2B technology, new interfaces will likely be required (Friede, 2017). As organisational interdependence will likely be high with B2B, any upgrades or changes in one organisation may adversely impact another organisation in terms of cost, time or data transfer. Organisations that are customers, or are otherwise in the more powerful positions, may be able to excerpt influence to avoid or reduce their share of change costs in B2B relationships.

B2B and even AI-to-AI may increase risk associated with the complexity related to so many interdependent systems required, where the information sharing and connectivity may require new IT approaches (Bandyopadhyay, 2012). A system change in one part of the interconnectivity in B2B may affect multiple other relationships, simultaneously affecting both customers, suppliers and financial institutions. Even the sales function will likely change in a B2B environment that may change the level of interactions direct with customers (Sharma, 2007). Organisations that cannot adjust to changes in time, or cannot manage the quality required, or cannot limit costs involved may incur loss in trade if they lose connectivity with others. Power may be enhanced with B2B (Joseph & Degabriele, 2001) and thus organisations with high influencing skills may achieve lower costs of change or diminishing risk than those without.

As B2B emerges into a more sophisticated tool in the new age, possibly enhanced by AI, it is possible that the less powerful small-to-medium-sized organisations will be forced to bear higher proportions of costs in connectivity advances. Divergence in B2B access or cost share may result in lower opportunity and market efficiency, despite the potential for improvement. The moral and competitive issues resulting from B2B developments may increasingly cause concern for society and law makers. Organisations of all sizes may require access to B2B in order to survive and thus identifying market improvements and interconnectivity may be new areas of skill required. Risk appreciation and appropriate mitigation or negotiations may be essential to avoid being disadvantaged as B2B continues to advance.

AI Creativity

There is likelihood that business-to-customer (B2C) will also utilise AI, despite its distinct differences to B2B (Iankova, Davies, Archer-Brown, Marder, & Yau, 2018). B2C occurs when the organisation directly interfaces with the customer be that via the Internet or social media. The emergence of B2C with AI will likely require sophisticated testing to ensure new product information is accurate (Iqbal, 2017). In recent times, there has been an explosion of apps, related logarithms and data mining emerging with new electronic products, advertising forms and customer intelligence gathering. AI may emerge in conjunction with B2B or B2C, where AI may commence with human commands and evolve into one of independent thoughts (Davenport & Kirby, 2016). The initial phases of AI may replace mundane and repeatable tasks; yet in the longer term, they may have a potential to eliminate whole industries and thereby affect society more broadly.

The new age business models may be vastly different to those of the past, as AI will by its nature cause disruption to past competitive value models. Organisations can already exist without sales of product or sales of services, where organisational value can even now be generated from the number of times a website or social media site is opened. Creativity may be essential in the new age in order to use the emerging platforms and generate value from them. It is already apparent that some apps may already be able to reduce costs, improve service and improve health care (Williams, 2012).

Advanced AI that rivals the human mind may likely require more proficient hardware and software that can perform fast calculations and be of a useful size. The full range of AI capabilities is still hard to predict with any certainty, yet it is likely that AI may yet transform human life as it replaces repetitive and mundane work, be it at home, at leisure or in the workplace. There is already a widespread speculation that AI may advance into driverless vehicles, self-functioning homes or robots that can perform household chores and thus there will likely be many

AI-associated new business opportunities associated with new product develop-ment, product sales, maintenance and integration. Organisations that are crea-tive, innovative or entrepreneurial may find significant advantage as new business opportunities present in this new age of AI.

Speed to market may be important in the new age, as organisational inter-connectedness may enhance the discovery of changes or opportunities to occur simultaneously. Organisations that are open and ready to understand AI may gain competitive advantages, yet they will still require sufficient skills and resources to achieve the gains. In order to identify AI early, organisations may need to regu-larly scan traditional and social media for new information, or attend trade shows or read conference proceedings. Failure to understand new AI in a reasonable time frame may leave an organisation vulnerable as competitors may implement AI before a late adopter and gain advantage.

Whilst robots have been discussed since the 1970s (Synnelius, 1974; Yone-moto & Shiino, 1977), the technology has largely been limited to the indus-trial sphere. Despite the hype around the potential for robots with AI in the past, it is only now that robots are emerging as a potential for the mass market consumer, where their potential uses include laundry folding (Kazuaki, 2015), personalisation (Miro Xavier, Kuhn, & Brayda, 2008), food preparation (Sony, U.S. Univ. to Develop Home-Use Food Preparation Robot, 2018), healthcare (Dahl, 2014) and even face recognition (Kwak, 2009). Robot proliferation may be dependent on social behaviours (de Graaf, Ben Allouch, & van Dijk, 2017), rather than just any technology capability. The rise of robots may be dependent on the emergence of capabilities that are perceived as useful and are offered at a reasonable price.

The advances in robots and AI are dependent upon future connectivity speeds, safety, accuracy and flexibility. Consumers are likely to require rigour-ous testing and proof before they step into driverless cars or trust robots to clean their house. Robot use will not likely be limited to the home as they may evolve into performing organisational tasks, such as workplace cleaning, replica-tion of repeatable tasks and even elementary maintenance tasks. Whilst it is not clear as to the exact timing of complete robot and AI capability, organisations may already wish to consider potential related implementation issues, technol-ogy issues and staff acceptance issues. Organisational opportunities arising from robots and AI are likely to be reduced costs of labour, improved processes and increased capabilities amongst others. The mere inclusion of connectivity, GPS and facial recognition may be insufficient for robot and AI advancement, as products using these new capabilities may have to be invented or developed.

Whilst robots and AI may replace human activity in a number of areas, there will be opportunities arising from their implementation. Until all facets of human work are replaced, there will be humans required for assessments, problem solv-ing and maintenance in respect to both AI and robots. Staff may seek to resist changes and job losses that may inhibit benefits associated with AI or robots, or they may perceive robots as impersonal and lacking human etiquette. There is high potential for environments lacking human interaction to be perceived by staff as lonely, lacking fun and meaning. Successful organisations in the new age may be those that are more creative and able to better satisfying remaining staff requirements.

The staffing skills of the new age are likely to be different than the past, as the inclusion of AI and robots may require more technical or analytical skills. Workplaces may have less humans, or less face-to-face interfaces and more electronic communication in the future, where not all personality types may be so suited to the new forms of work. Organisations may even have to consider specialised training and selection routines to ensure that staff are not stressed when working constantly with AI and robots. Whilst some may believe that the technology revolution has already occurred, it is clear that most computers are not AI, are still under human control and do not think independently.

Organisations that wish to retain or improve their competitive advantage will likely commence strategic reviews of AI and robot phenomenon early, identifying potential risks and opportunities ahead of the change. The nature of society is likely to be affected once AI and robots are widely adopted and thus early identification, consideration and planning for the future changes may greatly assist an organisation in preventing, or at least minimising associated disruption. Creativity may be a requirement for the future as the new age will likely change staffing skills and change human interface dynamics, whilst also influencing new organisational structures and processes.

Question 3.1. What sort of issues may emerge with the widespread introduction of AI and robots in to the workplace? How might an organisation prepare for the change and diminish negative effects?

Hint: Find and read current journal articles under new technology, AI or robots topics.

Androids, Auto-updates and Model Changes

The new age is unlikely to be characterised as a single event; rather, it is more likely that it will evolve over time as multiple waves of transformational changes. Any new systems or products of the future may involve continuous change between multiple versions, multiple systems and multiple models. Organisational success will not be limited to a mere single product or market as organisations will likely be multi-connected to customer, supplier and many other systems. As new and old versions of product or AI may co-exist, new complexity and issues are likely to emerge. Unlike most of the systems that are still currently under predominant human control, the future systems and new products may one day be under the control of AI or robots, where increased communication issues, connectivity issues and update issues may result.

Differentiation in product and systems may be required for manufacturers, programmers and product sellers to create competitive advantage. If a robot arm manufacturer produces a new more capable arm, it will have to choose how to integrate it with pre-existing robots and AI systems, choices will be required in terms of the hardware, software and interface technology. The future choices in relation to AI or robots may have serious secondary effects as there may be complex interconnectivity, where it may be unlikely for any single organisation will own or control the whole supply chain. The automobile industry has out-sourced many of its parts manufacture that required it to create its own systems to manage the related logistics (Trappey, Trappey, Chang, & Huang, 2010). As it occurs now, operating systems auto update constantly without intervention of the consumer, this approach may be problematic where AI and robots are heav-ily interconnected, as a simple system update may have the potential to inad-vertently leave pre-existing robots without a pathway to adopt a new capability.

The early adoption of AI and robots may have advantages associated with reduced cost, efficiency and customer service, yet early adopters incur increased integration and compatibility risk, error risk or communication risk. In order to organisations implementing, AI or robots will not only have to consider change benefits, but also have to consider potential downside risk, past and future tech-nology. For the risk averse, there will be temptation to be a late adopter, yet being last in the new age may also have heightened risk. These are considerable issues that the organisation will need to consider now and into the future, where the risk profile accepted will affect returns to shareholders and other stakeholders. The customer appetite for risk and new technology will also need to feature when an organisation decides how it will operate in the new age.

Organisations adopting either AI or robots, may find that their traditional governance systems unready or unwilling to support new age changes. Assess-ment of new projects or new products may currently involve the organisation calculating net present value (NPV) as a tool to assist decision making. Assump-tions required in NPV calculations include estimates of future costs and benefits, market penetration and competition where usually these calculations include parameters that are reasonably estimable. These calculations may be too diffi-cult or unreliable in the new age, as early adopters of AI or robots may find it extremely difficult to reliably estimate the parameters required and assign value to the associated risks. Risks required for competent completion of calculations may include assumptions around longevity, redundancy, maintenance, upgrades and future interconnectivity, in a fast-paced new age these may not always be known in time.

Assessment of new parameters and assessment of risk is not new to organisa-tions, it may be the pace of change and lack of reliable information that may add complexity to decision making in the new age. Redundancy may be difficult to assess also in the new age as advances may occur frequently and quickly. Organi-sations that accept risk without due assessment in the new age may open their organisation up to financial, reputation and survival risks. Governance and other stakeholders may quickly lose confidence in management, should unidentified risk lead to losses. Risk assessment in the new age should consider scenarios that are unlikely or potentially impossible to predict at the time.

Early adoption risk may occur when new technology does not perform to expectations, or if it is found to be faulty due to insufficient testing, or if it injures occur or if the technology frustrates the customers. Significant time and competitive pressures may tempt organisations to early adopt new technology, yet any consequential failure will likely be visible around the world through the Internet and social media. Entrepreneurs may be well positioned in the new age to promote new technology and gather support and funding for new ideas, where they may wish to take risks despite the uncertainty.

> *Question 3.2.* How might an organisation, as discussed below, implement widespread robot adoption in a retail environment whilst minimising risk? Identify the risks associated with this change and indicate how you may control and mitigate these. What residual risks may occur despite the control measures?

> *Scenario*: Imagine the scenario where new robots have been chosen to replace hundreds of employees across a global retail organisation. The robots will serve customers, wrap purchases and transact sales. The decision to change was based on perceived customer acceptance of the new technology, efficiency and reductions in labour costs. Senior management has recently received approval from stakeholders to adopt the robots, only to find after dismissing employees that the technology was flawed and the required fixes may be delayed for months.

An organisation today is likely to be quite familiar with the seamless software updates to their enterprise resource programmes (ERP), smartphone updates and associated complexity and risk. In the new age updates, version and model changes are likely to occur more frequently. There will likely be increased risk associated with changes that may occur simultaneously and not be controlled by any single organisation. The changes of the new age may be initiated by competitors, customers, banks and suppliers where the increased frequency of change and interconnectedness may create heightened risk exposures. New risk assessment and control measures may be required in order to satisfy internal governance, financiers or other stakeholders. Organisations with time pressures to cope with change will increasingly be required to choose between in-house or external resources, where each may have additional risk associated.

Communication and Information

Since the emergence of higher computing power, organisations over time have embraced the Internet, email and social media, where adoption may have been based on differences in cost, efficiency, customer or even brand recognition and advertising. The adoption of new technology has been so fast over the past 10 years that many of the inherent risks may not have been considered prior to adoption.

Many organisations now have a profile on social media including Facebook, where associated data may have been collected from the initial setup and posting of information. These social media accounts may have been set up for competitive reasons or to increase trade, where associated informational risk may not have been considered by many organisations. It was quite a disruption in March 2018 when Mr Mark Zuckerberg revealed the Facebook organisation had sold customer data without their knowledge, where some private information may have also been used to target individuals during the US presidential election. At US congressional hearings, later in 2018, Mr Zuckerberg was asked to explain about the sale of private customer information, where some now speculate new ethical standards may be required (Gross, 2018). It is clear now that information in the new age has value, where the new AI and computing power may be able to reveal trends and relationships. It is yet to be determined if any organisations previously assessed social media risk in relation to sales of private data, nor is it clear how organisations may identify and control similar risks in the future.

Data and computing power associated with the new age are already large and continue to grow, where, according to Moore's Law, it may continue to double every two years (Ramana, 2013). Whilst data of this new age may have benefits for society, the new technologies have seemingly been used negatively by Russia to influence a recent USA presidential election (Ziegler, 2017) and by the government in Myanmar against the Muslim Rohingya (Fink, 2018). The potential for data and social media to be part of fake news or used in more sinister ways presents important risks for organisations of today. It is now possible for organisations to associate, encourage or just like, social media posts that may eventuate in them inadvertently perpetrating or promoting an injustice. Some organisations are emerging to work against misinformation (Kuchler, 2017). It is also likely that a poor social media association may lead to the loss of public support, sales, reputation or value; therefore, organisations may need to be proactive reviews in attempting to mitigate this risk.

In 1950 or even in 1970 data could be secured through physical means through safes, security systems and security officers; yet today, physical controls are insufficient, due in part to interconnectivity of systems and availability of small storage devices like the USB. Employees, customers and suppliers amongst many others hold large amounts of data, which may be at risk of theft, public revelation via social media, Internet and email. Despite the risk that is inherent in the interconnectedness of the organisational systems, it may be argued that the transfer of corporate data illegally, or even inadvertently, is relatively low.

Competitive advantage may be inherent in the organisations systems, data and relationships so any revelation to the public or competitors of that data may leave an organisation open to legal claims if the use of private information leads to injury. Data can easily be collected on a USB, uploaded to the Internet or simply emailed out to competitors with relative ease and thus an organisation of the new age requires great attention to data integrity and security risks. Deliberate or inadvertent public data release by internal staff may be higher than that of the hacker. In recent times, several large organisations have revealed publicly that their customer data had been hacked, creating consequential risk that the customers affected. Some customers may choose to not trade with organisations that cannot manage their private data.

The systems and controls involved in securing an organisation's network are complex and resource heavy. Many managers of today, and into the future, may not have the skills to manage, mentor and control the IT department in their organisation, nor may they view the risk as core to the business. Professional standards apply to many including audit, accounting and legal that may also include government legislation to increase the importance. Small- to medium-sized organisations may not have the IT resources or skills to operate at high professional standards and this exposes them to an additional risk. Larger organisations may have risk committees and internal audit that evaluate and report on the organisation's IT standards. Data security is evolving over time and is increasingly emerging as a more complex organisational component to manage. The disruption involved in exposure of IT systems and data could affect organisational value, careers and markets and thus organisations of the new age will be required to assess risk and mitigate in order to survive.

Question 3.3. Assume that you are not from an IT-specific background or have qualifications in that area. What would your IT management plan include? How would you ensure that the organisation has adequate security systems? What key risks can you identify and how would you mitigate those risks?

As organisational data and communication is now inextricably linked and interconnected to internal and external parties, the IT department and associated controls may need to be considered as core to the operation. The costs and resources to manage the risks associated with IT and data may be considerable, although the effect of risks associated may be far greater. The issue may be greatest for the small organisation that may not have the skills or resources to manage the risk internally, where increasingly they may be required to use outsourced providers for security and the technical. Whilst some entrepreneurs or small organisations may seek to limit IT costs, or restrict related controls, the restrictions may need to be compared with the potential harm related, if key data are lost or stolen.

Workplace Standards and Collective Bargaining

Whilst AI and robotics may be introduced to an organisation as an efficiency or cost-saving exercise, the remaining employed staff may be unhappy with the changes. There is already speculation that law (Hildebrandt, 2018), accounting (Flesher & Martin, 1987) and other professional services may be replaced by AI in the near future despite those areas not having previously been considered for AI deployment. Whilst AI may be fast and able to offer new forms of knowledge in the future, there is little evidence yet that AI is capable of extensive creativity or providing opinion and advice.

Question 3.4. A business case indicates that 100 nurses and catering staff can now be replaced by AI and robotic combination. The funds saved from this change will allow the organisation to purchase additional life-saving equipment.

Write a detailed response to the board opposing the replacement of nurses and catering staff. In your response, please consider strategy, competition, customer, skills and risk. The operational and financial aspects of the business case strongly support the new AI technology being implemented.

Despite AI that is envisaged, humans will be employed in organisations to some extent for the foreseeable future, albeit in lesser numbers. Humans will likely be increasingly required to work with and around AI or robots, where in the long-run staff may be required to follow robot or AI instruction. Staff remaining in work after AI is implemented may do so only because the task cannot be performed by AI or it is not cost effective. As the new age is likely to be characterised by waves of change, the possibility of future redundancy may be high in the mind of staff, leading to constant stress and worry. If the change is not managed to the satisfaction of staff or society, unions and collectives may form to fight against the changes. Organisations will be challenged in their implementation of AI or robots, where maintaining healthy relationships with staff and society may be difficult.

Organisational Structures with AI

In the reduction of staff numbers over time as AI is introduced, various traditional organisational structures and processes may no longer be appropriate. Structures that previously required escalation from a front-line staff member up to supervisors for approval may no longer be required once AI is able to follow pre-programmed pathways and make independent decisions. The organisation may implement new process rules where AI is perceived as more efficient and reliable.

Once AI and robotics are able to recognise the human voice consistently further advances into call centres and helplines may be possible where even AI decisions may be more reliable, more efficient, with lower operating costs than their human predecessors. This is not to say that all AI and robots will work smoothly and be preferred by customers, resistance at the customer level is likely where they cannot understand or see benefits. As the new age will embody prototypes, new technology and new integration, the pathways to success will not always be smooth, where errors and issues will likely arise during the transition and thus requiring planning and management.

Until AI or robots emerge sufficiently capable to replace humans, it is likely that humans will be retained to programme software, integrate systems, wire hardware and investigate or fix any emerging errors. Remaining staff roles post AI are likely to be unique or situational, requiring thought and programming, where the human role may likely continue to diminish over time. Staff that remain in employment may never acknowledge AI as being able to perform tasks any better than humans, where leadership may be required to improve staff relationships.

Staff in the early phases of AI or robots may initially be more customer focussed, more empathetic and able to resolve complex issues the new age technology. Initially, staff may have authority to override and intervene in robot or AI routines and decisions, yet that authority may not continue once there is reliability achieved by the new technology. Robots and AI may follow strict guidelines, whereas the human response may be variable and able to attach emotions in order to resolve issues. There may even be significant value divergence between robots and humans if the staff cannot agree with the new stricter processes. The loss of staff authority to make change decisions may confuse or be perceived with distrust by staff as their opinions and recommendations may be held with less importance than those created by AI. Individual staff may no longer be measured not in efficiency, speed or cost as those may be under the control of AI, rather the human KPI may in the future be set towards process improvement, customer satisfaction or process instead. Organisations will need to consider the different responsibilities, measures and motivators as staff motivations and relations are likely to be quite different in the new age.

Staff may already be exposed to machines that act independently and activate bells or lights on factory floors or in control rooms that are based on criteria set in a programmable logic controller (PLC). Organisations have used PLC for controlling factories, power stations and mines for over 30 years, where the alarms are used to target investigation or maintenance to particular process points triggering the alarms. It is possible that AI may further disrupt those industries by replacing control room staff entirely as it may be able to resolve underlying issues autonomously. Staff remaining in such industries may only be retained only to perform tasks that robots may be incapable of or they may be retained to resolve new unrecorded issues. The staff required for factory and mining operations after AI is implemented may need to hold higher skills, with more flexibility, more creativity and more overall system knowledge than those employed previously.

Whilst the exact nature of the future is difficult to determine clearly, there is great potential for AI or robots to change organisations and replace staff roles. Organisations will likely require constantly changing processes, structures and delegations in an attempt to adapt and maintain competitive advantage. Staff that remain in the new age will likely be required to complete new tasks together with higher skills and knowledge than ever before. The nature of the new roles, structures and processes required in the new age will consequently affect stakeholders, customers and suppliers to some extent. The short- to medium-term will likely still require human oversight, intervention, creativity and risk identification and thus the implications and strategies arising from the impending AI emergence is further discussed in Chapters 4 and 5.

Service and Maintenance: Trades Requirements

All will not be lost in the emerging AI and robot new age, as for some time humans will be required to service, fix or perform upgrades that may still require skills of various trades, programming, testing and performance improvement. Organisations that currently service mechanical devices or machines may find new opportunity in expanding or changing their operations over to supporting robots. Software programmers that currently write apps or support large ERPs may find that the rollout of AI and robots creates new opportunities to programme and integrate. Robots will have working parts that will require greasing, testing or repair and replacement, where many of those tasks may need to be performed by tradespeople until robots can perform on themselves. The maintenance of robots will also likely require scheduling, logistics, tools and staff organisation. New opportunities may arise for organisations that wish to offer robot service scheduling, customer liaison and staff.

Forecasting an end to organisations and staff numbers as a result of any rise in AI or robots may be too narrow and pessimistic. Organisations that can assess their core skills and competencies, with an element of creativity, may well be able to change their operations into producers of robot parts or able to service their needs. In industries such as vehicle and aeroplane manufacturers, mining or farming many interrelated service, support and maintenance activities occur in order for the core activities to occur. In a similar way, it is envisaged that robot or AI organisations may wish to focus on core activities and accept non-core activities be supplied by others and thus presenting large opportunity for those organisations that are willing and able to make a transition in the new age.

Version Controls and Advancement

Once AI and robots are more sophisticated and further integrated with other systems there will be additional complexity in upgrading them. Upgrades are not likely to be simple events, where multiple integration points may include multiple operating systems, GPS and various programme versions to contend with. Organisations may have numerous choices between versions, models and products, where the choice taken will have implications to capability and cost.

Late adopters of upgrades may be quite exposed to risk if their competitors adopt a change and the new features advance them in terms of efficiency, cost or market share. When an organisation is a late adopter, they may find it difficult and more expensive to follow or catch up later, as there may be additional costs and resources required to shorten timelines. Although early adopters of new technology will incur costs associated with development, trials and new interfaces, where there may also be additional risk in market acceptance. The choice to early or late adopt change may be difficult in this new age due to lack of information and time and thus may hinder good decision making. Version control complexity may be significant if organisations own whole fleets of robots, driverless cars and other AI-based product, where difficulties may rise with the number of products and systems that need to be integrated.

> *Question 3.5.* Consider an organisation that may have 1,000 robots, across five cities that were linked with GPS, various phone companies and satellite operating systems. A new robot version emerges that is twice as capable and fast as the current version. The organisation can afford to replace one third of the robot fleet but cannot get all the funds now. It may be three years before the organisation can replace the rest of the fleet. Competitors are already successfully in implementing the new technology and finding that customers prefer the new features over the previous models.

There are significant integration issues in implementing the new robots, where running two versions of the robots simultaneously may be impossible on cost grounds. Failure to adopt the new robotic features may result in a 50% loss in market share as customers appear to prefer the new robot features.

Write a report to your management on how might your organisation prepare for the situations above? What advice can you recommend for the organisation – should you adopt part of the fleet or something else? The report should include recommendations, including risk and uncertainty that you foresee.

Hint: Be creative and innovative in your proposed solution.

In a retail situation, there will be more than mere integration issues to be mindful of, as robots have working parts that may have the potential to harm customers. Experimentation and significant testing will be required as robots and drones emerge in order to rate them as safe and capable. Organisations may be tempted to trial new technology or to partially adopt, where increased integration risk, or costs, or market share and customer acceptance will need to be considered. In the past, there may have been times to consider new technology before implementation, where social media and other internet communication may now enable the new features to be advertised and implemented faster than an organisation may like.

As the new age may be characterised by fast version changes to multiple systems, simultaneously there will be significant redundancy to consider. In the past, there have been opportunities to recycle physical items once there became redundant including phones, cars and various parts. The potential for re-use and recycling in the new age may be heightened due to the pace and quantity of changes that may arise. The quantity of redundant models in the new age may be so large that many new opportunities for entrepreneurs, engineers and tradespeople to retrofit, re-use or scrap the older models. There will likely be trade in older part, PLCs and computer circuit boards in the new age as a similar trade already exists for older factory parts and even petroleum bowsers. New markets, related to old parts and old versions, are likely to emerge in the new age. Entrepreneurs may also emerge to create new opportunity and take advantage of the redundancies created, where the advantage will be based on their abilities to educate and convince stakeholders and financiers of their business cases.

Organisational Improvements

As AI and robots emerge they may initially be expensive, yet once they are mass produced economies of scale may result in far lower costs, where the lower costs will assist organisations of all sizes to participate in the change. It is already possible that organisations may exist only digitally, without necessarily having a physical presence, where systems are already being created to understand new customer ordering processes on line (Awojide, Arikhan, & Adeosun, 2018). In the new age, restaurants without real estate may erode the traditional restaurant business models, or apps may compete with the traditional hotel market, where each new model may change the way organisations operate.

Agility is likely to be important in this new age of almost constant change, new apps and other new technology will likely need to be monitored and assessed regularly. Any new technology may have potential to grow or limit operations, where potential may be associated with the ability of the organisation to understand and be creative. Traditional taxi and hotel markets have already underestimated the potential for Uber and Airbnb, thus losing a part of their respective markets, the fast adoption occurring where customers may have perceived lower costs or convenience.

New age technology will advance once capabilities are able to deliver significant benefits in terms of cost, efficiency or improvements to the customer. Any new technology, be it in the form of software, AI or robotics, will likely replace human roles if the originating tasks were transactional and easily repeatable. Until AI can perform creative, risk mitigation and advanced problem solving there are likely to be roles for humans in the workplace, where the highly skilled may be highly sought and have require new environments to work in. This changed nature of roles will likely encourage the remaining staff individually or collectively bargain for commensurate higher paid jobs. At a societal level, the new age may result in higher unemployment and thus creating issues for government, tax collection and social cohesion. Organisations may need to monitor societal change rather than merely focussing on competition or new products in the new age, as society will also be closely interconnected.

Summary

It is clear that as AI continues to emerge, there will be great change for society and organisations in the new age. The ensuing change is likely to affect organisations of all sizes, types and across the world. Organisations will be confronted with choices on what to adopt, when to adopt and how to change, where complete information may not be available in time for decision making. Organisational decisions are likely to revolve around staff numbers, skills, training, structures and processes when new age technology decisions arise. Redundancy may be another key consideration for organisations as the new may be upgraded and redundant in short amounts of time.

Whilst organisations may operate with less staff in the future, the relative importance of the remaining staff may be heightened and their bargaining power increased. Organisations will need to consider carefully the staff relations as they amend structures and processes as morale, happiness and stress may result when implementing AI or robots. It is likely that in this increased complexity related to ongoing change that organisations may require new leadership and management in the future, where the related issues are discussed in Chapters 4 and 5.

Chapter 4 assesses how disruption and AI will likely result in changes to the organisational leadership, yet some of the past behaviours may still be required and relevant. Chapter 5 commences with a discussion of management fundamentals followed by discussion on how those may change in the new age. Chapter 6 considers how the organisation dynamics may be affected in the new age. Finally, Chapter 7 reviews modern research on change, where a range of suggestions are offered for those wishing to be in leadership and management roles in this new age ahead.

Chapter 4

Leading Organisations in the New Age

Leadership qualities in the New Age will be challenged like never before.

—Mathew Donald

As discussed in chapters 1 and 2 of this book, disruption has emerged after globalisation advanced in the past 20 years. Chapters 2 and 3 have discussed how disruption may form in relation to many changes in the world including geopolitics, financial markets, world trade and climate policy amongst many others. Artificial intelligence (AI) is a particular form of disruption discussed in Chapter 3 that may affect organisations transformationally, where significant changes in structures, processes and risks may occur. New leadership skills will likely be required as disruption and AI emerge.

Chapter 4 commences with a discussion of leadership fundamentals, included here as a useful beginning for those newly studying this field, yet also included as an update for those already trained and experienced. The fundamentals form a base to assist those in leadership roles understand how they may need to change in the new age once disruption and AI emerge. This chapter considers the likely issues emerging for leadership in the new age, where the discussion aims to be informative and thought provoking in respect to the consequential effects and options. Leadership is not necessarily a natural nor a single quality, rather it is a learned skill that is open to all to learn and use.

Leadership Fundamentals

Leadership is a difficult term to define in the business world where it may relate to a wide range of behaviours from that of charismatic or fun, through to one of decision maker. Definitions of leadership are not clear or agreed, where there are calls for new definitions and new research into the topic (Sutherland, 2018), as there is also a lack of clear meanings for associated terms (Counts, Farmer, & Shepard, 1995). Identifying and understanding the various elements of leadership are important in the modern organisational context as it has been associated with organisational change (Donald, 2014, 2016, 2017) or may even be associated with organisational culture (Donald, 2017, 2018).

Leading and Managing Change in the Age of Disruption and Artificial Intelligence, 75–92
Copyright © 2019 by Emerald Publishing Limited
All rights of reproduction in any form reserved
doi:10.1108/978-1-78756-367-420191005

Leadership may be an ability to gather the voluntary support of followers (Etzioni, 1965), where the response of the follower is not necessarily a result of higher or formal authority (Tolbert & Hall, 2009) as it is a different level of influence (Katz & Kahn, 1978). The topic of leadership has been defined with four functions that include the mission of the organisation, the choice of method to achieve, integrity defence and resolving internal conflict (Selznick, 1957; Tolbert & Hall, 2009). Leadership should be considered as relating to an ability to influence, rather than one of authority, logic or control.

Organisational change may require leadership to create a vision (Bass, 1985a), where culture and leadership are linked to organisational performance (Belias & Koustelios, 2014). Leadership may need skills of support for those at the bottom, rather than merely driving the organisation from the top (Coulson-Thomas, 2013). Kindness has not normally been associated with the topic, yet ethics has (Thomas & Rowland, 2014) and unlike other organisational activities leadership is not related to merely the allocating of resources, developing systems and controls. Leadership has the potential to influence employee feelings, behaviours and efficiency, by inspiring participants to share a vision and explain what the organisational future will be (Kotter, 1996).

Management and leadership may often be perceived as overlapping concepts, yet they are likely to be competing skills (Kumle & Kelly, 2006). Leadership may be an element of management, yet not all managers are leaders, nor are all leaders managers. The topics of leadership and management are quite often interposed, where managers are less trained on leadership than is required. Management fundamentals are discussed in Chapter 5 of this book in the modern context of organisational change in relation the new age of disruption and AI. There are many academic books dedicated to leadership, where this book is focussed on leadership in the context of organisational change (Donald, 2017) that is likely to be very important to organisations of the future.

Leadership may be defined as being those qualities that involve inspiration, co-ordination, credibility (Schultz, 2013) and influence (Skvoretz & Fararo, 1996), which may have a potential to improve organisational change (Stanislavov & Ivanov, 2014) by a person with status (Piazza & Castellucco, 2014) or social influence (Chemers, 2014). Leadership qualities of motivation, communication and team building may be factors that improve an organisational change (Gilley, McMillan, & Gilley, 2009), where the absence thereof may be a barrier to change (Donald, 2017). Leadership qualities that may assist in moving an organisation forward include communication, trust and engagement (Donald, 2017).

It is not essential that leaders be extroverts as might commonly be thought as even introverts can be good leaders. The ease by which the stakeholders engage and embrace the organisational direction may be one measure of leadership performance. Although personality may be important to some forms of leadership as transformational leadership has been associated with extraversion, openness, together with conscientiousness, where other personality types may be negatively linked to other leadership styles (Zopiatis & Constanti, 2012). For over 40 years, openness has been associated with leadership, where factors of information and enticement (Weinberg, Smotroff, & Pecka, 1978) may be useful.

Leadership requires communication skills as a means to explain and advance organisational objectives and direction (Bawany, 2014; Mayfield & Mayfield, 2017), where communication was the most common factor associated with organisational change (Donald, 2017). Communication has many elements to consider including that of type, regularity, content, language, length and verbal or non-verbal forms. A simple general staff meeting is unlikely to be sufficient communication by leaders as the matter may be more complex. When communicating with the range of stakeholders, it is important to remember that the various audience each have varying requirements, personalities and available time. Direct communication may sound appealing, yet in the new age that will not always be possible due to distances, separate locations, varying languages and varying time zones. Some staff may prefer to listen to their peers rather than others and thus it may be useful to identify and engage with sense-givers when disseminating information (Drori & Ellis, 2011). The leadership function includes many factors and thus those considering leading may benefit from developing openness, support, listening, influence, and respect and responsibility elements.

Leaders do not explain where an organisation is going, as they have other responsibilities including ethics (Moore et al., 2018) and strategy to consider. There is recent research indicating that leadership can influence the behaviours of staff through their own moral actions and ethical decisions (Moore et al., 2018). Unethical organisational behaviours are a current topic that society is debating (Donald, 2018), where governance boards may need to consider and monitor more ethical leadership qualities in the future. It may be that those with strong internalised morals may be the most influential in preventing deviant behaviour in the organisation (Skubinn & Herzog, 2016) and thus an organisation may be able to identify and hire for those qualities.

Leadership has been linked to engagement and thus there may be benefits of including staff in organisational direction setting and decision making through engagement (Hsieh & Wang, 2015). It may be insufficient for leadership to set directions at the top or merely explaining or influencing as modern research indicates that engagement is required to change an organisation (Donald, 2017). For well over 60 years, there have been calls for leaders to increase engagement if they seek to improve organisational performance (Rice, 2012), where it has also been associated with transformational leadership (Shaughnessy, Quinn Griffin, Bhattacharya, & Fitzpatrick, 2018) and resilience.

Engagement may be where an employee is both dedicated to superior performance as well as confident about their own personal effectiveness (Cole, Walter, Bedeian, & O'Bolye, 2012; Maslach, Jackson, & Leiter, 1996). To be in a position to change the organisation, the support of stakeholders may be required (Clayton, 2014), where the engagement of stakeholders may be a key project management skill (Walker, Bourne, & Shelley, 2008). Engagement has been defined (Donald, 2017) as including communication, training and decision-making tools (Kelleher, 2009) that influence trust and performance (Sloan & Oliver, 2013), skills and communication (Hauck, 2014) and effectiveness (Cole et al., 2012; Maslach et al., 1996). Organisational performances may be dependent upon all staff levels to take responsibility for their actions (Smith & Sharma, 2002), including those in leadership positions.

Staff connection and engagement may firstly require leadership to be trusted by their staff. Trust may influence change implementations when combined with communication (Della Torre & Solari, 2013) or may be a factor influencing change itself (Donald, 2017). This is a particularly difficult matter for people in new leadership positions as trust is not automatic, likewise trust may not easily be improved if it has historically been low. It is particularly important to listen to staff if they disagree with a leadership position (Sheldon, 2018), as employee commitment may be dependent upon trust in the leadership (Xiong, Lin, Li, & Wang, 2016).

Whole courses and books have been written on leadership, where this section was included here as a refresher for the trained and as an introduction for the new learner. As a general guide, those with leadership ambitions should develop self-awareness of the topic and should consider developing the skills discussed in the previous section. Ongoing feedback from peers, subordinates and superiors in relation to leadership performance may greatly assist in improving self-awareness and other perspectives. Whilst leaders may on balance be quite confident and well communicated, they may lack skills of encouraging others for opinions or may not seek feedback from peers. Knowledge of one's own leadership skills and perceptions may assist the leader in changing their approach and potentially gaining additional influence. Mentoring programmes for early leadership roles may be very important in the early phases as discussion on improvements may be more difficult for the more experienced.

A summary of leadership qualities discussed above is included in Table 4.1, provided as an aide to those seeking leadership roles and as a checklist for those seeking to hire or mentor leadership staff in their organisation.

Table 4.1 indicates the task of the Leader is far more than just talking to staff and thus is more comprehensive than one may first expect. The LQAT could be used in the hiring criteria for new employees or be used to assess, mentor and feedback processes for those already in leadership positions. It may be considered that this sort of table is subjective and may be biased, depending upon the personality and agenda of the assessor, where additional value may be achieved if the tool is completed regularly over time or completed by multiple staff and peers. It is highly recommended that in using the LQAT, examples of behaviours should be given as a way of justifying the ratings and as a way to communicate the reasons. Those assessing leadership positions may find that they can create a gap analysis using the LQAT, where it may be possible for those in leadership positions to set improvement goals as a result.

Whilst some may hold characteristics of charisma or extroversion, it does not mean that they are necessarily leaders as leadership involves many aspects that are distinct from that of management. Leadership is more focussed on unifying the organisation, building harmony through respect, ethical behaviour and engagement. Whilst the topic is still yet to have a unifying definition, there are clear leadership factors that leaders can assess, develop and improve on. Organisations that can appreciate linkages between performance and leadership may

Table 4.1:   Leadership Qualities Assessment Table (LQAT).

Leadership Quality	Description	Assessment Score (Out of 10)
Support	Ability to gather positive support from followers (Etzioni, 1965) skills of support for those at the bottom, rather than merely driving the organisation from the top (Coulson-Thomas, 2013).	
Influence	The ability to influence (Katz & Kahn, 1978; Skvoretz & Fararo, 1996) without necessarily using power.	
Direction	The nature of the mission of the organisation, the choice of method to achieve, integrity defence and resolving an internal conflict (Selznick, 1957; Tolbert & Hall, 2009).	
Culture	The degree of shared assumptions, beliefs and values that are held dearly (Schein, 1985) including that of power and structure, performance and risk based on relationships (Koberg & Hood, 1991; Wallach, 1983) as defined by Donald (2017).	
Inspiration	The ability to inspire participants to share a vision and explain what the organisational future will be (Kotter, 1996).	
Communication	Breadth and effectiveness of communication type, regularity, content, language, length and verbal or non-verbal forms.	
Engagement	The ability to achieve staff dedication to superior performance, or the level of staff personal effectiveness (Cole et al., 2012; Maslach et al., 1996).	
Trust	The ability to listen to staff if they disagree with a leadership position (Sheldon, 2018), or the level of employee commitment (Xiong et al., 2016).	
Respect	The ability to acknowledge work performance and recognition including a quality of interpersonal treatment (Grover, 2014).	
Responsibility	The ability to take responsibility for actions (Smith & Sharma, 2002).	
Sense-giving	The ability to identify sense-givers within the organisation and to engage the sense-givers in disseminating information through the organisation.	
Ethics	Ethical behaviour (Moore et al., 2018; Thomas & Rowland, 2014).	

choose to adopt an assessment tool (Smith & Sharma, 2002), where leadership improvement and mentoring may result. The rest of this chapter assesses the leadership fundamentals above in respect to change in the new age. Whilst the new age may affect all organisational leadership, it may not be necessary to alter all of these leadership fundamentals in response.

Communication

As was noted in the leadership fundamentals section, communication is a core element of leadership (Donald, 2017) so may be required for staff happiness, or workplace harmony, or efficiency and productivity. Research interviews with senior change managers in Australia identified communication as the most common factor related to organisational change success (Donald, 2016, 2017). Chapters 1–3 of this book earlier characterised the new age as one including disruption and AI, where ongoing rapid organisational change may occur, assisted through globalisation. Leaders will likely find that past communication strategies may no longer be as effective in this new age, where new pathways may be required.

Communication processes that were very slow and dependent upon human involvement in the 1980s and 1990s, are now fast processes. The originator of communication is now likely to type their own information where they have a choice to post it publicly on blogs, Internet, email or social media. There are now so many communication forms available that an organisation not be aware of poor publicity unless it particularly monitors. Any unfavourable publicity has the potential to generate reputational or financial loss, where the poor publicity may not receive any direct verification or response. Whilst laws exist to protect organisations from fraud, slander and libel, there is potential for false news and reputational damage to occur from indirect and unknown sources.

There will likely be constant pressure to change and respond as disruption and AI emerge across the world. As communication has been associated with organisational change (Donald, 2014, 2016, 2017) those in leadership positions may be required to explain regularly about changes that are happening and why they occur. Staff and other stakeholders are unlikely to automatically follow the constant changes in direction characterised by the new age, as they have choice between following change or not. In deciding to support the leadership or not, staff require information on the logic and reasoning of any new positions or new directions taken. Information gaps arising in communication may be interpreted with distrust, leaving potential gaps to be filled by sense-givers who may not be knowledgeable of the matters.

In an attempt to improve communicative reach, the leader could increase the number of communication messages, yet the issue may not be the quantity that causes the recipient to not hear messages. As stakeholders and staff are not homogenous in their communication needs, it is unlikely that any single message type will be sufficient. In the new age, there will be almost constant change, where the frequency of changes may be so high that stakeholders may not be willing to accept them without good explanation from their leadership.

Leadership will need to spend time understanding the diversity in their staff and stakeholders, possibly preparing detailed analysis of their fragmentation and various communication needs. This detailed understanding of communication may enable leadership to build communication plans that are relevant to stakeholders that are being targeted. It will not help an organisation if the leadership continues along with a rigid, blanket top-down communication style. Increasing the quantity of verbal or written communication will be insufficient if the staff prefer pictures and graphs for information sources. Top-down communication may be insufficient if staff prefer to gather information from colleagues with sense-giving skills. There will be many possible paths for the leadership to communicate with the staff and stakeholders, where analysis and planning may be more effective than trial through error.

Stakeholder diversity creates a number of challenges for leadership that need to explain organisational change as messages to shareholders, customer, banks and staff need to be consistent so as to not confuse. Despite the need for consistency messages should be developed in order to target the recipient's specific needs. Any technology adoption or disruption may need to be explained to customers, staff and other stakeholders, where despite varying language, form and frequency, the core message needs to be consistent in order to build trust. To succeed an organisation requires leadership that can gain stakeholder change acceptance, where failure to explain messages in an appropriate way may diminish stakeholder support and may limit change implementation.

A large dilemma for leadership of the future is that stakeholders may not like continuous change, especially where changes occur in vastly different directions. In the new age, it is quite conceivable that an organisation may choose one AI platform or product internally approved, only to find shortly after that a new more appropriate technology has emerged, where new approvals may be required. Rather than explaining each individual action and change to the stakeholders, it may be better for the leadership to explain the environment of change in the context of the new age, disruption and AI, as then individual changes may be merely individual steps along the path and may not be so confusing. Partnering and disseminating information to stakeholders in the broader context of change may be better communication than individual explanations of each change one by one. Stakeholders may prefer higher levels of inclusion about organisational decision making and broader information on market, AI and disruption. The sharing of organisational processes and information may improve stakeholder trust in the leadership, where Trust is discussed later in this chapter.

Irrespective of the type or level of communication chosen, there is no guarantee that staff will engage and follow messages from the leadership. To improve the communication process, it is recommended that leadership regularly perform a gap analysis, where the gap information can be used to assist identify further leadership action. The below communication analysis tools shown at Tables 4.2 and 4.3 may help target the type and regularity of information required by stakeholders. The gap analysis could be performed informally through conversation with staff and management, or formally through survey,

Table 4.2:   Communication Regularity Table (CRT).

Stakeholder Category Name :-_____ Communication Type	Regularity Preference Daily, Weekly, Monthly, Annually
Email	
Newsletter	
Social Media (list preferred form)	
Blogs	
Advertising	
Other written form (describe)	
Interview	
Face to face (formal)	
Face to face (casual)	
Group or individual	
Phone	
Audio visual	

where multiple tables are provided below to improve the comprehensiveness of your analysis and response.

In Table 4.2, a range of communication types are considered in relation to each stakeholder type be they customer, staff, supplier or bank or others. The purpose is to formally consider what types of communication may be most suited to each stakeholder type rather than communicating in set intervals that may not be to the stakeholders liking. As further new types of communication may emerge from time to time, they should be added to the CRT to ensure that it remains relevant. The nature of the constantly changing new age will require communication assessments be performed regularly, certainly more than merely annually. Stakeholder preferences and requirements for information and communication on the ensuing disruption and AI will change over time and thus those in leadership positions that embrace a broad and regular communication assessment may position their organisation ahead of others in the market.

As communication has various elements, it is important that leadership evaluate needs of the organisational stakeholders from various perspectives. Table 4.3 considers the style of communication, where each fragment of the organisational stakeholder may have varying preferences that should be considered when communicating. Whilst some leaders may intuitively understand the audience variations, it will still be useful for leadership positions to consider communication as a way to improve messages or understand any lack of influence in the organisation.

Many organisations continue to elevate employees with technical skills, experience and performance, where many in leadership roles in organisations spend little time in broadening their understanding of communication. The linkages

Table 4.3:   Communication Style Table.

Communication Style	Description	Daily, Weekly, Monthly and Annually
Simple language, short form no graphs	May be useful for fact-based information that is clear when read quickly or by those less able to read.	
Mostly graphs, simple language	May be useful to communicate more complex data including trends or comparisons; graphs should be used to simplify messages and enhance understanding.	
Message with argument, some graphs	May be useful for the audience that prefers to read and take messages away for further consideration; useful for an audience that may be negative towards the message/direction.	
Message with argument, high graphs volume	May be useful for the audience that prefers to read and take messages away for further consideration. Useful for an audience that may be negative towards the message/direction. Higher graph volumes to assist the sense-givers explain to other stakeholders.	
Message with argument, some data tables	May be useful for those with mathematical backgrounds including accountant, finance, banks and engineers.	
Message with argument, high data usage	May be useful for those with mathematical backgrounds including accountant, finance, banks and engineers.	
Message linked to organisational values	Useful for situations when the change may be different to stakeholder expectations. Values in mission and vision will assist in explaining why certain directions were chosen.	
Message linked to high level strategy	Useful when the strategy has previously been explained and accepted. May reduce confusion if the new direction may not be clear.	

between communication, trust and engagement, which form critical elements of leadership, are very important, where leaders of the future should consider building improved communication skills early. In this new age, leaders may have to regularly explain linkages between AI or disruption and organisational change. Those leaders that can communicate in a meaningful way reasons for organisational change, redundancy or rapid changes in direction may be better positioned to influence shareholders, banks, staff, customers or suppliers.

The communication content requirements of stakeholders will likely vary over time, where their interest in material may vary between historical, current and future information. An organisation that has recently been losing money and redundancy may be required, may need to explain what has happened, or may need to give assurances about the future employment or direction. Banks may be interested in understanding how the organisation direction will yield profits and guarantee cash flow that will secure debts. Customers may require organisations to justify their directions and positions as there will be linkages to market.

There is likely to be increased changes with disruption and AI that were Chapters 1–3, where new leadership skills may be required to communicate effectively with stakeholder. The increased pace and change regularity may limit the attention stakeholders may be willing to dedicate to understanding the matters. Leadership communication may influence organisational change in both positive and negative directions (Donald, 2017) and thus due consideration of the communication options may be important. Leaders may not be effective if they communicate without preparation or planning, or where due consideration has not been taken as to its language type, length, style and regularity.

Leaders will need to consider how a positive message could still be negated if it is presented too late, too long or of a wrong style for any particular audience. So, messages delivered in large cold halls, with insufficient seating or poor sound may also diminish communication effectiveness. The communication method should be considered an essential business tool as it may be an important factor in changing an organisation (Donald, 2017). Communication sessions may be best delivered in good temperature ranges, in comfortable surrounds with food, whilst ensuring appropriate acoustics and relevant information, including explanations. Whilst organisations must monitor their resources in order to achieve financial outcomes, where increasingly communication should be considered another important business tool worthy of resources and monitoring.

There is little point in the leadership developing good strategy or action plans if the messages are lost due to poor or lack of appropriate communication, resulting in stakeholders rejecting the proposals. Key stakeholders require information and data in order to analyse and support organisational change. Banks and shareholders may require financial tables, assumptions and details of the strategy. Staff, customers or suppliers may require information and data of the benefits of the strategy towards their interests. Leadership is responsible for influencing the stakeholders, gathering support and support in order to move an organisation forward, where failure to gain agreement may negatively impact or inhibit the preferred direction.

Question 4.1. You have been asked to deliver the organisation's latest budget; you started the new job just this week, where the presentation is to a call centre team in your organisation that is a large water utility provider. The arranged time is 4 p.m. on Friday and today is Thursday. The organisation is in the middle of a restructure due to competition in the market and financial results have been well below budget. There are rumours in the market that the CEO may soon be replaced and the organisation may be subject to takeover if things do not improve.

Describe the sorts of messages that may be important to the call centre staff. Would you deliver the presentation at short notice? Why or why not? What options do you have for the presentation? What communication style, regularity and content would you include in this presentation?

In the new age of disruption and AI, the leadership will be challenged more than in the past as the changes will be fast moving and potentially transformational, where the desired information and full understanding of the implications may not be known. In this new age, there will be a reason for the organisation to adapt to the surrounds, where the direction of the organisation may need to change regularly. In these rapid changes, staff and stakeholders will likely be more dependent organisational leadership to communicate as other information sources available to stakeholders, like social media, may lack reliability. Confusion may occur when an organisation moves in directions that are alternate to the formal publicly issued information. Leadership communication may likely be the most important element in rebuking rumour and setting clear messages for stakeholders.

Question 4.2. An organisation has recently received approval to expand due to a new AI development that they have purchased. Prior to the arrival of the new technology, the organisation becomes aware of competitors purchasing a newer more capable model. The organisation cancels the purchase with supplier agreement and decides to wait until the following year when even more capable AI may be available.

Discuss how a Leader may approach this matter. Include, in the discussion, how the stakeholder perspectives on this change may fragment. What options may exist for the leadership in relation to explaining the matter? Should the leadership proactively request meetings with stakeholders or something else?

Organisations of the future are likely to confront ongoing change that may be sudden and fast paced, be it from disruption or AI. There will likely be a large quantity of changes occurring, sometimes simultaneously others crossing over one another, where the change effects may be that of efficiency, cost, staffing, product or services, market and financial reasons. It is the skill of the leadership that will influence whether the changes are successfully implemented. Communication may be associated with organisational change, where it is likely to be merely one factor (Donald, 2014, 2016, 2017). It is unlikely that communication will be sufficient to prepare an organisation for change as additional factors will likely be required, especially one that encounters ongoing and regular AI or disruption.

Trust

Organisational change success may not occur through merely an improvement in communication as other change factors may be required, including trust (Donald, 2017). Organisational resistance has been associated between information supply, employee participation and employee trust (Bordia, Hunt, Paulsen, Tourish, & DiFonzo, 2004; Oreg, 2006), where increased participation may increase trust and inhibit resistance (Giangreco & Peccei, 2005; Lawrence, 1954, reprint 1969), leading to higher employee commitment levels (Giangreco & Peccei, 2005; Pugh, 1993). Despite any improvement in communication, the organisation may still not change successfully where trust in the leadership is low or absent. Staff may not accept messages in communication merely from listening, as they also require trust. Despite messages from the leadership containing various compelling arguments and messages, staff may not listen or be open to the messages until there is sufficient trust in the leadership.

A dilemma for the leadership is that staff and other stakeholders may prefer consistency and clarity in order to trust, yet the increased number of changes in the future may cause that to be impossible. Leaders will need to explain the context of decision changes and directional change as individual changes may appear as confusing without the additional information. It may be difficult for the leadership to explain why a new direction is so different to any previous messages, where linkages to the broader environment may assist in trust development.

Question 4.3. An organisation spends months building relationships with a European or Asian supplier, signing an exclusive supply agreement on price and quantity. The country of receipt later imposes a 20% tariff on goods. The tariff now makes the new arrangement unprofitable, where reverting back to the original supplier may be more prudent and may enable a return back to profit.

How might the leader use communication and trust to quickly renege this new deal or change its terms? How should the leader communicate the tariff issue to staff, shareholders and customers without losing face, or causing the stakeholders to lose confidence in the leadership? If damages or contract breaches may cost additional funds, how should the leadership communicate the loss to stakeholders?

Trust is a leadership factor that is built up over time; stakeholders may not have high trust in leaders just because they appear honest. Past behaviours, past messages and past results build knowledge about the leadership, where too much past confusion or poor past events may erode trust. It is important that even when past events have failed to deliver. Leadership should explain the variances in an open way to stakeholders. If the leadership previously promised that staff numbers would not be reduced and yet were reduced later, the matter cannot be ignored, it would need explanation and context in order for it to not appear as a trust matter. To avoid trust erosion, leadership may need to clarify and explain direction changes in the context of disruption or AI as they occur, whilst confidentiality is important it may not be more important than stakeholder support. Traditionally, organisations may have withheld information on market grounds and commercial in confidence reasons, where in the future stakeholders may be confused if not appropriately informed.

Question 4.4. The past leadership has not explained two major restructures for an organisation. In the first restructure, the organisation moved the organisation into a product based structure. The second change was to move the organisation into a matrix style (Williams et al., 2016). Now only three months after the last change, it is intending to change to a hybrid structure for competitive reasons. What levels of trust may exist towards the leadership by stakeholders of this organisation?

What strategies and actions may be deployed to improve trust in this situation? How might the leader mitigate past behaviours to improve the likelihood of stakeholders supporting another change in direction?

Leadership that explains that disruption will be sudden with impacts that potentially threaten the organisation survival may find that they achieve higher levels of trust than those that withhold information. As trust in the leadership may be vital to organisational change and cohesion, the increased sharing of market and strategy with stakeholders may be imperative. There will be risk in competitors hearing about the changes in direction and following where the organisation is more open with directional changes, one that leadership may be willing to take in the new age. Confidentiality may be controlled through confidentiality agreements with suppliers and customers. Customers may find it difficult to relate to disruption or AI, although they may accept a change and increase their trust in the leadership if the context and benefits are well explained. The various communication forms and regularity discussed in the previous section of this book may assist the leadership in adopting the most effective communication form. There will be trade-off required by the leadership in forming communication for stakeholders, where privacy and market confidentiality are traded against understanding, acceptance and trust in the leadership.

Failure to warn stakeholders of new emerging disruption or AI may lead to diminished trust, particularly where the leadership was aware of the change but failed to notify. There may be requirements for listed organisations to inform the market of real and probable significant changes, yet disruption and AI may be remote possibilities that do not need to be reported and thus market rules in the new age may need to be changed. Even if information is not required to be disclosed to markets, information of new age events may be required to be discussed to improve trust with key stakeholders. Financiers and insurers may require an understanding of how the organisation may react should new technology emerge or if tariffs are applied to imported goods, they may also require reassurance of what the reaction scenarios may look like if new age disruption emerges.

AI developments may be quickly introduced to markets, where customer interfaces may require the organisation to adopt quickly, where failure to do so may lead to financial losses or loss of market share. Early adoption of new technology will be associated with increased risk that it is not successful, or too expensive to integrate or is quickly made redundant. Stakeholders may have different appetites for risk, where failing to explain risk and value may be perceived as unfair or mischievous. It is conceivable that organisations failing to identify or share new age risk may leave themselves open to legal claims if leaderships fail to openly share information.

Leadership may choose to be cautious in the light of new age changes, yet delays in making change or general conservatism may cause additional risk in themselves. Organisations may need to hire and retain leadership that are able to operate in the fast-paced new age, requiring leadership that are able to manage risk and communicate related messages well. Trust will likely be improved if the leadership can effectively communicate change logic or reasons. Whilst it may be impossible for leadership to know when a government will impose tariffs, there is a real possibility today that they may occur as discussed in Chapter 2 and thus planning and communicating on the matter may be prudent.

High levels of trust in the leadership are required in the new age, as changes will need stakeholder support. Disruption may erode organisational profits, product or relationships, where stakeholders may require new financial forecasts, analysis, remedies or risk analysis. Assumptions and data may be difficult to estimate in the ensuing new age change, where openness and trust may be required before stakeholders accept changes. Leaders will likely need skills to explain and rate risk if they are to convince stakeholders to trust and support changes. Overly positive messages without open risk assessment may be appealing, yet such unbalanced behaviour may erode trust in leadership over time.

Staff, financiers or even customers may not be willing to listen or engage with leadership that is not considered trustworthy and thus even a well-positioned, open and fair plan may not be accepted if leadership trust levels are low. Organisations should consider that poor behaviours and low trust of previous leadership is not automatically elevated when new people are appointed. New leadership may require time and new actions to build trust before it can influence stakeholders to accept their new directions.

Culture has been identified as a potential influencer in organisational change (Donald, 2017), where the term culture has been defined as those shared assumptions, beliefs and values that are held close (Schein, 1985), including power and structure, performance and risk (Koberg & Hood, 1991; Wallach, 1983). An organisational culture that historically produces low levels accurate data, poor analysis or poor past decisions may also suffer from low levels of trust in the leadership. Stakeholders may rate and perceive the organisational trustworthiness by how promptly the organisation responds to questions, how well-attended meetings are or how it treats its staff. Leadership will likely need to consider a wide range of factors in order to improve culture and trust.

Innovation

As discussed earlier, the new age will likely create new opportunities and risks for organisations. Communication, trust and culture are but some of the leadership responsibilities that may need to alter in this new age, as other leadership tools may also be required. Innovation has been associated with globalisation and change, where the way innovation is implemented may determine its success (Kim & Chung, 2017). The term innovation refers to the implementation of new ideas that may benefit the organisation (West & Farr, 1989; West, Hirst, Richter, & Shipton, 2004), also associated with decision making that is dispersed with formal structures and written plans, albeit more prevalent in new technology organisations (Cosh, Fu, & Hughes, 2012).

Innovation may be required in the early phases of the new age as past structures and processes may no longer be appropriate for the fast paced, sudden and unexpected changes. The lack of verifiable information and clear directions of the new age may require new ways of interpreting data and setting direction by leadership. Leadership may be commonly be associated with those of power or direction setting, yet there is research indicating that traditional consensus or domineering leadership environments do not yield innovation (Davis & Eisenhardt, 2011). Any rigid top-down structures of the past may no longer be appropriate in the new age, as change may occur almost constantly.

Past organisational structures and processes may have existed to provide controlled and valuable information to leadership in order to set organisational direction and influence stakeholders. In the new age, the time to gather and complete reliable or verifiable information may be far too slow in order to react to future changes like geopolitical change or trade wars. Leadership may have to prepare stakeholders about change well in advance of it arriving, where advance information may not be accurate nor complete. A leader's ability to attract sufficient information, verified by some means and move the organisation forward without delays will likely be required in the new age. Successful leaders of the future may be those that are able to gather, understand, decide and bring their stakeholders forward faster than their competitors, yet also ensuring that identified and treated.

Innovation in the age of AI and disruption will require prompt identification of the emerging change, requiring understanding of the change size, type and impact on the market. Traditional organisations may have waited until their product sales were impacted before preparing for change, or others may have waited for change financial returns before reacting to change, in the future these methods may be far too slow and late. Modern organisations may seek to understand change earlier and thus place more effort and resources into data gathering, verification and analysis. Organisations that move in the correct direction early may minimise negative impacts of the new age, whilst potentially being early to capitalise on any related opportunities.

Processes in organisations of the new age are also likely to be altered as past processes aimed at controlling processes and limiting deviations may too restrictive or rigid. The entrepreneurial aspect of the organisation may influence product innovation and creativity (Bisbe & Malagueño, 2015). The leadership of organisations will likely need to introduce innovation to many aspects of the organisation beyond merely products and services, where influencing skills may also need to change. Chapter 7 explores more on organisational change based on recent research (Donald, 2017), where new concepts and methods are discussed.

Leaders may wish to assess their organisation for innovation based on characteristics of the new age. To assess leadership innovation, leadership dimensions may need to be assessed against their abilities to improve speed or flexibility in the organisation. There are insufficient measures of innovation (*Measuring innovation: a new perspective*, 2010) and they may be difficult to determine (Nelson, Earle, Howard-Grenville, Haack, & Young, 2014), yet the practitioner may require measures for leadership innovation to enable comparisons. Table 4.4 is designed at improving leadership innovation by providing dimensions and ratings, where a score out of 30 may allow comparison between various leadership actions being considered.

Table 4.4 can be used to assess leadership initiatives that may be aimed towards innovation. Each of the potential leadership dimensions are listed in the left column of Table 4.4, where the three columns to the right require a rating as to how a leadership initiative may improve speed, flexibility and improvement. A number of alternate leadership initiatives can be assessed by placing scores into the rows and columns and totalled, where assessment of the initiatives may be used in

Table 4.4:   Leadership Innovation Assessment Tool.

Leadership Dimension	Improves Speed (1–10)	Flexibility (1–10)	New or Improved (1–10)	Total Innovation (30 Max)	Comment
Support	2	8	3	13	
Influence					
Direction					
Culture					
Inspiration					
Communication					
Engagement					
Trust					
Respect					
Responsibility					
Sense-giving					
Ethics					
Total					

assessing innovation based on the totals. Further research is likely required to enable leadership to be assessed against innovation.

This section on innovation is not comprehensive, as it was included here in order to introduce the concept and begin thought on how leadership may need to respond to the new age. As the pace of change will be broad and fast, the leadership has a unique and important part to play in influencing, co-ordinating and moving the organisation forward.

Transformational Leadership

Transformational leadership has generally been associated with positive employee outcomes (Bono & Ilies, 2006; Montano, Reeske, Franke, & Hüffmeier, 2017; Niessen, Mäder, Stride, & Jimmieson, 2017), where training on the topic has improved organisational outcomes (Mason, Griffin, & Parker, 2014). Transformational leadership may be associated with how employees may thrive when exhausted (Niessen et al., 2017). In this new age, leadership may be more important to the organisation than in the past as changes in direction may confuse staff and stakeholders, so they require explanation and understanding of the changes. A transactional leader may focus on transactions, structures and performance, potentially spending too much effort on the day-to-day for the future ahead. The alternate, transformational leadership, changes an organisation through a vision, where staff interact and follow in a meaningful or creative way (Bass, 1985b; Niessen et al., 2017).

The issue for transformational leadership in the new age is likely to be in the setting of the vision, where being specific may lead to confusion due to the number of times it may need to change. Stakeholders may prefer visions are specific in order to measure performance, yet despite specific goals leadership may not be so measurable if disruption eliminates and significantly changes markets. Leadership measures for the future may need to relate to their negotiation skills, cohesion generation skills and agreement achievement due to the high level of risk and uncertainty. The leader may need new skills to create a vision that can be understood and accepted by stakeholders in the new age, where flexibility and ongoing changes may compete against the stability of message.

The transformational leader will need to set and explain an overall vision before setting out to influence and receive support from stakeholders. Failure to explain and satisfy the stakeholders may result in organisational changes not being approved or may yield a loss of confidence in the leadership. Messages that are not conveyed fast and accepted may incur risk or loss of value if competitors are able to react faster or receive more support. The choice of leader and good assessment of their skills will in this new age increasingly be an important role for organisational boards. Leadership without new skills for the new age may well leave the organisation vulnerable to significant value loss.

New Age Pressures on Leadership

Leadership as the responsible party for setting organisational direction, communicating the vision and building the stakeholder engagement will be challenged as the age of AI and disruption emerges. The processes historically developed to change organisations may be insufficient, as other factors may be interdependent (Donald, 2017) and thus is discussed further in Chapter 7. Organisational direction setting will not likely be as controlled as in the past, as multiple scenarios and alternate strategies will be required regularly. Despite data potentially being incomplete and unverified in the new age, a level of risk and uncertainty assessment will likely be required.

Rather than an organisation setting a mere single budget, an organisation may need to set goals that vary in ranges, or be based on contingencies in order for leadership measures to vary as new AI or disruption emerges. In the emerging AI and disruption, many of the base parameters and assumptions of market, volume and prices may regularly and significantly be affected in many directions, thus measurement against an annual budget may be unfair or impossible. Failures against annual budgets may lead the organisational stakeholders to lose confidence with the leadership, if explanations are not considered adequate. Fixed medium-term goal setting may be too difficult or uncertain for the leadership to hold the goals set or maintain engagement of stakeholders.

It is clear from this chapter that leaders of the future will be under significant pressure to set organisational vision, monitor, change and explain, irrespective of any sudden and ongoing change related to disruption and AI. Leadership likely will be required to have excellent communication skills that promote trust and engagement with stakeholders, despite stakeholder needs not being homogenous. The leadership influencing skills will likely be required in introducing innovation into the organisation to enable new ideas, new structures and processes to emerge. Chapter 5 continues discussing the new age, reviewing management aspects rather than the leadership aspects discussed in this chapter.

Chapter 5

Managing Organisations of the Future

> The New Age will require reassessment of what Management is and how to perform it.
>
> —Mathew Donald

This chapter will commence with a review of management fundamentals to cover essential elements and definitions of the topic, where the initial discussion is not intended as a comprehensive coverage as there are many complete books and subjects written on the topic. Management fundamentals section explores the relevant theory of the topic, as a modern update for the practitioner or as an introduction for the new learner. The new age is likely to influence and affect the various aspects of management, where the remainder of this chapter goes on to explore changes in management practices that may be required in the new age.

Management Fundamentals

Management is the combination of processes, structures and resources that the organisation relies upon to achieve the goals required by stakeholders, yet it has been defined as the activity of completing tasks, concerned with efficiency and effectiveness (Williams, McWilliams, & Lawrence, 2016). As was discussed in Chapter 1 of this book, management is not leadership, despite any perceived similarities and overlaps. It may be desirable that a manager have leadership skills, it will not always be the case that leadership skills will be bestowed to those who are in management. This section discusses modern literature and thinking on management, where the knowledge will be used later in this chapter to explore how it may need to change in light of the new age.

Management has a wide range of responsibilities that are quite distinct and separate to that of leadership, these include the way work is distributed, monitored and the way that employees interact with the tasks (Donald, 2017). After a review of the literature, management was defined as a skill of making decisions (Sadler-Smith, 2008), thinking (Khandelwal & Taneja, 2010) and alignment of input and outputs (Donald, 2017). Management task alignment involves efficiency and competitiveness (Singh & Shoura, 2006), people (Seilby, 2014), plans (Ketter, 2014) and control (Griffin & Van Fleet, 2013). Tasks expected to

Leading and Managing Change in the Age of Disruption and Artificial Intelligence, 93–120
Copyright © 2019 by Emerald Publishing Limited
All rights of reproduction in any form reserved
doi:10.1108/978-1-78756-367-420191006

be managed are often not structured nor routine and thus cause difficulties that require resourcefulness to overcome them (Kanungo & Misra, 1992). Owing to the fast turbulent world that face managers today they may need to use intuition when making decisions (Sadler-Smith, 2008), rather than purely facts or data.

The concept of management was derived from a systems perspective to organising activities (Likert, 1967), where the concept envisaged management as being responsible for the conversion of inputs into business outputs, allocating resources including capital and employees (Bordley & Pollock, 2012). The required skills of a manager are considered wide (Griffin & Van Fleet, 2013) with difficult choices and thus they often allocate resources to issues rather than opportunities (Drucker, 1963, 2006). Others have defined management with four functions of planning, organising, leading and control (Williams et al., 2016). Many managers do not know how to implement change successfully, despite understanding change importance and the expectation that they lead the change (Rosenberg & Mosca, 2011). New concepts are emerging for management, including elements of ethics and corporate social responsibility, yet the definitions are still broad and open (Nonet, Kassel, & Meijs, 2016). Specialised roles were created to manage risk, yet they failed to prevent the Global Financial Crisis (GFC) (Dionne, 2013).

Managing may be said to be the process by which the organisation appoints positions within the organisation to achieve its long-term goals, where in order to achieve the goals they are further broken down into medium- and short-term goals. In order for organisational positions to support any goals they likely require plans that are supported by job descriptions, individual goals and instruction on priorities. The way the organisation converts inputs to outputs occurs in work processes that are defined and controlled in order to improve efficiency and effectiveness of the organisation. This is not to say that managers provide all instructions and decisions in the organisation, rather they are responsible for the outcomes, processes and structures. There are many aspects to management roles, where behavioural descriptions may be better than those based on position or function (Stewart, 1991). Management political skills may be just as important as their technical skills in relation to their performance (Bedi & Skowronski, 2014), where they are now also expected to have conflict resolution skills (Thomas, 1992).

Organisational control is traditionally important in delivering outcomes that are aligned to expectations, yet more creative organisations may use their budget control systems more interactively than those that are less creative (Cools, Stouthuysen, & Van Den Abbeele, 2017). Situational differences may affect a departments knowledge of management (Bresnen, Hodgson, Bailey, Hyde, & Hassard, 2017). Management styles may differ between male and females, between those that prefer efficiency and those that do not, or where elected managers use democratic styles (Kocher, Pogrebna, & Sutter, 2013). Managers may have different characteristics based on the level of the role, varying between those in top, middle and lower levels (Williams et al., 2016), although roles have also been classified into three groups, that is, being interpersonal, informational and decisional (Mintzberg, 1971).

When managing in risk environments, it may be preferable to manage by exception, where the context of the environment may be important (Henry, 2001). It has been proposed that there may be two responses when management anxiety emerges, one response being that of opportunity for engagement, the other response being one of detachment (Segal, 2011). The skills for management may not be homogenous, yet recruiters may seek human, technical, conceptual and motivational skills when hiring (Williams et al., 2016). Human, technical and conceptual skills have been associated with experience in management (Ermasova, Nguyen, Clark, & Ermasov, 2018) and thus indicating that it may be a learnt skill. Despite the potential for management to be a learnt skill, ageism is prevalent in society and organisationally, where a number of policies and factors may be required to extinguish the discrimination (Vasconcelos, 2015).

The remainder of this chapter will discuss the various aspects of management in the context of the modern new age involving both disruption and artificial intelligence (AI). These aspects of management are not likely to disappear in the new age, although the concept application may alter. The very nature of management as a concept of delivering controlled and dependable outcomes to stakeholders, may be seriously challenged in the new age as the future may be an environment of fast paced and unreliable information.

Strategic Management

Organisations are built upon processes and resources, where goal alignment is necessary to prevent confusion and inefficiency. Strategy may have emerged over 2,000 years ago based on skills of administration, power, communication and leadership (Mainardes, Ferreira, & Raposo, 2014; Quinn, Mintzberg, & James, 1988). Whilst strategy can be disunited, it has been successful (Nag, Hambrick, & Chen, 2007) and is often used by organisations to develop long-term goals. The topic emerged in the last 40 years, derived from a number of fields including finance, marketing and economics, where disparities remain on the definition (Hambrick, 2004; Nag et al., 2007). Strategy definitions may require amending as students have found it a difficult concept to apply (Mainardes et al., 2014), where it has been described as being the conduit between the inner organisation and the outside world (Mainardes et al., 2014). The topic is concerned with the long-term survival and growth of the organisation rather than the many other management aspects (Bao, 2015). It is also important to assess and understand existing strategic management systems prior to introducing new systems (Melander, Löfving, Andersson, Elgh, & Thulin, 2016).

The process of setting strategy varies between organisations, where some update the strategy annually and others less frequently, some set a strategy for a next five-year horizon, whilst others set it for 10 years. The process may start differently in various organisations, where strategy may be described as having five elements and the plan arising is aimed at gathering competitive advantage (Mintzberg, 1987). The mission and vision statement for an organisation is often an area where the planning may commence, descriptions and forecasts reviewed for the potential competition type and the competitive advantage. The forecasts are rarely unique or in a single direction in the early phases, as there may be alternate paths and scenarios to rate before deciding on a particular one to use in the more formal strategic plans.

The strategy development has historically been completed by small groups that may have worked autonomously, hidden away in an attempt to keep the longer-term organisational directions and assumptions confidential. More recently, there have been discussions about opening up the strategy process to deliver new benefits (Hautz, 2017). There are clear benefits in setting a strategy as it enables the organisation to coherently set goals that can be communicated with staff and other stakeholders. A strategy, once agreed with shareholders and financiers, can be a reference point to use in investment decisions as they occur. Organisations that do not set strategy formally, may lose the support of stakeholders and appear to be confusing, where ad hoc decision making may occur due to the lack of cohesion between ideas and plans.

The process of approving strategy is important to most organisations as it clarifies stakeholder expectations and informs the stakeholders of the potential options and reasons for direction. There would be little point in management setting a 10% return on equity as a vision if the shareholders or banks required 15%. The goal gaps and subsequent alignment may be just as important to the organisation as the numeric targets finally set. Usually, if there is a gap in stakeholder expectations and those offered by management, there will be a time of review and justification on top of a discussion about the assumptions and reasonableness of the direction. The required return for the organisation to achieve is a weighted average between shareholder requirements and that required by the financiers. The average return parameter required is a base for management to build strategic plans to achieve those returns, where the final plans include a blend of assumptions around customer, new products and innovation, or suppliers.

An evaluation of risk may be essential when setting strategy, where integrating risk management with strategy may be of benefit in times of high change (Gibbs & Deloach, 2006). Strategy development is one of blending the stakeholder expectation with the market opportunity, where the risk appetite may be a limiting factor to what is acceptable. Setting strategy, is for some like 'crystal balling' the future, trying to guess the market position, the environment, technology and other factors before then setting a strategic plan to achieve the goals. Whilst there is no single way to write a strategy there are some principles that organisations may normally follow, presented later in this chapter. Traditionally, organisations that set strategies regularly may find minimal changes are required on an annual basis. Significant strategy changes may often involve large amounts of time and money to prepare. Organisations that do not achieve financial targets may come under higher scrutiny from stakeholders, and thus may review their strategy in more detail when that occurs.

A strategy is often required by shareholders and other stakeholders so they can understand the logic and position that the organisation is taking, often linked to market conditions and probabilities. It is unlikely (unless dealing with entrepreneurs or gamblers) for a stakeholder to invest or release funds into an organisation if they do not agree with the direction and assumptions. Larger stakeholders usually prefer to be able to analyse, test and confirm strategy as their way into an organisation, rather than merely a passive investment. Strategic plans may commence from a number of techniques, where each may include some form of gap analysis, potential scenarios and a preferred or most likely direction.

Strategic planning techniques may include the following techniques shown in Table 5.1.

Table 5.1:   Strategic Management Technique Checklist.

Technique	Details	Completed (Y/N)
History	Review of historical results, data, trends and relationships. This form of strategy build believes that there is some insights in the past that may assist the organisation predict or assess the future directions for the organisation to take.	
New products or services	Review of new products and services in the local market or related markets that may be used to indicate future changes.	
Overseas trends	Review current and related markets in other countries for developments and changes.	
Competitors	Review the nature, size, structure and financial accounts of competitors against the organisation to identify gaps and opportunities.	
Related industries	Review related industries to see what changes are occurring, what their new products, technologies or innovations are being adopted. Review markets to see if they are growing or decreasing in size.	
Current strategy	Review current strategy with an open mind, identify pros and cons.	
Strengths Weaknesses Opportunities Threats	Review the current market and current organisation in particular for respective strengths, weaknesses, opportunities and threats.	
Innovation and Developments	Review market and unrelated markets for new innovations and changes.	
Staff	Perform a gap analysis against the desired staff skills, training, structures and efficiencies to identify improvement areas.	

Each of the areas in Table 5.1 may be useful to gather information on what is happening in and around the organisations market. The nature and scope of work performed in preparing strategy is limited to the resources available for the task, the time allowed and the creativity in pulling all of the potential information together. In performing each of the analyses in Table 5.1, the data and analysis may be substantial and even confusing, where multiple directions and options may appear. Organisations have often had iterative meetings to cut down the options to a preferred version, after careful consideration of the parameters, calculations and financial numbers. There will often be a risk review of the scenarios before the final version is accepted (Gibbs & Deloach, 2006). A comprehensive review of the organisation strategy, as shown in Table 5.1, may be a long and detailed review that essentially results in boundaries as to where the organisation may go or not go in the future. In deriving the final strategy, each of the options and parameters will be assessed for logic, likelihood, past performances.

The new age creates new issues for strategy setting in organisations, where the nature of disruption and AI may be too sudden and fast paced for normal strategy setting to comprehend or react to. Annual strategy setting for long time frames of 10 years may be inappropriate for a future that is fast paced, where it may be far too long to wait up to 12 months to change a key strategy after a disruption emerges. Likewise, it may be inappropriate to have a 10-year plan as new AI may result in immediate and substantial changes in customer perceptions. Globalisation, technology and social media have changed the way information flows and the way it is shared, possibly rendering the past strategic processes as void.

Strategy that is developed from the likely rather than the possible, or the seemingly impossible may result in plans that are irrelevant or out of date before they are even approved. An organisation that bases a new car strategy today on petrol or even electric vehicles, could in the new age find that other forms like hydrogen vehicles have emerged, or that flying driverless drones are adopted in just a few short years. The timeline and probability of these options may be very difficult for an organisation to determine and set for a long term, where any locked in position may also be difficult to reverse. Just a few short years ago, the possibility of drones flying driverless around the world may have been thought to have been impossible to occur this century, yet today that is a regular event for some military.

Organisations may choose to update their strategic plans more regularly in an attempt to keep them up to date and be relevant in the new age, whilst others may question their usefulness and thus may decide to cease strategy setting. The dilemma for the organisation of the new age is that whilst long-term detailed strategy development may be inflexible and too slow, an organisation devoid of strategy may suffer poor decision making due to lack of forethought and consideration. In this new age, the organisational data integrity may not always be clear, possibly clouding any authenticity and applicability so potentially confusing decision makers.

Strategy may simply be described as a process to set the organisational direction, after stakeholder agreement. A strategy direction is determined based on analysis and options derived from perceived competitive advantage, opportunity and potential financial results. There may be advantage in being first to respond in disruption or early adoption of AI be that from cost, competition, functionality of risk. Waiting for additional reliable information may at times be a satisfactory reaction to the new age, as at times the information on changes may be too remote. At the same time, waiting for changes to be confirmed, analysed and understood may place the organisation behind competition and lose advantage.

Whilst strategy is about building long-term plans for the organisation, it is often traditionally based on facts and trends that are fairly reliable. The strategist for the new age may be one that has to spend considerably more time verifying potential events or emergences, checking data and trying to determine what may or may not happen. The likelihood of any event in the new age may be more difficult to assess and predict, where even having a long-term plan may be useless. Strategy may be useful for disruption and AI as it enables preparation for the change, although the change may not be clear as it emerges. The very nature of strategy may need to be overhauled for the new age, where strategy may be more of one attempting to survive and thrive, so being more about the systems and structures. In the new age, change direction and actions may be left, waiting for the new change to emerge. Perhaps the future of strategy is more about preparing for a range of possibilities rather than preparing for the most likely scenario.

There are multiple steps involved in developing strategy as shown in Table 5.1, where the new age may require more time and effort being spent on identifying potential future events, verifying data and analysis. New age strategy may be less about setting a direction and more like a war setting, where possible and probable changes are identified, analysed and a range of reactions are listed, without necessarily choosing a direction during the strategy setting. The strategy of the future may be like looking for a needle in a haystack, as one knows it exists but unable to know when or where it will emerge. In a traditional six-part strategy process (Schendel & Hofer, 1979), internal and external environment scanning often forms part of strategy development (Robinson, 2015). In the new age, creativity and thought may need to be developed in an attempt to identify and prepare for disruption and AI that may not have emerged as yet.

A proposed strategy process model for consideration in the new age is shown in Fig. 5.1, where the lack of verifiable information on the changes ahead may be one of the highest risk factors in the strategy process. As discussed previously in Chapter 2, there are a number of disruptions currently occurring or that may emerge in the future, where they may not traditionally have been considered in strategy development, including those of geopolitical and climate changes. The future new age changes have potential to emerge suddenly and fast paced in this globalised environment so strategy development will likely need to be broader than in the past.

The new age proposed strategy process outlined at Fig. 5.1 emerges from the traditional model (Schendel & Hofer, 1979), where additional steps have been included. The new steps shown in Fig. 5.1 seek additional verification on emerging data and information that has been identified in the scanning process. As no single organisation is likely to dominate the markets in the new age, a single

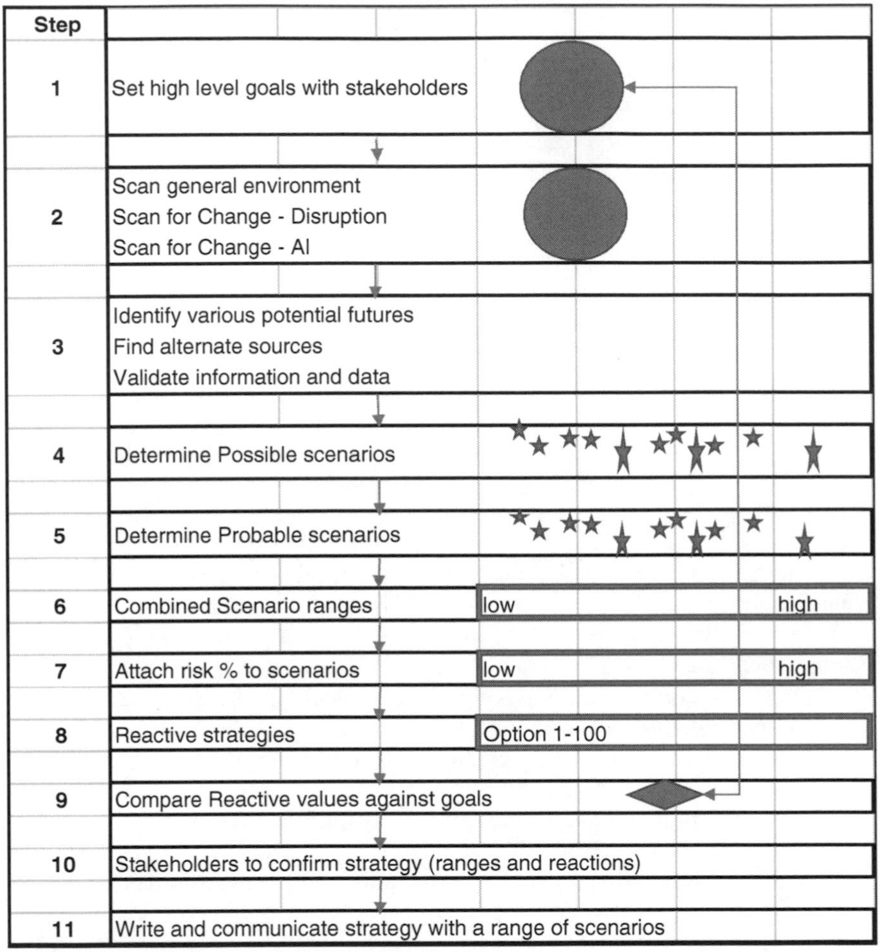

Step								
1	Set high level goals with stakeholders							
2	Scan general environment Scan for Change - Disruption Scan for Change - AI							
3	Identify various potential futures Find alternate sources Validate information and data							
4	Determine Possible scenarios							
5	Determine Probable scenarios							
6	Combined Scenario ranges	low			high			
7	Attach risk % to scenarios	low			high			
8	Reactive strategies	Option 1-100						
9	Compare Reactive values against goals							
10	Stakeholders to confirm strategy (ranges and reactions)							
11	Write and communicate strategy with a range of scenarios							

Fig. 5.1:   Proposed New Age Strategy Process.

strategy may not be prudent for an organisation despite the ease of understanding it. The new age may require many alternative options, based on possible and probable emerging events, where multiple scenarios and responses may be resulting strategy. Whilst stakeholders may prefer to hold one strategic direction, it may not be possible with the interaction of markets, globalisation and various communication forms, including social media.

There may be debate and eventual improvement to the process defined above at Fig. 5.1, where the process has been proposed here for initial thought by academics and professionals to consider any differences and even relevance for strategy in the new age. It is envisaged that the strategy developed using the process at Fig. 5.1 may have many possible pathways based on possibility and probability of the options included. The strategy emerging in this new age may be more like a reckoner or list on what to do if scenarios emerge, rather than being a clear stable direction to be followed in the long term.

Clear issues emerge in the new age if the future is far less certain than in prior times, where the first issue may be around accountability for results. If no single scenario is locked in and agreed with stakeholders, it may be difficult to measure and reward management for organisational results. Other issues may surround the treatment of scenarios that occur outside the strategy. Organisations may require new assessment tools and policies on the treatment of unforeseen gains and losses or may require discussions around new rewards, bonuses and pay systems.

Question 5.1. An organisation is in heavy transport that has over 100 vehicles in the fleet that cost over $US 100,000 each. The investment needs to take place in three years' time due to redundancy in the current fleet. You have been asked to develop the organisation's next 10-year strategic plan. Consider the organisation industry and perform scanning of the environment, including various disruptions and AI.

Write a paper on what your scan discovers and what the strategy options may be for this organisation. Include elements of Fig. 5.1 in developing options. Discuss how risk is assessed in developing your strategy options.

Hint: Be creative in your scan, consider the possible rather than merely the probable scenarios.

Competitive advantage is a primary goal of setting strategy, yet in the new age advantage may disappear quickly (Giurgiu & Borza, 2015). Organisations that fail to identify and capitalise on advantage in some form or another may result in lower earnings or even failure. Failure to identify and use advantage may see the organisations products or services without differentiation, reverting to lower prices and lower volumes than their competitors. Some may argue that organisational advantage will arise beyond the traditional market environment, where some call for specialised management roles to be focussed on the external, politics and societal change (Doh, Lawton, Rajwani, & Paroutis, 2014). Chapters 2 and 3 explored disruption and AI as a way of showing that the external environment is interlinked to organisations, where globalisation has increased the speed and effects over the past and thus organisations may need to include disruptions and AI in their mainstream strategy processes.

Competitive advantage is related to holding advantage in the market, including dimensions of location, intellectual knowledge, patents, skilled staff, processes, finances, customers, suppliers or even reputation. The competitive advantage may lie intrinsically around the organisational setup (debt vs. equity) or be one that is built over time (e.g. staff skills, processes and customer relationships) and thus even if an organisation does not start with competitive advantage, it may develop and build it over time. Once an organisation has competitive advantage, it may be able to increase its market size or increase prices and/or increase margins, yet there are limits to organisational advantage.

In the case of early adopters of AI change, the actions taken may not always be hidden from the other market players. Early adoption is already available as an opportunity for organisations, as robots are also already being adopted early in the industrial lift truck market to gain advantage (Trebilcock, 2013). Early adoption may occur if there are predictions of lower running or capital costs, improved efficiency or perhaps reduced taxes. In any early adoption, the first organisation to adopt the new product, service or technology may achieve advantage until the competitors follow or catch up.

This section has explored strategic management and its historical processes, where it has been argued the process needs to change in the new age. Strategy has often considered only market or the probable events rather than those in the geopolitical, societal or AI amongst other new age topics considered in Chapters 2 and 3. In a time of disruption and AI, changes may emerge that are sudden and fast paced, where the traditional annual or irregular strategy update may no longer be appropriate. The role of the strategist may necessarily become involved in data collection or information verification, creativity and critical thought.

A strategy may no longer be a simple direction that rarely changes once it is approved, rather there is likely to be so much change in the new age that the strategy becomes more of a set of alternatives. Organisations, may in the future, refer to their strategy more often as it may include data, analysis and predictive thought that can be referred to and implemented quickly as change emerges. The nature of change in the future will consequently impact the way that stakeholders are informed, where failure to adequately address their issues and requirements may lead to distrust and loss of confidence in management.

Stakeholder Management

Stakeholders include a variety of groups including customers, employees, competitors and elements in the broader society that may have a level of interest in the organisation (Kaler, 2006; Verbeke & Tung, 2013). The various stakeholder groups interface have diverse or competing goals that interface with the organisation, yet despite the potential incongruence, competitive advantage may arise from the relationships (Verbeke & Tung, 2013). A lack of homogeneity in the stakeholder group creates challenges for management to effectively influence and control the diverse group. A number of stakeholders have authority in the organisation, where the shareholder or owner that can appoint and change the management of the organisation, whilst banks may have direct or significant influence over loans and financial parameters.

A number of stakeholders have indirect influence over the organisation including customers, suppliers and staff, each trading with the organisation through contracts and laws, each excerpting some influence over the organisational direction. Other stakeholders are broader and more remote, yet may also have influence over the organisation, including the society, government, compliance organisations, local communities and environmental groups. Owing to divergent stakeholder interests, management has to consider their competing interests against organisational goals, where an optimised position may not be possible. Banks for instance may be conservative, seeking security and stability, whereas customers may be seeking new, innovative or more risky solutions. Staff may want stability and longevity of employment with reasonable pay rises, yet shareholders may want higher returns or more change in the organisation. Managers that fail to make appropriate decisions despite the competing demands may lose their tenure or lose authority.

Society may not always understand organisational directions, where complaints may occur if the change is not completed in a balanced way, measured by social effects rather than purely financial effects (Zhao, Park, & Zhou, 2014). Failure to understand the broader requirements of society and broader stakeholders may cause protest or financial loss. Whilst for some organisations a financial result may be important, others like charities or non-government organisations may rate reputation and operational success as important. Management should be cognisant of the competing stakeholder interests, being aware of their thresholds, so considering and bargaining in an effort to gather support.

Management do not necessarily manage or control stakeholders as they do with other aspects of the organisation, this is due to the stakeholder having a choice to accept and follow, to challenge or reject decisions. Stakeholder management requires an element of influence, yet is required to bargain and achieve agreement that enables the organisation to move forward and achieve the goals set. This type of influence relationship relies on elements of leadership including those elements of trust, communication and engagement. The management aspect of stakeholder management is one of controlling and minimising any potential for escalation, protest or loss of support.

Stakeholders require trust in management as they may not always be familiar with the topics, the data, or the analysis that underlies the decisions and directions. Past organisational or relationship failures may reduce stakeholder trust in management so increasing the stakeholder requirement for additional information and verification in the future. Management should, as far as possible, ensure that agreements, data and analysis are accurate and timely, presented in an open way, irrespective of the stakeholder. Failure to openly present accurate information to any stakeholder may impede acceptance of future information or support, yet this may be more difficult in the new age as information may arrive faster and be more difficult to verify. Openness may assist in keeping trust with the stakeholders and thus management may need to declare their sources and the verification processes.

As was discussed in Chapter 4, the leader will have to consider the level, type and other elements of communication, yet it is management that will have to consider the content of the information. There are always decisions about commercial confidence and privacy when communicating, this is especially difficult with external stakeholders. Staff may require information about sensitive decisions or financial data, customers about product longevity and price, banks about financial forecasts. Failure to supply relevant information to stakeholders, will likely lead to the loss of relationship or support. The choices on what to communicate to stakeholders may be an important skill for those in management in the new age.

Organisational management should consider building a stakeholder management policy that sets out what they will communicate with stakeholders, and when. The policy should consider a wide range of stakeholders and recognise the potential for loss of sensitive information being offset with their need to know. The lack of predictability and verification of change in the new age may be problematic for good stakeholder relations.

The relationships may benefit from a stakeholder management plan that sets out likely information requirements and assesses accordingly, an example is shown in Table 5.2.

Table 5.2 has been prepared for use in identifying stakeholder information content requirements and may be used in conjunction with Table 4.2, as it focussed on the nature rather than the content of stakeholder. NSAT at Table 5.2 should be used is to first consider all the potential stakeholders of the organisation, using a very broad and indirect criteria and potentially naming each organisation. The second column of the Table 5.2 is to identify the potential information content requirements for the particular stakeholder group, the third column is included as a specific prompt to any emerging new age matters that stakeholders are likely to require information on. Potential responses for management to consider in relation to the content requirements are listed in the final right-hand side column. Once the NSAT has been completed, reviewed and approved, it can provide a checklist for management to consider when dealing with stakeholders or a list of interested parties once disruption or AI emerges.

Market Management

Management in the new age also need to consider the market, as new processes may be required during elevated new product risk, where the acceleration of information may improve strategic decisions (Proff & Fojcik, 2015). An organisation that implements marketing dashboards may find that there is improved speed and capability, where these may also improve performance (Krush, Agnihotri, & Trainor, 2016). In market disruption, management may require new mindsets to gain competitive advantage in terms of what is offered or marketed (Strandvik, Holmlund, & Lähteenmäki, 2018). There are clear differences in the new age for those involved in new products and services.

Traditionally, the marketing of the organisation, its values and direction is geared towards customers and other external parties, yet the connection with employees may be a critical part of the offer. The staff have influence on quality, timeliness, service and reputation and thus should not be underestimated. Staff are touch points for many stakeholders including customer, supplier and financiers to name a few. Whilst the staff are clearly a stakeholder, as discussed in the Stakeholder Management section of this chapter, they are also influential to product and service delivery that can affect the organisation's market position.

Once an organisation has identified a market advantage it may seek to announce and promote that advantage to the market, competitors and customers. The timing of market announcements as well as their content are critical to the success of any changes or improvements. Promotions that are too early to market

Table 5.2:   New Age Stakeholder Assessment Table (NSAT).

Stakeholder Group	Information Requirements (Likely)	New Age Gaps (Likely)	Actions to Mitigate Negative New Age Responses
Customer	• Product or service life cycle • New products or services • Product or service competition • Supply quantities and prices • Organisational reputation • Compliance with laws and society expectations	• Disruption and AI or robots' effects on relationship • Lack of verifiable information • Social media fake news or unreliable • Other new technology	• Information source verification • Detailed analysis of effects of disruption and AI shared • Openness of information • Sharing of risk assessments • Partnering relationship
Staff	• Job security • Financial results • Forecasts • Career, training and pay rates • Change — industrial or societal	• Disruption and AI or robots' effects on relationship • Lack of verifiable information • Social media fake news or unreliable • Other new technology • Competition with technology	• Information source verification • Detailed analysis of effects of disruption and AI shared • Openness of information • Sharing of risk assessments • Partnering relationship
Government	• Legal compliance • Industry changes • Society changes • Environmental compliance	• Employee relations • Financial stability • Corporate governance	• Advertising • Community and industry partnering groups • Responses to government enquiries
Community groups	• Legal compliance • Industry changes • Society changes	• Disruption and AI or robots' effects on relationship • Lack of verifiable information • Social media fake news or unreliable • Governance	• Advertising • Community and industry partnering groups • Responses to government enquiries

or that differ markedly to the actual features may not only affect product or services sales, they may also affect reputation and overall value. Management need to constantly assess market needs and organisational offer in order to promote and improve the market position. In the new age, these management requirements will be particularly changed and challenged, particularly on time and scope. One can imagine offering a new product or service to the market, advertising and promoting the offer, where shortly thereafter a tariff emerges to make the sale impossible. Alternately, imagine promoting a new product that will help customers only to find that competitors are now offering a robotic version that the customer likes better.

The concept of product or service, market position, offer and advertising are not new for an organisation to introduce or promote new products. In the new age, there will be increased uncertainty around the future, uncertainty around trade, politics, climate and technology as discussed in Chapters 2 and 3. Management will have to work closely with all stakeholders when committing large sums towards improvements and change in their organisation as the future may not be as predictable as it may have been in the past. The task of understanding market, disruption and AI from many sources of data and information will be a new skill for management in the future. Understanding what new products or services to develop and promote in what time frame will be more critical than ever. Management will need to develop sound systems to reduce risk and convince stakeholders that investment is not overly risky in this new age, where risk-averse organisations may perceive uncertainty as too high to invest at all. Risk management is discussed separately later in this chapter, as it is an important issue for the future of management in the new age.

Determining market position and estimating product acceptance may also be difficult to determine for management in the future, this is particularly difficult if past disruption or AI has impeded organisational results. Management may become focussed on their personal reputation or trust profiles within the organisation if previous changes approved have not been successful due to disruption or AI. There is potential for competition between the organisational interests and the self-preservation of management to occur when past decisions have been unsuccessful in the new age. In order to maintain stakeholder trust and engagement, management will likely need to include updates, assumptions and openness beyond what may have been usual in the past. Failure to provide sufficient detail to stakeholders at times of risk, for some may sound conservative and prudent, yet, in the new age, it may be perceived with distrust. Decision-making skills of management will be heightened in this new age as decisions may have to be made in short time frames, without full information integrity.

Organisational value and reputation may be lost if market position and profile are not controlled and managed. Management need to have systems in place to ensure that information circulating in the market is accurate and open, noting that with social media, email and Internet the control may be more difficult than ever before. Failures inside the organisation in terms of quality, quantity or supply may quickly be spread to customers and competitors if the management is not able to control information and data. Management may also need to have real-time systems in place to monitor and address fake news, erroneous customer queries or media reports. Systems and communication paths will likely need to be constantly open and ready for use in the new age, as change from multiple sources and multiple time frames is possible.

Management have multiple decisions to make about how their advantage can be marketed, how the information is disseminated and in what language or form. The cosmetics industry for instance has historically performed its marketing through print in magazines, often joining up with actors and celebrities. Car part manufacturers and fuel organisations have often supported car racing sports and activities and large sporting events. The range of marketing promotion methods, forms and outlets is almost endless, where the cost of each form may vary widely. Sponsoring an event like the football World Cup may involve millions of dollars, a sponsorship of a local football team may only involve hundreds of dollars. As large marketing campaigns often have long lead times, high cost and will be linked to future sales plans, so any change or risk may be costly for the organisation in terms of financial and reputational loss.

Despite the risks in market and marketing outlined above, there is potential for opportunity to be associated also in the new age. It may be possible for organisations to deliberately cause market disruption to gain advantage (Paetz, 2014), where innovation may be an essential element in that disruption (Denning, 2016), where multiple approaches may exist to the innovation (Leavy, 2017). Organisations that are creative and risk takers may be designing new AI or robots that will transform markets or they may be interested in causing disruption through working with governments or other means. Creating disruption in an attempt to gain advantage is a legitimate approach for management to support, although in taking this approach there is heightened risk due to the lack of control or knowledge on how the market may react to such disruption. There is argument that lean (Krafcik, 1988) can be used to introduce innovation into new products where testing the market often may be a good strategy when disruption and risk occur (Cooper, 2013). Smaller innovative organisations may be able to out manoeuvre more established organisations during disruption, where all markets may be at risk of associated face-paced change (Denning, 2014). In larger organisations, there may be a number of inhibitors to innovation including their higher levels of governance (Roundy, Harrison, Khavul, Pérez-Nordtvedt, & McGee, 2018), where the lack of organisational processes in smaller organisations may be an innovation advantage in the new age.

Product or organisational marketing and advertising may also likely change in the new age, as the traditional large advertising campaigns may no longer be relevant. Historically, some advertising campaigns may be planned over eighteen months ahead, new products and services designed even earlier. The increase in technology and its ease of use some has already led many organisations to plan and organise their own marketing and advertising, without the need to engage expensive large marketing organisations. There may be considerable losses if an organisation continues to formally plan advertising and spend large sums on the advertising if disruption or AI emerge suddenly and make the new product or service irrelevant. The traditional marketing and advertising organisations in the new age will need to broaden their skills, rather than merely being the conduit to printers and publishers they may have to show more insight into markets or more effective campaigns.

This section has discussed how disruption and AI may change the nature of marketing and advertising, where both activities are often critical to positioning products or services into the market. Management may have to consider innovation as one way of addressing the higher risk when disruption emerges as the higher risk levels may erode much of the traditional market activity. In order to survive and yet maintain presence, organisations may choose to perform advertising and marketing online on their own. The new age disruption has the potential to eliminate or drastically change those organisations in the traditional advertising and marketing roles, where reinvention and higher service levels may be required to survive.

Operations and Project Management

The above sections have discussed the management requirement to set strategy, manage stakeholders and set market position for an organisation. Another component of management is that of running the operations and completing projects, otherwise known as operations and project management. The term operations management has been argued to be associated with customer responsiveness, where agility and flexibility may be subsets of that concept (Bernardes & Hanna, 2009). The element of operations may be interpreted as all of the systems and resourced used presenting the organisational offer of product or service. Project management has been described as a particular temporary task that may include support and inclination as important factors, where the process may include internal and external staff (Nesheim & Smith, 2015). Both operations and project management may use process maps in order to control and improve processes (Muincu & Comanescu, 2015; Project Management Institute, 2004). The process map is a visual tool that assists management and staff identify and eliminate, redundancy or inefficiency in processes (Nascimento & Silveira, 2017; Rowell, 2018).

Once an organisation has set a strategy, had that approved and started to market the offer and direction, the next consideration for management is how the organisation will produce and operate to achieve those goals. Operations management may be an area of the organisation requiring layers of management that are interconnected, producing a system to produce the product or service in the way that the strategy imagined. Operations management is classically about managing the trade-offs between time, cost and quality in order to deliver the product or service on time. In order to improve efficiency, organisations may seek to minimise inventory through just in time or introduce lean (Krafcik, 1988) to reduce waste and complexity in their processes (Muincu & Comanescu, 2015). There are other trade-offs for management to consider including competing stakeholder expectations, financial outcomes, safety or reputational outcomes.

Process feedback loops and communication are often used in to improve or ensure quality, where four particular types of communication are important to success (Zeng, Phan, & Matsui, 2013). A feedback loop inserts a step into processes that reviews deviations and seeks improvements, where the loops may be essential for organisational knowledge (Akbar, Baruch, & Tzokas, 2018). Despite the widespread use of business process as a tool, success may depend on the inclusion of formalised role definitions, ownership and governance (Goeke & Antonucci, 2013). It is traditionally rare for organisations to review their processes often, as there is considerable time and effort required to understand processes and to document, although some may do it as part of their process improvement or quality process.

In order to manage an operation or a project, the process commences with organisational vision and mission that is translated into strategy. The strategy is often broken down into annual budgets that determine the required financial returns as well as the marketing or sales goals that set price points and volumes for product or services. Operational and project management often set key performance indicators (KPI) as a way of monitoring performance, where deviations are monitored and reacted to as required to achieve performance. During a budget-setting process, operations management determine and highlight constraints based on the capacity of people, machine, knowledge and skills. There will often be negotiations required within the organisation and with stakeholders in order to resolve capacity constraints identified, where actions may include increasing the capacity or reducing the sales offer.

A general overview of the operations process described earlier is shown in Fig. 5.2, being a graphical summary of the operational cycle described above.

As can be seen in Fig. 5.2, the operational cycle is iterative, where, once the operation has begun, there is constant monitoring and adjustment through feedback to ensure the process remains likely to achieve the goals and KPI set earlier in the process.

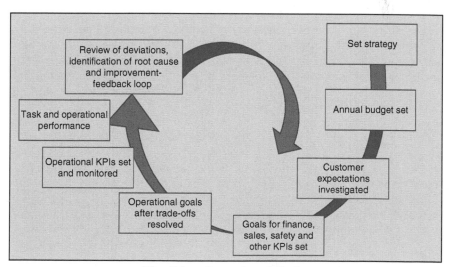

Fig. 5.2: Operational Cycle.

To avoid chaos in the operational task performance, both operations and project need regular short-term planning to ensure that tasks are arranged logically and are likely to achieve the KPIs required. Operational and project management organise and communicate daily expectations, resources and sequences so that the organisation can produce and sell the outputs expected. Operational managers are responsible for deciding who does what and when in the organisation, yet regular relationships with other parts of the organisation are required to include variations in customer requirements or plans. The supply of resources needs to be finely tuned between outputs and times, where the aim is to meet expectations on time, quantity and quality. The management style and organisational culture, structures and processes may each be important to the success of delivering plans.

The style of management may be very important to the way operations and projects are conducted. The research of Brazilian project managers indicates that they were focussed on people interactions, exhibiting a style that was reactive yet tenacious (Ramos, Mota, & Corrêa, 2016). Whilst autocratic styles in the early part of the twentieth century were successful in building the likes of the Ford motor empire (Clarke, 1987), it is unlikely that employees of today would accept autocratic styles of management. There is a research that shows how personality preferences towards efficiency may bias management towards autocracy, yet when elected, management may prefer to use democracy and consensus styles (Kocher et al., 2013). In research of the construction industry, management conflict resolution skills are important to relationships, where a compromising style may be harmful to contractor relationships (Lu & Wang, 2017). In these examples, it is clear that the authority of position is no guarantee of operational management success, where the management style chosen may influence the reaction and performance of staff.

Whilst a policy is usually general and behavioural in nature, procedures are almost always specific to a task and detailed, yet despite this distinction they are often confused in the workplace. A procedure will have been developed by management, often after technical advice where multiple perspectives should have been considered. Procedures may need to be reviewed and approved by a range of experts or advisors in safety, environment, engineering and staff amongst others. Failure to include employees in procedure development may cause disharmony between staff and management leading to sub-optimal adherence to procedures. Procedures, if not designed well, may result in poor practices, injury, poor quality or loss of financial outcomes, where considerable time is required to develop effective procedures. Policies and procedures are included in the organisational framework in an attempt by management to communicate expectations and control performance towards expectations.

The importance of delegation is more pronounced when the organisation is large, complex or has multiple locations and divisions, yet even in a very small retail organisation, the management may have to delegate responsibility to others. Staff roles descriptions are usually required to maintain some order in the organisation as well as setting out skills required during staff hiring. Job descriptions are also required to set out authorities and delegations so that the staff member is clear. Authorities that are set too low may cause low morale, staff feeling untrusted or without control so need to be cautiously considered.

Organisational structure sets out the hierarchy of control, where structures as organisations seek to gain competitive advantage. An analysis of thrifts in the USA across the nineteenth and twentieth centuries shows that structures may vary over time according to government legislation, market situations and even fraud (Mason, 2012). Structures may exist in several forms including that of regional, customer, product and mixed (Williams et al., 2016), where there may be benefits and risks in each type. Competitors may have very similar structures or be completely different in the one industry, where the nature is decided by management through their perception of competitive advantage. Where organisational performance is below expectations management and stakeholders may seek, as one reaction, to change organisational structure and restore performances or competitive advantage.

Operational management, like others in the organisation, are responsible for ensuring quality in their staff, resources, processes and outputs, be that for a service or a product. Quality may have various measures including (but not limited by) time, cost, look, feel, information, image, etc., where the operational manager in conjunction with marketing and others needs to define those measures that link with customer, reputation and strategic advantage. Failure to maintain quality on the required factors may impact reputation of the service or product or the whole organisation. Whilst quality and process control may tempt the operational manager to control and define all processes, there are times when this approach may not be of advantage to the organisation. Staff involved in services direct to the public may need to have a level of delegation and authority to improve service or improve product delivery, be that in the form of process redefinition, one off deviation or process improvement. Failure for staff to be engaged in quality improvement may be perceived as inflexible, tight control leading to a lack of staff motivation.

Improvement processes are well defined for organisations and projects (Project Management Institute, 2004), where the aim is to reduce deviation, waste and cost. In order to improve processes, there needs to be KPIs defined and monitored before analysis and correcting actions can be formulated. Where corrective actions do not appear to improve processes as expected the management will cycle back to defining more of the process and setting of KPIs; this usually continues in an iterative process until the quality required is achieved.

The above poses difficulties for management as the past procedures, processes and structures may be too slow, too inflexible or too complex for the new age. Past management practices have evolved in order to increase control and the achievement of performance on target, yet those practices may be no longer be appropriate during the new age that is characterised by sudden and transformational change. To reduce the unpredictability of change in the new age, management will need to consider buying in or internally generating ideas, monitoring and confirmation processes. Whilst organisations may already have strategic or marketing and product development functions, the existing ones may be far too focussed on the predictable or likely rather than the improbable or invisible changes. The new function required in the new age is one named here as the new idea generation function (NIGF). One may argue about the name or the exact role description, yet there is clear belief that organisations of the future must consider and prepare for disruption and AI that is unlikely to be predicted and understood within the old structures and processes.

Management, in preparing for the new age, will very likely need to generate new ideas in order to identify and prepare for disruption and AI before they emerge or become possibilities. Sitting back and waiting for the customer or competitors to introduce change will not be appropriate when change is so sudden and fast paced. In any case, the new age change is likely to come from far beyond the current market or competitor and thus waiting until it is imminent may not be sufficient time to react. The traditional iterative improvement process may be too slow for the new age. New elements to be included in the new NIGF function will likely need skills in monitoring and understanding, gathering data and analysis, verification and investigation, scenario planning and decision making under high risk and uncertainty. Table 5.3 shows the elements that may be required in the new function, where some of these skills may exist in organisations today. Although organisations of today, and historically, may have omitted changes that were hard to understand, predict or thought to be only possible. In order for an organisation to form the NIGF function, they may need to hire and develop new skills as analysis and understanding of disruption may not be skills that they readily hold today.

Question 5.2. Choose an existing organisation and review its structure and processes. Determine, through a comparison analysis, what elements of the NIGF may already exist in that organisation. Describe how any missing elements of the NIGF could, or should, be included into the existing organisation. How should the organisation set out to be forward thinking and ready for disruption or AI and robots of the new age? What are the advantages of including NIGF in an organisation for the future?

As was discussed in Chapter 1 of this book, the new age will occur with fast pace, being assisted by globalisation and new forms of communication. Any simple adoption of new skills or merely the NIGF in any organisation is unlikely to be sufficient for the organisation to thrive in the new age. The rigidity of organisational processes, structures and job descriptions may be counterproductive in the new age. In disruption and AI, management may need to work in uncertainty with less definition, whilst more data than ever may be available there will be far less time to analyse it. Management may also seek new staff skills in response to any emerging disruption and AI as the organisation will be required to operate faster, with less definition or controls in place than ever before. The following Human Resource Management section of this chapter and the rest of this book considers and discusses how management may decide to respond to the change of the new age.

Table 5.3:   New Idea Generation Function.

NIGF Element Name	Disruption	AI and Robots	Internal
Monitor	Review newspapers, social media, analyst reports, currency, election analysis, political reports, trade reports, government advice.	Trade shows Science journals Social media Other industries Technology magazines	Identify products, processes and structures that are sub-optimal or may be affected by disruption or AI if they emerge.
Verification	Seek additional sources of information and data that confirms emerging changes.	Seek additional sources of information and data that confirms emerging changes.	Compare internal data with external to see if the change is likely to occur.
Data Analysis	Seek data from significant data sources so that trends and analysis can be determined.	Review science journals for data reports on new AI and robotic capabilities.	Review external data against internal data to see what impact there may be on the organisation operationally or financially.
Understanding	Discussion groups Media reports Industry groups Analyst briefings Political analysis groups	Review prototypes Trade shows Direct questions with designers and manufacturers.	Review internal capabilities and design against the new change, build gap analysis.
Scenarios	Build scenarios from best to worst, with a few disruptions to a multiple.	Build scenarios for new AI or robots from best to worst case.	Consider and build scenarios of internal responses to each disruption and AI.

Human Resource Management

As discussed in the previous sections of this chapter, management may need to adjust many aspects of the organisation in the future in response to change in the new age. The operational and project management are responsible for setting processes and KPIs to ensure the quality delivery of product or services, where staff may be the most important element to adjust. Staff in most organisations may be an important part of the operation in terms of significance, relevance and cost, where the staff may also be an important element for customer or other stakeholder engagement.

The human resource management (HRM) function has emerged as a specialist position that assists the more generalist and functional management in dealing with staff-related matters due to their importance in organisations. The HRM often assists or leads in industrial negotiations, employment law, recruitment and possibly training. The HRM role, with its specialised technical skills, allows management to focus on tasks involving work allocation, process, structure, performance and improvement. At times, the HRM role may negotiate on behalf of the organisation or at other times they may advise management of laws and processes and act in staff disciplinary matters. At other times, the HRM may advocate for employees or organise training. The HRM function may also act as mentor to line management in relation to employment law, employee relations, employee training and even employee safety matters.

Management, through their relations with HRM, determine policies and employment agreements that attempt to control costs and align with the organisational performance requirements. However, today the HRM role is often the recruiter, the negotiator and the contract proposer. For larger organisations that may be multi-divisional or multi-country, the HRM role provides consistency in contracts, terms and policies rather than allowing each area to negotiate different terms and cause conflict. In recent times, there has been a reduction in collective unionism in a number of countries (Cristiani & Peiró, 2014; Verma & Fang, 2002), where reduced focus by HRM on industrial relations over time may have been the result.

In the new age, several new matters in relation to staff may present that will affect the nature of the HRM role in the future. As AI and robots emerge, there may be wide spread staff losses, those remaining staff may need to work directly with robots and certainly with less people overall. The staff may be unhappy with the changes and protest, revolt and likely reform into collective groups to gather power in the changing new age. This will require the HRM role to firstly be good at negotiation with the staff being made redundant and ensure that the payouts required are both legal and fair. Secondly, for those remaining employees, they may need to be reskilled or reselected to ensure that they are appropriate to work in environments devoid of humans that may require high analysis skills. The HRM role will be required to assist the other management roles understand the changing environment and requirements for new assessment tools, failure to address this may leave operational management to choose employees that remain based on past rather than future skills.

Disruption may or may not lead to sudden mass loss of jobs as AI or robots may and thus it will be the sudden and fast paced nature of disruption that may affect the staff relations. Currently, workplace agreements and structures may pay people based on skills and roles, in disruption those rigid structures may have to change suddenly. There is potential for great upheaval with staff when disruption causes an organisation to change suddenly or perish. Staff may be unsupportive of sudden changes to job descriptions, tasks and structures and so may even form stronger collectives to halt and prevent change. Resistance to change is not merely a staffing matter as other factors are involved (Donald, 2014, 2016) and thus the matter is discussed further in Chapter 7 of this book. Great leadership and management skills will be required to address staff issues during disruption as the current systems are built around stability.

Employees that remain employed after disruption and AI will be relatively more important due to their ratio inside the organisation. This will require management to reset the training and skill development of staff. The HRM role may well become more important to the organisation in satisfying and resolving staff matters of the new age. The past inflexible, control systems of the organisation may be challenged in the new age as staff request and require additional flexibility to work from home, to be trained in data analysis, for more breaks due to stress caused from working in AI or robotic environments. The list of staff issues in the new age may be complex and vary widely, thereby creating new and increased issues for management and HRM to resolve. The flexibility requirements will go both ways, where the organisation may require workplace change quickly without full documentation, whilst staff may want new pay rates and terms in order to agree.

Management and staff may need more information on the new age in preparation for the changes ahead. The organisation may need more measures for staff and management in order to understand gaps and opportunities. In the past, many organisations have adopted systems like circular feedback surveys to assist in management development, where considerable benefits may have arisen if deployed with training and career development (McCarthy & Garavan, 2001). The staff group in any organisation will not be homogenous, where there may be varied competing demands based on the changes expected. There is the evidence of staff that identify strongly with an organisation being more focussed on the change process than the outcomes, whereas staff identifying less with the organisation may be more interested in results of the change (Van Knippenberg, Martin, & Tyler, 2006). There is a high relationship between management quality and their readiness for the future (Rank, Unger, & Gemünden, 2015), where the readiness trait may be important in hiring management in the future. Awards may be used to improve motivation and performance, yet those may not always be successful, hence requiring new factors (Gallus & Frey, 2016) to be considered.

As discussed earlier in this chapter and in Chapter 4, there is high likelihood that significant changes in leadership and management may be required during the new age. In order to cope with the new age of change, management will likely need to alter processes and structures, where there will be significant impact on staffing numbers, roles and responsibilities that may flow into staff relations. Satisfactory responses to staff requirements may assist the organisation change when required, where failure may result in considerable issues including reformation of collectives, power struggles and dissent. The HRM role may be more important in preventing and resolving the staffing issues that may arise in the new age, where creativity in developing new arrangements that are acceptable to employees may be critical. Further discussion on staffing matters in the new age are done in Chapters 6 and 7.

Risk Management and Control

The origins of risk management began after World War II, initially associated with insurance, where it now covers operational, financial, liquidity and market risks (Dionne, 2013). Others have commented that risk management has broadened due to many failures, now covering all organisational risk (Power, 2004; Vinnari & Skærbæk, 2014). For the purposes of this book, risk management is concerned with the identification, valuation and mitigation of organisational risk in the attempt to restrain or inhibit organisational risk effects, where the risk origins include disruption, AI and robotics. Risk management may also include market, financial or even safety risk as required by a range of stakeholders including auditors, banks, shareholders and government. Many risk management practices of today may still not yet include geopolitical, currency, trade war and other changes of the new age discussed in Chapters 2 and 3.

Risk management requires a process to identify risks, followed by a process to estimate their value that enables management to assess and rank any risks based on the multiplication of risk percentage with estimated value. The assessment of risk is the primary responsibility of management, where organisations often appoint others to review and mentor risk decisions. In the case of traditionally structured organisations, governance boards appoint auditors to review risk, insurance companies require forms and processes be followed and verified. In the case of projects, governance boards may appoint Project Management Offices (PMO) to review and oversee projects, where they review project processes, forecasts and risk. Overview of risk assessment is required as identification and likelihood assessment is subjective, where staff or management alone may not always identify appropriate risk or may be biased.

Management of risk is important for controlling and performing up to expectations as once the risk is known, various actions and preparations are put in place to minimise or eliminate the consequences of risks identified. Reactions towards risk vary according to the industry, market, risk aversion of stakeholders as well as management attitudes and experiences. Organisational size has been shown to influence capital investment choices when facing risk (Doshi, Kumar, & Yerramilli, 2017) and thus indicating that decisions on risk are not uniform. Project structure may be the most important characteristic influencing risk in a project (Tomasz, 2014). As uncertainty and risk cannot be eliminated it may be advisable in high risk environments to make incremental decisions to limit the size of any potential losses (Vahlne, Hamberg, & Schweizer, 2017).

Risk assessment bias may occur due to the lack of data or information, or through over optimism, where so many organisations now require risk to be assessed by a peer review or cross section of the organisation. The additional oversight by senior management review or the PMO review may add an extra layer of quality to the process. The process of identifying risk needs to be open so as to minimise bias, assisted by including a range of people in the process. Working in a team has long been associated with idea generation (Deichmann & Jensen, 2018) and thus identifying risk through brainstorming may be an appropriate,

Table 5.4:   Risk Register Table.

Risk Identified	Description of Risk	Likelihood %	Consequence Value $	Risk Value $	Potential Mitigation
Competitors decrease price by 10%	Increase in sales volume of competitor offset by losses in our organisation.	Based on history 25%.	$4 Million	25% × $4 million = $1 million	Change our offer to include new ancillaries so customer can see more value in our offer.
Staff demand 10% pay rise	Competitors have offered 8% that was recently accepted.	80% based on competition behaviour.	$2 Million	80% × $2 million = $1.6 million	Consider efficiency requirements to offset the value loss, counter claim.
Product recall	Risk of quality systems failing and resulting in all product recall. Loss of reputation value.	5% Based on no recent history.	$5 Million for 1 off recall $15 Million for loss of reputation	5% × $5 million + 5% × $15 million = $1 million	Audit of quality systems by external party. Communication to staff as to quality importance.
			Total risk register =	$3.6 Million	

Source: Project Management Institute (2004).

as brainstorming is already used in auditor fraud investigation, where structure to the process may yield improved identification (Chen, Khalifa, Morgan, & Trotman, 2018).

Risk registers are a way that organisations often keep track of their identified risk, where these are taken to review meetings with stakeholders, auditors, mentors and governance reviews. The registers can take considerable time to create, manage and update, where the stakeholders may be very reliant on the information contained therein. Project and operational management may not always have the skills, time or resources to maintain the risk registers as required, or may be biased in their preparation. The governance and process around risk register completion and assessment is one that stakeholders and senior managers should consider greatly when designing processes in an organisation.

Risks may emerge faster than ever in the new age, as information may not be reliable or verifiable and may be generated in large volumes. In December 2018, trade wars had broken out, where the extent of tariffs and implications are yet to fully emerge, including trade wars between the United States, China and Turkey, or between Europe, Russia and the United States. Any organisation, trading across borders that may be involved in any upcoming trade wars, is likely to incur additional risk on supply, price and currency amongst many other associated risks.

In traditional risk registers, disruption events such as trade wars, sanctions or tariffs may not have been included, considered improbable or insufficiently controllable by management. The new age will likely present as many disruption events, where ignorance or avoidance may no longer be an appropriate response. Globalisation and changed communication processes and enabled disruption to emerge quickly without too much warning. Management are responsible for delivering organisational performance, tasked with identifying risk, analysing and mitigation so despite the uncertainty of the new age they will need to find appropriate responses. These new risks will likely be problematic as the likelihood and consequence are far less predictable than those considered in the past.

The pace of change may increase significantly in the future, arising from increased speed of technology, speed of communication assisted by the interconnectedness of globalisation. The increased pace may bring forward the adoption of robotics or AI ahead of current predictions, or the pace of change may accelerate new unknown disruptions. Organisations of today may not readily include robots, AI or disruption discussed in Chapters 2 and 3 in their risk-assessment processes, where increased risks may arrive as they emerge. Risk registers and responses do not guarantee risk avoidance but they do inform stakeholders and assist understanding.

Question 5.3. Various aspects of trade wars have commenced in 2018, where some have already imposed tariffs. The Brexit vote in the UK parliament was not taken in their parliament in December 2018, where the UK currency fell considerably after the delay was announced. On the 11 December 2018, it is unclear if the UK government will remain, whether a deal on Brexit will be agreed or what it will end up containing.

Imagine now that you are running an organisation in December 2018. The organisation purchases parts from the UK that are assembled in Europe, where the finished pieces are destined for your customers in Russia, China and the Middle East.

What might be the risks that should be included in your organisations risk register? What issues do you see in assessing the likelihood and value for the risks? How might the organisation best mitigate the risks? How might the management inform stakeholders of the risks without losing their confidence in your organisation?

The new age will present many new difficulties for management as risk is naturally associated with disruption, where reasonable estimates of likelihood may be difficult to achieve. Climate change is one disruption that most organisations will need to consider, where some position as to its likelihood will need to be taken along with some estimate on start time. One could ignore the matter or leave the issue for another 25 years, yet an organisation, whilst going on, will be making decisions about location, plant, staff and operational matters. Organisations that may buy land and buildings near the sea or airport, may find that sea rise of say 50 centimetres, in say three years' time may render their investment worthless. The time forecasts on sea rises may be later than a three-year period, yet the exact timeframe the risk may enter the market prices is unknown. There is a wider political argument as to whether climate change is real or not, yet an organisation is deciding around risk on an almost daily basis.

Whilst climate disruption is just one disruption to consider, there is more than property to consider. Should climate change emerge with real evidence, there is potential for rapid currency losses or mass migration away from lower areas of the world and some countries may close borders and trade. Irrespective of one's political belief about climate disruption, rapid change and even panic could arise without verified fact based on mere perception, fake news or social media. Management should consider included climate change risk registers, yet there may be very few that currently do. If climate disruption is left untreated then risk may grow where at some point staff may even boycott organisations located on coastal areas.

In future, it is quite likely that stakeholders, insurers and government may require organisations to disclose their risk registers and defend their mitigation plans. It is probable, at a future point in time, that failing to consider disruption or AI or associated risks, may open the directors and senior management to claims of unprofessionalism or even negligence. Assessment of risk registers may be difficult if the mere possible is included in with the probable, yet organisations attempting to assign value to an organisation may require such information. The risk averse may decrease their value of organisations where new age risk is identified, yet others may see opportunities and assess value more positively. It is envisaged that disruption, AI and robotics or other possible events may be best collated and reported on a separate table, discussed later in Chapter 7. The traditional risk management processes may also not be appropriate in uncertainty, where a more heuristic processes may be more appropriate (Mousavi & Gigerenzer, 2014).

Where risk registers are reviewed by auditors, accountants, senior management, PMO or governance parties there are often rigid processes and times applied. The inflexibility of these traditional controls may be counter to the flexibility and speed required of the future new age. Stakeholders may require the organisation to be evolving and flexible to change in the new age, yet current processes and change methodology may be too slow and inflexible. Risk register preparation and response may need to be far faster and more organic changes in the new age, where too late or too early may change the risk profile of the organisation.

This section discussed how risk is often managed in organisations, where traditionally the risk included for review was probable and could be valued. These traditional practices for managing risk were aimed at controlling and delivering performances to expectations. Independent review of risk is a common process in organisations today be that from internal or external sources, where the independence is aimed at ensuring risk is appropriately identified and managed. It is clear that the nature of the new age the past risk management processes may no longer work or be appropriate as globalisation, disruption and AI will likely affect risk in less predictable ways at a faster pace than ever before.

Summary

There are many traditional structures, processes and tools of management that have evolved and since the industrial revolution. Whilst management tools do not always achieve their goals for specific organisations, the overall system and integrity are achieved for the most part. Exceptions to the system integrity are rare as shown by the GFC, Asian crisis or the great depression. Investors in organisations, through their due diligence and oversight, take risk and earn return that is based on organisational controls. Organisations of the new age will likely need to be more flexible and responsive to change whilst managing heightened risk. New tools and techniques will likely be required for management in the new age as change will be faster, include less information reliability, far more data that will threaten organisations more than ever before. All will not be lost as management will likely respond to the challenges and seek opportunity as change ensues. Chapters 6 and 7 explore potential organisational responses that may be adopted in order to survive in the new age.

Chapter 6

Organisational Implications

Organisations will not be able to avoid the emerging New Age:
failure to respond may lead to organisational failure.
—Mathew Donald

As has been discussed in Chapter 1 of this book, there are important differences in the new age that will affect organisations for a long time into the future. This chapter aims to assess some of the more important aspects of this change as a means to enlighten management and leadership of the impending change. The new age will likely be characterised by sudden and fast change aided by globalisation, associated with the various forms of data and communication that may not always be reliable or verifiable. Management and leadership will likely need to sponsor organisational change in order to prepare and respond the new age of change, where the slower controls and processes of the past may have to give way for the change ahead.

In the new age, data and information will likely be more readily available, in vast volumes, in almost real-time based on new technology, Internet and interconnectivity. Yet, despite the speed and volume of data available, a great deal of the emerging data may be unreliable or unverifiable, varying in form from fake news, social media, blogs to mere rumour and speculation. Organisations with leadership and management that can cope with the pace and uncertainty may be able to assist their organisations adapt to the new age change ahead. The new skills, structures and processes required may likely relate to the organisations need for data, trends, patterns and information. The staff skills required may be significantly different to those currently held, where leadership and management may have to adapt to their new requirements. Chapter 6 is neither predictive nor prescriptive in nature; rather, it explores with critical thinking potential organisational considerations in response to the new age. Chapter 7 explores current research on the topic and proposes new ideas and methods that may be useful to monitor change.

Strategy

As was tabled in Chapter 5 of this book, strategy may be defined as an organisational activity that occurs less frequently than others, where the identification of advantage is determined after a review of markets, history and emerging

Leading and Managing Change in the Age of Disruption and Artificial Intelligence, 121–141
doi:10.1108/978-1-78756-367-420191007

change. The advantages identified in a strategy are later formed into detailed long-term actions and targets that set the organisation forward, where the presence of the plan assists in creating short-term targets and synergies for organisational decision making. A key issue in the development and setting of strategy in the new age is that strategy may become redundant quickly as new disruption and the artificial intelligence (AI) or robots emerge. Current strategy setting processes, in larger organisations especially, take long amounts of time, involving intense reviews and resources before they are confirmed and adopted.

Organisations may currently have small teams that develop strategy based on a specialised understanding and reading of the particular industry, markets and trends. The strategist of the future may need to be familiar with social media reports, fake news, politics and many other sources of ideas and information that may be relevant. In the new age, rather than generating ideas in isolation, it may be better for the strategist to use teamwork as that has been associated with ideas generation and innovation (Deichmann & Jensen, 2018).

The recognition of AI and robotics into a strategy for many organisations today may be too remote to consider, although over the next 10 years some form of AI may likely emerge in many industries. Drones are already emerging as toys for the mass market, regularly used by militaries, photographers and real estate agents, thus the wider industrial and organisational use may not be so far away. For strategists of the future, there are questions about how the drone may evolve and be used in alternate ways, questions about when the new use of drones may emerge. The mere existence of drones today does not necessarily mean that they will automatically be used commercially for drop offs of parcels or pizza, yet those are possibilities. The strategist that forecasts drone use or robotics in the next five years may be too early or too late, where it is not yet clear if government or consumers will embrace the technology and open up markets.

Many organisations may not include AI or robotics in their current strategy as there is considerable risk in terms of the size of the investment and uncertainty around the benefits, their likelihood and the value. In only the last few years, Uber-type organisations have taken considerable taxi market share worldwide with Internet bookings and independent owner drivers. Despite the recent Taxi changes, many taxi owners may still not be planning for the emergence of driverless cars or automated flying drones taking passengers. Whilst there is likelihood of drones cannibalising the taxi product, many strategists may perceive risk and uncertainty as too high to consider, be that by drone or driverless car.

Organisations of the future may benefit if they include some formal review of emerging technology in their strategy preparation. The strategist to maintain confidence may need to show that the unusual or less possible have been considered, explaining reasons for their inclusion or rejection. It may be quite uncertain as to when AI or robotics may emerge, where advantages and reliability may be difficult to assess. Timing of new technology adoption is important as being too early may incur high development costs or not be successful, due to the lack of testing. In the assessment of risk, it may be prudent for organisations to estimate and understand costs involved in reverting back to the pre-implementation stage. A formal review of AI may be required to assess risk and uncertainty thereto related.

Table 6.1 is an example of how AI may be assessed in the new age, where the pace of change may be high as well as the risk and uncertainty. Whilst the table is merely a summary, it is envisaged that considerable robust debate, data and analysis would support each line in the NASAT table. As can be seen from the above, there are many aspects to assess AI at a strategic level, where the true costs and details may only be known when implementation occurs.

An organisation may perform review processes in their Research and Development (R&D) where they develop new products or services. In considering new products, services or internal processes changing as a result of new AI or robots, the organisation may benefit as perceiving those with similar risks to any current R&D. As AI or robots are likely to filter throughout the organisation, it may be prudent to assess AI and robotics carefully, formally in order to better understand and decide if the time is right to include them in the strategy.

The high risk in AI and disruption may require management to build processes that are iterative rather than transformational so that the size of the risk is minimised, where the next iteration is only committed to once the previous one is shown to be successful. This approach may minimise long time frames in development and reduce the risk of technical failure. Stakeholders may be more positive towards an iterative approach as they can measure success more easily and be in a position to control using milestones. An iterative approach may be slower than a full-scale implementation; however, it may be easier to slide back to an earlier version or the pre-change state. The additional time involved may also benefit integration and testing as the complexity involved in iterative change may be less than that of transformational change.

Data integrity in the strategic process may be difficult to capture as the new technology may be merely reported in journals or trade shows and magazines, where protypes may be the only examples, or competitors may have all the new data. The strategist and the stakeholder will likely have to work with poor data integrity or sub-optimal data when assessing new AI or robots, where the lack of data and high risk may inhibit change for some. Creativity in data analysis and data sourcing may be critical for the early adopter of new AI, where negotiation with suppliers and customers may be required in order to gather sufficient data for valid analysis. There will be great temptation for the risk takers and the entrepreneurs to work with insufficient data and information, taking advantage through innovation and creativity. Challenges for the entrepreneurs will be to gather sufficient stakeholder support whilst declaring the assumptions and risks.

It is already clear that disruption has increased risk and uncertainty, where changes in geopolitics, trade wars and tariffs at the end of 2018 are identified, yet the direction and resolution is quite unclear. Those setting strategy at the end of 2018 may find that the risk and uncertainty is so high that planning for each scenario may be too difficult. In later December 2018, it is unclear in the UK if the government will fall, unclear what Brexit will end up like, unclear what the currency will be in one year's time. At the same time, widespread protests in France have occurred, where government reform may stall or reverse as a result. Investing in Europe, the UK or the USA to name a few disruptions towards the end of 2018 may be too uncertain and unclear that organisations may not be able to set clear

Table 6.1:   New Age Strategy Assessment Tool (NASAT) for AI/Robotic.

AI Aspect for Consideration	Comment	Metric to Consider	Risk %
AI availability (time from now)	Consider the time to develop scope, design and implement AI or robotic.	Time required to implement AI from scope, design to implementation.	Show the likelihood of this AI being available in the timeframe.
Verification	Consider verifying the technology or data from multiple sources, check the scope and functions.	Estimate how many cross confirmations of function and capability can be confirmed.	Determine a risk of the capability not being ready or not functioning as advertised.
AI adoption cost	Value the full cost of AI or robot including implementation and any redundancy costs.	Value including internal labour to adopt.	± Risk % of the adoption cost varying.
AI adoption benefit	Value of associated business benefits in adopting AI/robot.	Value of benefit and/or costs avoided.	± Risk % of the adoption benefits varying.
AI conversion time	Value of activities to convers from current technology to new AI or robot.	Value of conversion including internal labour.	± Risk % of the adoption cost varying.
Integration complexity	Rating of technical risk in design and/or in integration.	Estimated human hours to integrate new technology.	± Risk % of the integration hours varying.
Customer Impact	Estimate of integration impact on customer and interconnectivity.	Estimate importance or value of AI/robot to customer.	Risk that the customer will be adversely impacted by AI/robot.
Advantage versus competitors	Is this AI/robot to gain market advantage or to follow competitors.	Value of market advantage.	Risk of market advantage not being reached.
Ease	Detail how hard it may be to revert back to status quo if AI/robot is unsuccessful.	Value or hours required to move away from AI or robot if it is unsuccessful	% likelihood that AI/robot will not meet expectations

strategy, or invest in those regions without taking considerable risk. Yet, in order to trade and take advantage, organisations will already be setting plans and directions in their strategic plans.

In order to satisfy the stakeholder requirements a range of strategies may be required for presentation. In the past, offering several scenarios for approval to stakeholders may have been perceived as weak or confused; yet, in the new age, such may be required in order to clarify risk and uncertainty. In order to create sufficient scenarios in the new age, idea generation may be required that may require creativity and openness of thought. Whilst the concentration of ideas may be beneficial in stability, diversity may be required in unstable times (Strandvik, Holmlund, & Lähteenmäki, 2018). Management may have to seek new process and structures in order to create an organisation that is able to be creative and generate ideas appropriate for the new age.

In the new age, information proliferates informally and may often be unverified through social media, Internet and emails. A reduction in demand for information sourced from newspapers and television has occurred in recent years, despite those historically being prepared by professional journalists that verify information before publication. In the new age, that may be further disruption and AI, where timely accurate and verifiable information may be more important than ever to enable management to analyse emerging issues and improve decision making. If reliable news is less available overall in the new age, organisations may seek to purchase independently verified information, or they may seek to hire those with skills useful for verification, including journalism, political advisers, ex-diplomats, analysts and risk assessors.

Stakeholder support is required for strategy to be adopted. The way strategy is developed, analysed and built is the responsibility of management. Leadership is responsible for communicating the messages and arguments in the strategy, where failing to gather support may leave even the best strategy un-actioned. Stakeholders will require the various forms of communication and argument in order to understand the strategy direction. Openness and trust will be required between the leadership and stakeholders in order for information to be appropriately communicated and accepted in the new age, as the suddenness and pace of change may be significant and confusing when direction alters. Those in leadership roles of the future may also require negotiation and influencing skills in order to explain the reasons for variable scenarios, risk and uncertainty in ways that stakeholders can understand and support.

An iterative approach to strategy may be required in order to maintain the support of stakeholders in the new age. The strategy of the new age is not likely to be a mere high-level financial plan produced annually, as it is may be needing constant review and amendment. Organisations managing large or multiple projects may already use gates and milestones as a means to manage through risk and uncertainty. It is proposed here that managing through milestones or gates may assist organisations operating in the future. Long-term strategy may be significantly reduced to possibly no more than a simple statement of goals, where anything more detailed may be inappropriate during rapid and sudden change.

Strategy is likely to be more flexible, with multiple scenarios in the new age as it will need to include possibilities with ranges of likelihood and uncertainty

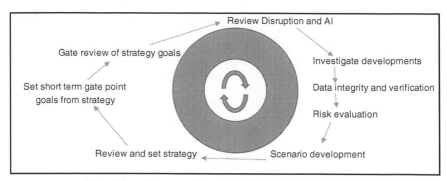

Fig. 6.1:   Strategy Iterative Gate Process (SIGP).

attached. The set and forget type of strategy of the past may no longer be useful or relevant to the organisation of the future. Continually setting strategy, re-evaluating and re-setting at fast pace may be very characteristic of the new age, where new consideration may be required as new information emerges. An alternate way to assess and re-set strategy may be that of a gated approach, where new directions are not confirmed until they have been reviewed and formally approved.

As can be seen in Fig. 6.1, it is proposed that strategy in the new age be iterative, where it is assessed and amended regularly based on set gates that are linked to strategy goals or timeframes. At each gate, there is a review of performance and information against the strategy goals, before the next iteration of strategy is set there would be a scan of disruptions and AI to understand emerging data and information.

Question 6.1. Your organisation currently sets and updates its 10-year strategic plan annually. The current process takes six months to complete involving over 50 staff members and 300 spreadsheets. The review with senior management, shareholders and banks takes on average two months to complete.

Write a business proposal to this organisation setting out reasons why the existing strategic planning process is no longer appropriate in the new age. Include in this proposal a critique of the SIGP versus the current process, recommend any changes to the SIGP or the current process setting out reasons and benefits of your proposal.

This section has reviewed the strategy process in light of the emerging new age, where it is argued the strategy development process may change in the future. Annual long term, slow processes used traditionally to develop strategy may no longer be appropriate. The strategy setting of the future may need to be iterative and gated to ensure that it remains relevant and is flexible to the sudden and fast-paced disruption and AI of the new age. The following section of this chapter reviews how the organisation's structures and processes may need to evolve in response to the future ahead.

Structures and Processes

Organisations develop structures and processes in order to achieve performances expected by their respective stakeholders. Stakeholder performance expectations are likely to be varied, where shareholders may expect reputation and financial return, or customers may expect great prices and quality product, or local community groups may expect low environmental impacts. Management is responsible for designing the appropriate structures and processes, where the design process may be formal or informal and related changes may occur frequently or infrequently. The systems deployed by management may prevent or constrain organisational change (Smith, 2008). In the new age, change will be much faster and constant than in the past, thus may influence and force changes to the way organisations operate.

Organisational structures are the formally defined lines of authority and control within the organisation. There are five main organisational structures are recognised in the literature being those of business unit, divisional, functional, matrix and those less defined being hybrids or other alternates (Steiger, 2013). Matrix structures organisations have been found to have the highest level of knowledge sharing when compared to the other types (Steiger, 2013). When the organisational environment is frequently changing, organisations are more likely to be responsively structured with a customer focus (Lee, Kozlenkova, & Palmatier, 2015). Business performance may also be enhanced if a market-driven structure is adopted (Lee et al., 2015). Adopting new technology may require an organisation to change its own internal processes, where that is often difficult and benefits are not always realised (Gans, 2016). In an unstable environment, the support of a vigorous learning process by management may assist an organisation change (Herrera, 2015).

Formalised structures are used in an organisation in order to clarify who is in control of what and to communicate delegations and authorities. These structures assist all staff as they communicate lines of control that may historically improve efficient processes. The organisational structures are usually quite rigid and take time to change due to the process and associated approvals required. The historical rigidity and slowness in the change of organisational structures and processes may have existed in order to ensure changes were satisfactory and well communicated. The new age may require changes to processes and structures more quickly and less defined in the past in order to maintain competitive advantage.

Traditionally, staff may have understood and followed organisational structures and processes based on their formality and documentation, where fast change of these tools may cause confusion for staff that may not be willing to change flexibly. Where there are high amounts of change and uncertainty, an organisation may not have the time nor the resources to adjust all of its formalised processes, thus may seek shorter changes that include flexibility and organic change. International organisations may have evolved and survived using some form of hybridisation (Schemeil, 2013), where the future new age change may require new structures in order for organisational survival.

The new age will not just be about sudden and fast change as there will be technology that will capture more data than ever before. The emergence of big data may soon affect decision making and power in the organisation of the new age (Bratasanu, 2018), thus new skills, structures and processes may be required. This increase in data, combined with less reliability may increase stress on staff and management alike as decisions will likely need to be made swiftly in order to maintain advantage or gain improvement. There will likely be staff action to prevent or inhibit change if they perceive effects for their position, livelihood and standing (Cox, 1997; Hoag, Ritschard, & Cooper, 2002; Kanter, 1995; Klein, 1970; Maslow, 1970; Watson, 1970; Zaltman & Duncan, 1977), where past change experiences may influence employee stress levels (Bruckman, 2008).

Organisational authorities will likely need re-adjusting in the new age as there will be heightened unreliability and uncertainty in the future. The new age authorities will need to be appropriate for the inevitable requirements for flexibility and shorter decision time frames. Decision models that are too slow or too early may expose the organisation to additional risk if not set with skill. Internal governance, control and management may be unwilling to take sufficient risk where information is unverified or data are lacking, yet failure to take a decision may be equally risky for an organisation trading in multiple simultaneous disruptions.

Managers may seek data, business proposals, discussions and meetings in order to assess decisions and apply due diligence. Decision making can be informal or formal, where the formal process is more likely to occur when decisions are of larger value, are of high risk, or where the decision effect may have a large effect on the organisation in some way. Informal or even verbal decisions, on the other hand, are often made without documentation where the decision may be considered ordinary, routine or with little risk. Decision-making pressure and stress occurs when a short time frame for the decision presents, where the decision moves from one of optimisation and analysis to that of trade-off between time, significance, information and data required, feedback and options.

Some managers, due to experience levels or personality traits, or those with more entrepreneurial traits may be more willing to make decisions with risk. Although research suggests that entrepreneurs may be rather overconfident with their own abilities and are more risk averse for market risk (Wu & Knott, 2006). Senior managers take risk when they delegate their responsibilities or hire staff, where risk control is attempted through job descriptions, process definitions, controls and monitoring. Entrepreneurial may be attracted to new organisations that match their personality type, where their management style in start-up organisations may be influenced by their traits (Dvir, Sadeh, & Malach-Pines, 2010). Entrepreneurial creativity, commitment and ambition was heightened if they operated in start-up or were intensive technology organisations (Dvir et al., 2010), indicating that entrepreneurs may be useful for organisations in the new age.

To improve decision-making reliability, the manager may seek corroborating information or more reliable sources or expert opinion. The traditional media of newspapers and television has diminished in size over recent years, where many journalists have lost their jobs as a result of new age media emergence. The investigative journalist may often possess skills that an organisation of the future may need including those of information verification, analysis and interview. In order to reduce risk in the new age, management will seek the corroboration of information, new sources and cross-verification, as failure to do so may leave the organisation vulnerable to fake news. More investigators, data analysts, political analysts and strategists may be required to improve the lack of reliable information available in the new age, as traditional organisations and management may lack these skills in sufficient quantities. The manager of the future will need to verify sources, opinions and rumour before evaluating risk and probability and taking decisions. Failure to address information unreliability may expose the management to poor decisions and loss of trust by stakeholders.

It may be depowering, embarrassing or disengaging if management are measured against changes they cannot influence or forecast. If a trade war commences across an organisation's market and losses ensue, it may be difficult or even unconscionable to withhold performance bonuses from management. New control and measurement systems may be required in the new age as changes may occur faster than traditional systems can monitor and report, where many disruptions may occur outside of the managers control or knowledge. Management cannot completely be removed from poor performance responsibility as they are responsible for risk identification and mitigation, thus new systems that can apportion responsibility may be required. Organisations of the future may have to evolve and debate how management can be motivated and monitored in times of great uncertainty, where traditional fixed annual budgets may no longer be appropriate.

The traditional methods of setting slow to react and inflexible systems, structures and processes may be incompatible with trade wars, robots, data management, technology changes of the new age. Current management of any organisation will be required to ignore the new age change ahead, or to embrace the concept and commence reframing their organisations. The adaption of the new age may require fast-paced change and decisions, where many today may not be willing to adapt when, thus much uncertainty exists. Disruption and AI are already emerging as major changes and issues for organisations globally, thus management may be need to act.

Question 6.2. A recent trade war and tariffs has reduced the sales opportunities for your organisation by 50%, where the probability trade war between those two countries had not been discussed publicly or appeared in any social or other media previously.

Discuss how fair it may be if the shareholders chose to withhold the management bonus based on a significantly reduced profit for the year and reduced organisational value in the market. How might management react to such an action? How might the behaviour affect management behaviour in the future? Will new staff be attracted to management positions in this organisation?

Should this organisation consider flexible or milestone type budgets in the future? If so, please describe any issues in setting and monitoring a new form of budget process.

The fixed and logical process definitions often used by organisations, to control processes and to assure quality, may no longer be appropriate once disruption or AI emerges. Processes may need to have alternatives included so that staff can keep processes running during times of instability or high risk and uncertainty. Processes that are altered due to any emergence of robots may need to include allowances for staff conflict or the lack of human interaction. Staff may also need to be trained in dealing with change, difficult situations, contingency and dilemma, where past system stability may not occur as regularly in the future. Staff confusion or inability to adapt to a faster, more organic or more transformational new age may be a key inhibitor in the organisations of the new age, where management will need to consider appropriate actions to prevent such inhibitors from taking place.

A new age function (NAF) may be required to identify, analyse, verify and respond to change in the new age. Management will need to consider what the details of these new functions will be and to where in the organisation will they report. If the new functions are not integrated with the current organisational structure, they risk being irrelevant and unconnected to the existing knowledge and structure of the organisation. Although if the new functions are too integrated into the current structures, they may lack the focus and creativity required to identify and analyse new disruptions or AI as they emerge. Processes for the new functions may be best defined, reviewed and approved in advance of AI or disruption emerging. These NAFs may benefit if practised and ready for an event to occur, perhaps similar to how emergency services prepare for natural disasters.

Many of the new age changes identified and monitored by a NAF may not eventuate or emerge in different forms to that expected, or may be completely incorrect due to wrong analysis or fake news. Those employed in a NAF need to hold high levels of conceptual abilities, excellent analytical and investigative skills, yet be resilient to scrutiny and ridicule if chasing ideas that others see as ridiculous. To that end boundaries and budgets will need to be set by senior management to ensure that this new function does not become overly expensive or mis-directed. Controls on a NAF may be akin to those for R&D activities, appreciating that they will be monitoring new AI and disruption that may or may not impact the organisation, its market or country. Whilst disruption or AI may be difficult to identify, there will be limits to the resources that an organisation has to apply to the NAF, thus management may choose to set guidance or scope for the NAF in relation to how creative, opportunistic or entrepreneurial it should be.

It is clear that upon the emergence of the new age, characterised with disruption and AI or robots, organisations will need to respond. As the changes are likely to be far reaching and transformational so too are the organisational changes, where traditional structures and processes are unlikely to be appropriate in the future. The organisation may have to create new functions like the NAF in order to elevate the identification, verification and analysis of new age change within the organisation, where management will need to decide between scope and resources to dedicate towards this new function. There will likely be other changes required to the organisation that are discussed in the remaining sections of this chapter.

Market Dynamics

Products, services, financial and other markets are likely to change the way they operate once disruption and AI emerge. Competition will be no easier in the new age, as there will be difficulty for many in understanding, scoping, analysing and making decisions in the fast pace of change. There will be additional risk in the market over and above the individual organisation, as the new age changes may affect complete industries and market segments. Organisations may have traditionally attempted to gain advantage in markets by evolving their structures and vertically or horizontally merging, be those advantages as cost, price, volume or other means. There is now every likelihood that organisations of the new age will continue to seek advantage versus their competitors, where the decision making and competition methods may need to alter and be faster.

Innovating around existing base products may be more successful than transformational or incremental changes, where the featuring an existing product highly may not be required (Leavy, 2017). Additionally, a competitive innovation strategy may be important in a new age type environment (Notarantonio & Quigley, 2013) that may include high-speed change and uncertainty. Flexible processes may be useful for the new age as discussed earlier in this chapter, where flexibility may also be useful for product development when undergoing change, or it may be used to create and lead disruption (Smith, 2008).

Dynamic market instability may require mindset diversity in order to create new ways of thinking and create challenging assumptions (Strandvik et al., 2018). In digital disruption, organisations may benefit if they focus on new customer segments rather than cost cutting (Vanzeebroeck & Bughin, 2017). Managing through uncertainty, making decisions based on a clear customer focus may enable the management to make appropriate decisions without the complexity, inflexibility and delay that traditional organisational workings may involve. Although there is research indicating that not all customer focussed strategies are right for all organisations, especially those that are product focussed (Sousa, 2003). If an organisation focusses on its own existing technology and compares that to where innovation may affect value creation, they may be able to identify disruption early (Nagy, Schuessler, & Dubinsky, 2016). Thus, in order to gain advantage, some organisations may choose hybrid structures to gain market advantage, where customer and an employee focus may have already been successful in at least one technology organisation (Menon, 2011).

At the moment, there may not be a designated easy to follow pathway for operating in the new age, yet flexibility and fast change may be the essential elements. Organisations that wish today to change prices, change product, change operations or merge may currently be inhibited by their own internal slow decision making, slow approval processes, slow negotiations and legal documentation. Disruption and AI may affect whole markets and even countries simultaneously in the new age, where the changes are not limited to single organisations. Organisations are more likely to have to adjust to new age change than more traditional market related product and demand changes (Wieteska, 2016).

If an organisation believes that a market is going to be adversely impacted, by say a disruption like a trade war, they may decide to leave a particular market.

A significant market change like an exit will be more easily visible to suppliers, shippers, forward orders, warehouses, staff and customers based via the array of communication sources including social media email, Internet and B2B connectivity. This is not to say that the new age will result in increases of collusion or insider trading, rather it will be the interconnectivity, technology communication sources and ease of analysis that will enable information to flow fast into analysis and use by others.

Question 6.3. Your organisation has discovered and is implementing a new robotic solution. The old product will be dropped and the new robot will be adopted in its place. Your organisation currently buys parts for the old technology on a regular basis from suppliers that also supply your competitors. Additionally, your customer base buys from your direct competitors and it is not clear that they will accept your new robotic solution.

Write a briefing paper for this organisation that considers the information and competitive issues surrounding the introduction of the new robotic solution. List strategies that may be useful in preventing information about your new robot being leaked to the market. Would you deploy any disruption actions with the market to hide and confuse? If so, describe the ethical concerns of such action and how they might be mitigated.

Whilst risk and uncertainty may be key characteristics of the new age, opportunities will still present for the entrepreneurs, the creative and risk takers. Whenever a new AI or robot is adopted in a market with customer interface, there will be an opportunity for niche players to offer high customer service alternatives, despite any cost differential. If a department store adopts robots as the service and selling points for their stores in order to reduce cost, there will be opportunities for competitors to offer high customer service, niche alternatives. The alternative may be successful if offered to customers that have high propensity to dislike robots or that prefer human interactions in the sales process. In this example, it is important for the organisation to be aware of their advantage and understanding of the market fragmentation that may appear during any new age change. Small organisations could even poke fun at the robotics in advertising, whilst promoting exceptional staff, knowledge and service to gain advantage, yet remaining a niche player.

Question 6.4. Your organisation is a small take away food business that is now concerned that their larger competitors may erode the business through their adoption of drones that enable faster delivery times at lower cost. Customers of yours a reporting that they like the competitor app that was rolled out with the drones, where they can now get chicken or pizza at the football, at work or almost anywhere in the city.

Write a business response plan for this organisation listing explaining why the customers may be prefer the competitors new offer. Your organisation would prefer to remain as a niche market player in take away food market and does not have funds to adopt wide scale drones and apps. How might this business build a competitive advantage in the new market without reducing prices?

The risk and uncertainty in the new age may make large-scale acquisitions and new launches too difficult for many organisations, where stakeholders may be averse to the risks and unwilling to invest in new operations. Smaller organisations in niche markets may be able to survive in symbiotic positions against larger competitors, offering products and services their larger rivals are not able to provide due to their relative inflexibility, or slower reaction times. Due to the fast paced, sudden nature of the new age flexibility and niche offers may be a good survival strategy and as a way to reduce risk and gather stakeholder support.

Many management students have been taught to use strengths, weaknesses, opportunities and threats (SWOT) for over 40 years (Galvin & Arndt, 2014), it is still often used in practice as a quick and easy way to identify market issues. Whilst market scanning in order to find and understand competition strategy (Porter, 1980) and advantage (Porter, 1985), these historical models may not be appropriate in the new age. Neither SWOT or Porter's five include disruption and AI type uncertainty or risk in their approaches, where new models may be required in the future. Disruption for instance may be more readily found in smaller subsidiaries than in their larger multinational owners, where the subsidiary characteristics may be the determinant to success in finding disruption solutions (Cowden & Alhorr, 2013).

Organisations that remain on older, trusted market models may find over time that they miss out on opportunity or are not reactive enough to change in the new age. Flexibility, combined with new ways of identifying opportunity are the likely characteristics required in the future, where there is increased potential for marketers, innovators and entrepreneurs. This is not to say that all new age organisations should be risk takers, rather it may be that those seeking to understand and pre-empt disruption or AI may simply not find those in traditional, slow and low-risk processes of the past. New creative market models are required in order for organisations to identify both risk and opportunity when fast paced, high risk new age change presents. The following section of this chapter pursues these themes in respect to change in staff skills and requirements that may feature as a result of the new age.

Staff Requirements

The above sections of this book make a case that the new age of disruption and AI that may occur in a fast paced, risky and uncertain environment will likely change the traditional strategies, structures and processes of the past. There will also likely be changes to the ratios between staff and machine, computers or AI in the new age, yet at the same time skills required of the remaining staff may be quite different. The change ahead will not be limited to staff, where the HRM function itself will likely adopt new technology in its processes (Larkin, 2017). Staff responses to change are not isolated as their response is often influenced by the leadership context that is experienced (Bommer, Rich, & Rubin, 2005; Van Dam, Oreg, & Schyns, 2008). It is important to consider staff in the response to change in the new age as individuals are not uniformly satisfied with the direction, pace or outcomes of organisational change, where commitment can affect change outcomes (Bennett & Durkin, 2000).

Staff may suffer anxiety, stress and confusion if the organisational processes of change are not appropriately explained by the leadership or controlled by management. Staff reactions may vary based on personality, expectations or past change experience, where the variation may be difficult for management. Technically superior staff may be less required for the organisation if knowledge is transferred to AI or robots, as other skills may be more appropriate in a changing environment with uncertainty. Management assessment and choice of those staff to retain and hire will be critical decisions as any organisation transitions with disruption and AI or robots.

The new age skills required of staff will likely require abilities to work in environments absent of humans, or those requiring more analysis and large data volumes or requiring staff to follow AI or robotic decisions or directives. The technical or analytical employee may be better positioned to the new work environment than those requiring process and regular human input. Organisations may need to hire, procure or outsource new age skills in order to identify disruption and AI, or to analyse and verify, where some level of creativity and thought will be required for each new function employed. Management will likely require staff that can consider new ideas, develop strategy quickly and invoke change quickly without necessarily removing all of the governance controls, where these skills may be required to be included in screening criteria.

New skills will not only be required of staff, as managing in the new age has been associated with uncertainty and risk, where project resilience may be required to keep things on track (Blay, 2017). Management have traditionally been responsible for organisational performance, where processes, structures and authorities have been used to control and deliver results to stakeholder expectations. The new age will likely involve fast and sudden change of events and new technologies that may be difficult to assess and predict. Management will likely remain responsible for performance outcomes, where the lack of time and accurate verified information may be too uncertain for the traditional manager to use to form decisions. The lack of decision-making skills in uncertainty and risk environments may result in no decisions, late decisions or decisions in error, thus may be a key focus required by organisations in the new age, either through recruitment or through training and development.

Leaders will be particularly challenged in the new age as their skills in explaining and positioning the organisational direction will be more important than in the past. Staff will require understanding and satisfactory explanation of why the organisation is changing direction so often, or why staff ratios are in decline with the emergence of AI, or they may require an understanding of geopolitical changes in faraway places. Staff may be more challenging to deal with in the future as they may no longer be merely satisfied to sit back and follow, they may question the leadership far more as they seek answers and understanding. As discussed previously in this book, staff may seek flexible arrangements more than ever as technology improves their ability to work from home, to be on line and work with AI or robots. Leadership will be responsible for listening, engaging and providing satisfactory negotiations and outcomes to reduce the potential loss of key staff and knowledge.

Whilst leadership engagement may be useful in retaining and satisfying staff more may be required as skills for the new age are important to the organisation and the staff collective. Firstly, staff will need be prepared for change, including an understanding of the underlying parameters and the potential for future change that may not always be predictable. Staff may require training on working with stress, training on analysis, verification and even working with robots. The future organisation will need to envisage change as continuous and normal, where staff embrace change and are able to flourish as it occurs. Each of these staff changes will require engagement and trust in their leadership for success to be achieved.

Staff and management alike will need to be selected or trained to work in a less certain world, where analysis and abstract concepts may need to be prepared for despite their unlikeliness. Organisations of today may be more used to dealing with possibilities and control than uncertainty and risk, where some level of entrepreneurial and risk-taking skills may need to be included in the mix in an effort to foster creativity for new solutions. The hiring management of the future should consider these skills in order to gain advantage rather than merely hiring the technical skills in isolation.

Knowledge may be the most important element to develop in the new age that is characterised with so much change and competition (Huarng, Mas-Tur, & Calabuig Moreno, 2018). Those with lower skill levels may benefit most when knowledge is shared and may have limited benefits when skill levels are high (Dong, Bartol, Zhang, & Li, 2017). Employee creativeness may be instrumental for the success of an organisation, where training and mentoring may also be useful in generating creative ideas (Dong et al., 2017). In Pakistan, employee intentions to leave an organisation have been associated with employee perceptions of future training opportunities (Rahman & Nas, 2013).

The structures for staff may need to be different and more flexible in order to adapt to disruption and AI, where it is already reported that autonomous teams may be have better performances and satisfaction levels that historical structures (Cohen & Ledford, 1994; Gallie, Zhou, Felstead, & Green, 2012). As learning may be important to the future organisation in adapting to change it may be important for the leadership and management to foster openness as that has been shown to be related to employee desire to learn (Maurer, Lippstreu, & Judge, 2008). Executives may need to learn or be hired with emotional intelligence as that may improve their success, where they may need to include the skill of empathy (Hacioglu & Yarbay, 2014).

From the above, it is clear that management and leadership skills required to engage and manage staff of the new age will be significantly different from the past. Staff will likely be challenged as staff ratios decline with AI or robots, or be confused when organisations change quickly from disruption, thus the organisation will either need to explain and engage or seek coping skills by training and selecting staff with those skills. Staff that are retained in times with AI may require analysis skills, higher knowledge skills and abilities to work with technology with less people. Management will have to consider the ways that they may want to convert and assist staff that suffer from stress due to change in the new age. Failure to address and satisfy staff may lead to some staff leaving, whilst others may stay on as with disengaged attitudes, each potentially harming the organisational reputation or culture. Staff that are disengaged or leave have the potential to harm the organisations reputation and relationships with customers, suppliers and other stakeholders, thus the issue will need to be addressed in some form by the management and leadership of the future.

As the staff of any organisation may be significantly impacted by change in the new age, it may be important for staff management to build plans and strategy that includes specific staff response plans. Table 6.2 shows new parameters that may be included in roles of the new age.

Table 6.2 lists skills that management and staff may require in the organisation of the future. Individual skills may also be required to be assessed against

Table 6.2:   Staff Considerations for New Age.

New Age Staff Consideration	Explanation/Description
Change	Explanations linked to the broader environment including disruption, AI and robots. Explain advantages and disadvantages of the change as well as any uncertainty or risk that may result in future change. Seek input from staff as to how change is implemented.
Skills	Assess and hire staff with skills of analysis, creativity, entrepreneurial flair that are comfortable working with lower staff ratios. Bias roles towards higher skills and knowledge roles. Assess staff flexibility and ability to adapt to rapid change.
Communication	Communication using various forms, regularity and language deployed by a variety of levels in the organisation. The information may contain reasons for the change, discussions around what will happen if not change is deployed.
Trust	Management and leadership to follow on through on promises and guidelines. If not able to deliver promises then explain the reasons step by step. It is important that staff do not perceive management as incompetent, irrational or not in control, especially where change moves in alternate directions to previous expectations.
Openness	Management and leadership to foster openness with staff. Let staff know the full story, the risks and the opportunities.
Emotional intelligence	Hire management and staff with empathy skills.
Training	Include training programmes for all staff, where training is targeted to new age skills of knowledge management, analysis, verification and working with lower human ratios.

Table 6.3:   Individual Change Skills Table.

Change Criteria	Description
Uncertainty	Perceived level of uncertainty related to the role activities in the near term (say 6–12 months).
Control	Perceived level of control in the role activities for the near term.
Documentation	Level of documentation required for this role in the near term.
Structure/ creativity	Level of structure and/or creativity required for this role in the near term.
Intuition	Level of intuition required for this role in the near term.
Analysis	Level of analysis required for this role in the near term.
Decision making	Level of decision making required for this role in the near term.

the likely change environment of the future, be they a new or existing employee. A range of performance criteria for use in the assessment of staff against new age change in the future are defined at Table 6.3, later shown for use in Table 6.4.

Table 6.3 attempts to tie several of the topics discussed earlier in this book, where the change criteria skills may be required to be known when assessing staff for roles. Uncertainty is listed in Table 6.3 as some roles may be affected by disruption or AI early, where staff that prefer certainty may not be appropriate in the new age. Some staff may prefer roles that are structured and controlled with high levels of documentation, whilst some of those roles may continue to exist in the new age they may be scarcer in the future. The last three criteria to be assessed in Table 6.3 surround marking roles in terms of their analysis and decision making combined with intuition, where roles may be increasingly required to make decisions with intuition and partial analysis in the new age.

Table 6.4 has been created as a template to show how an individual staff member may be measured against the change criteria shown at Table 6.3.

In the above SATNA tool, roles are assessed specifically against criteria that is likely to be less controlled and defined as in the past. The tool may be used as a way of explaining the role requirements or as a way of tabling what someone in that role may need to improve on. This tool could also be used to assess current staff against new roles and used to determine if people should be retained in new structures or let go, where applicable. Management should ensure that the assessment of staff to roles is performed rationally and openly to assist in maintaining Trust rather than making decisions that are less structured.

As shown in Table 6.4, four columns have been added to the criteria of Table 6.3 to make a comprehensive assessment tool. The first column for level shows the management assessment level of uncertainty, control and documentation, where the other four criteria can be assessed similarly, a score of 1 is for low levels of uncertainty and control, and 5 being high levels. In column two of Table 6.4, it is proposed that management assess the likelihood of the criteria changing in the next 12 months to new age change. The third column added to Table 6.4 is

Table 6.4:   Skills Assessment Tool for New Age (SATNA).

Change Criteria	Level[a]	Likelihood	Current Performance (Adaption)[a]	Improvement
Uncertainty	1	50%	5	
Control	1	30%	3	
Documentation	3	80%	1	
Structure/creativity				
Intuition				
Analysis				
Decision making				

[a]1 is low and 5 is extremely high.

Table 6.5:   SATNA Example – Low-impact Change Role.

Change Criteria	Level[a]	Likelihood	Current Performance (Adaption)[a]	Improvement
Uncertainty	1	50%	5	
Control	1	30%	3	
Documentation	3	25%	2	
Structure/creativity	1	30%	3	
Intuition	1	30%	3	
Analysis	1	30%	3	
Decision making	1	30%	3	

[a]1 is low and 5 is extremely high.

related to the current performance of the criteria in the role, based on management assessment and discussion with staff. A rating of 5 in the current performance adaption column would indicate a currently high adaption to change by an incumbent staff member, where a three would be a mid-range adaption performance. Colour has been added to Table 6.4, which shows that red is high-risk cells, orange is mid-range, and green is low change or high performance in the last column. In this way, the less green that is shown for a role the more risk, uncertainty and change it may likely encounter.

To apply SATNA, a stable large grocery organisation, which controls its market due to size, may expect a role to be less impacted by the new age. In Table 6.5, an example of a store person role is rated (hypothetically) to show how the role may appear in a lower change environment. As can be seen in Table 6.5, the colours are greener than red, indicating less new age change likely.

To further show how the SATNA may be used to assess change applicability for roles of the future, Table 6.6 is shown below for a role that may be involved in

Table 6.6: SATNA Example – High-impact Change Role.

Change Criteria	Level[a]	Likelihood[a]	Current Performance (Adaption)	Improvement
Uncertainty	4	50%	5	May need training on dealing with uncertainty.
Control	4	75%	3	May need templates to cover scenarios that need control.
Documentation	2	35%	3	Documentation exists may need updating.
Structure/ creativity	4	70%	3	New structures required post-robot installation.
Intuition	3	40%	3	Operations not expected to require any additional.
Analysis	4	75%	2	Data from AI will need review and analysis.
Decision making	2	15%	3	Decisions will be data driven and acted upon by robots.

[a]1 is low and 5 is extremely high.

new age change. The role shown in Table 6.6 may be a similar stores role that is in another industry where robots and AI are emerging fast, where the role may have considerably different new age change issues to consider.

In the above example, Table 6.6 appears to have higher levels of change that are more likely than those for a similar role with less change that is shown at Table 6.5. The levels of change are indicated by the scores and the colours, where red and orange colour indicate more change versus another more stable role. It is envisaged that the HRM may need to integrate new age changes into the staff roles of the future, where the action may assist staff in understanding the context of their individual role. The SATNA is considered an early development in the process to integrate and inform staff of the change in the new age.

Question 6.6. Consider various roles in a department store that has just purchased sophisticated AI to integrate with robots that will perform activities of unpacking boxes, emptying delivery trucks and serving customers. Staff after being informed of the impending change have asked for an assessment of their individual roles and the impact the robotic changes will have on their roles.

Complete a SATNA for several of the department store roles and write a business response to the staff collective summarising the robotic changes ahead. Critique the SATNA as a tool that may assist in explaining the changes ahead. What other considerations should you consider in this response?

This section has set out the case for an appreciation from leadership, management and the HRM role that the new age will involve great changes to the organisation. There will likely be significant issues and change for staff in the future, including redundancy, lower staff ratios and new skills, where appropriate responses may reduce or eliminate adverse stress on existing staff. The skills of old may leave an organisation vulnerable to disruption or AI as they emerge, it is recommended that staff be re-assessed on new age criteria now so that organisations can be ready for the new age of change ahead.

Customer Service

There is great potential for customers, like staff, to be impacted by the new age, where they may lack sufficient information or warnings about likely changes emerging. Customers may lack skills, time or focus to identify new age change that may emerge and affect their organisations. Customer service may traditionally have been providing goods or services that the customer may want. In the new age, the customer may value advice, forewarning and information either before, during or after a significant change.

Management has the responsibility to identify and react to new age change in their pursuit of organisational performance towards target. The customer relationship and requirements should be considered in the pursuit of targets as the customer is an important stakeholder. In considering the customer, management should consider the type, price, quantity and quality expected by the customer, where changes to the organisation and its offer consequently often affect the customer. Organisations that fail to build good relations with their customers or fail to integrate and influence with the customer potentially may suffer lost customer sales.

There may be real benefits in the new age where organisation chooses to work closely with their customers, as the customer can assist in organisational creativity (Bellingkrodt & Wallenburg, 2015; Chesbrough, 2006; Tether, 2002) and assessment (Bellingkrodt & Wallenburg, 2015; Grawe, Chen, & Daugherty, 2009). Technology organisations may already need to innovate and build customer service in order to survive (Shrivastava, 2017), where the two skills may be more required in the new age. Customers may not take up new disruptive products until they have sufficient quality, thus organisations may benefit from focus on potential opportunities arising from disruption instead (Christensen, Raynor, & McDonald, 2015).

Customers may be aware that new technology vehicles are being developed as they may read social media, news or online forums on those matters. The customer may not on the other hand keep abreast of the technology evolution and may not know what will or could happen, how that may impact them. The customer may be an individual consumer or that of a large organisation in regards to their lack of knowledge on new age change. The organisation has a tacit obligation to forewarn and explain to the organisation of the impeding AI and disruption that may affect the customer relationship, yet there is also an opportunity in this relationship. Organisations that are best to predict and explain AI to their customer base may build trust, may be more valued and create more opportunities with customers than those that do not engage in this type of relationship.

As discussed earlier in this book, technology and globalisation now position organisations into more interconnectivity and dependencies than ever before. In customer sales relationships of B2B both parties may have invested considerable funds in creating system linkages, should either party move to a new technology there will likely consequent changes to the other party. The leadership skills of any seller may be heightened in importance as the change of this new age will be significant, where leadership will be required to build relationships on communication, trust and engagement. Communication in the new age should be aimed towards building knowledge and relationships as disruption and AI may be difficult to detect and change with, where customer understanding may assist in the change process.

Summary

This chapter has discussed how the new age will impact the way organisations operate today, where many of the traditional tools may no longer be valid or may require rethinking and change. Strategy that has been a mainstream way of directing an organisation, may be too slow or too inaccurate in the new age, where disruption and AI may occur at a fast pace and suddenly. Structures and processes of old may also be too inflexible and slow for an organic change to occur, where failure to change may also cause harm to an organisation. Market and customer relationships will be significantly changed by the disruption and AI emerging around the world. It may be the reduced staff ratios and the potential staff confusion around the endless change that may be one of the most difficult issues for leadership and management to resolve, where continued support from staff may be critical for the organisation to move forward in the new age. Chapter 7 considers current research and recommends more actions for organisations of the future to consider as they seek to survive and prosper in this new age.

Chapter 7

Organisational Change, Tools and Measures

> Organisational change practices must evolve: understand, measure and improve.
>
> —Mathew Donald

In reading earlier chapters of this book, it should now be clear that organisations in the new age will likely result in unexpected and hard-to-predict change, characterised with fast pace and sudden change. This rapid unpredictable change is likely to require organisations to change in ways that may not have been experienced in the past. Leadership and management may need new skills and practices in order to achieve the requisite changes in stakeholders, staff, processes and structures. Change in this new age is likely to be continuous and multifactored simultaneously, where new paths may be required in order for organisations to change and even survive.

This chapter commences with a review of research and literature on organisational change that indicates that it is not a simple process. This chapter goes on to use many of the concepts discussed earlier in this book to propose a range of actions for those in leadership and management positions to consider in the new age of disruption and the artificial intelligence (AI). The changes proposed later in this chapter may be summarised as increasing the flexibility of organisations whilst integrating them into society values, whilst applying new governance and ethical frameworks. This chapter finally discusses how organisational culture may be a new direction for leadership and management to consider when taking their organisations in to this new age.

Change Factor Research

This section discusses recent research by the author of this book, Donald (2017), into organisational change, seeking here to understand current thought on change and how it may be applied in the new age. As discussed previously, change may be continuous in the future new age, where the organisational interconnectivity may make the avoidance of change impossible (Shah, 2010). It may be that

---

Leading and Managing Change in the Age of Disruption and Artificial Intelligence, 143–167
Copyright © 2019 by Emerald Publishing Limited
doi:10.1108/978-1-78756-367-420191008

organisational survival may even depend on change (Burnes, 2011; Company, 2008), or that without change a competitive advantage may be lost (Kotter, 1996). The origins of organisational change may include market forces, corporate rationalisation, operational efficiency or deregulation (Bennett & Durkin, 2000). There are many organisational change factors researched over the past 80 years, where considering each factor individually during change may be confusing or even invalid (Donald, 2017).

It is important that organisational change be understood further and included in future research, as it has been reported that the fail rate may be as high as 70% (Burnes & Jackson, 2011; Senturia, Flees, & Maceda, 2008). Some suggest that the change failure may relate to resistance to change (RTC) (Georgalis, Samaratunge, Kimberley, & Lu, 2015), although others indicate that it may be employee resistance as the main source of organisational change failure (Danisman, 2010). Despite change increasing in pace, there is still little empirical evidence to track and measure the various theories (Todnem, 2005). As change outcomes vary, some already argue that a multidimensional approach should be adopted in future research, where even variances in human predispositions may explain some variances in reactivity to change (Taylor & Cooper, 1988).

In recognition of calls to research change and RTC in a multidimensional way, recent research was conducted using a mixed method, attempting to determine if RTC factors were co-existing and interrelated (Donald, 2017). This was important research for the academic and the professional organisational change practitioner, where the interactivity of change factors may alter the way organisational change should be approached in order to improve success rates.

The research commenced with 25 interviews of managers responsible for some form of organisational change, where the interviewees were selected upon self-nomination and snowballing from invitations posted on various LinkedIn groups. The selection method for this phase of the research was aimed at gathering the experiences and thoughts of those involved in and responsible for organisational change, seeking to identify the most common factors influencing change. Employees were not approached directly in order to avoid ethical selection and stress issues that may have occurred if invitations had been routed through employers. The participants in this first research phase were from a wide cross section of backgrounds and industries.

Data that were collected from the interview phase of the research were analysed in Nvivo10, where the data revealed a number of important findings that were used in the second phase of this research. In support of organisational change being common, six of the 25 participants (or 25%) reported that their organisations had more than 50 changes in the past three years. The data also indicated that the change factors may have influence in a positive and negative direction, rather than being merely negative.

A further review of the data using the Nvivo10 word frequency function was used over the interview data. As shown in Fig. 7.1, the most common words of people and change were introduced in the interview script.

As indicated in Fig. 7.1, the most common interview words as positive influencers of change were communication, management, project and process.

These words and concepts were at odds with a generally held view of many that staff may be the most influential component in change and for RTC in particular.

Further word frequency analysis of interview data in Nvivo10 this time for negative references to organisational change is shown below at Fig. 7.2.

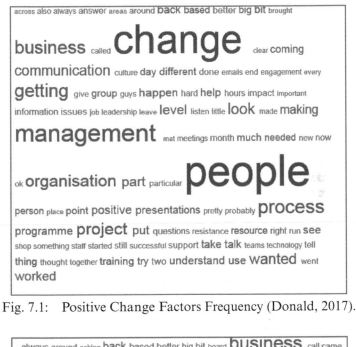

Fig. 7.1:   Positive Change Factors Frequency (Donald, 2017).

Fig. 7.2:   Negative Change Factors Frequency (Donald, 2017).

Fig. 7.2 indicates that the factors of management, communication and process are important as change factors, where their relative importance appears to align with their importance to positive influence shown in Fig. 7.1. Resistance did not feature strongly as a concept in the positive factors of Table 7.1 but is shown with relative importance in Table 7.2. The participation in the interviews was relatively evenly split based on gender, where the perception of change influencers did not appear to be different. Interview data after coding were compared for bias towards negative or positive change factor nodes, where interviews appeared to be relatively balanced as shown in Fig. 7.3.

As Fig. 7.3 indicated no relative bias towards negative or positive influencers of change references in the interviews, the data were reviewed for interrelationships. Using the word cluster function of Nvivo10, the data were analysed separately between positive and negative references as shown in Figs. 7.4 and 7.5.

Fig. 7.4 indicates that stakeholder engagement may closely relate to communication, where these may then link to politics and power followed by management. These positive change factors appeared to be linked differently to those negative factors shown in Fig. 7.5.

The cluster in Fig. 7.5 shows different factor relationships to those shown in Fig. 7.4, where leadership appears to be closely related to culture, management and politics/power closely related. The interview data shown above could not confirm interrelationships between RTC factors in a statistically significant way, yet the analysis of the interview data did suggest co-existence of RTC forms.

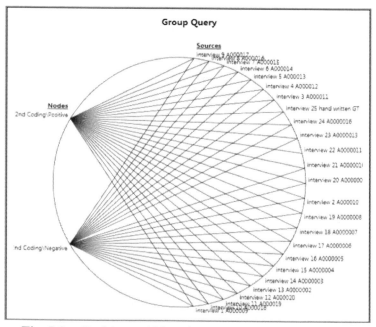

Fig. 7.3:   Positive and Negative Interview (Donald, 2017).

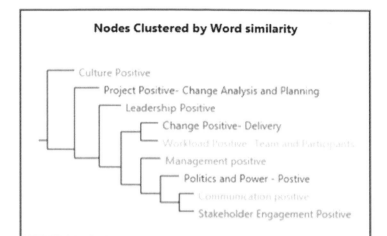

Fig. 7.4:   Word Similarity Clusters – Positive Factors (Donald, 2017).

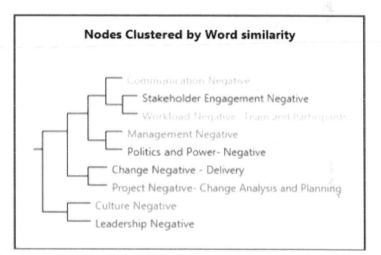

Fig. 7.5:   Word Similarity Clusters – Negative Factors (Donald, 2017).

Owing to limited suggestions of change factor interrelationships in the first interview phase of this research, the second phase of survey was developed to gather quantitative data on the topic. Several of the factor concepts were omitted from the second phase of the research in order to ensure the survey was not overly long. The interview data indicated that communication was the most common concept in all interviews, where culture was low in frequency and was not included in the survey phase.

Second phase survey questions were designed from the interview data factors and concepts, where the data were analysed in SPSS. Prior to analysing the data for interrelationships, the data were tested as shown in Table 7.1.

To generate the data shown in Table 7.1, each survey factor was optimised through the removal of various questions, achieving the highest score possible for each factor. Table 7.1 shows that all Cronbach's alpha scores were above 0.7 and thus were considered good. The stakeholder engagement factor being above 0.9 was considered as excellent. The lowest Cronbach's alpha scores, representing the factors with the least internal reliability, were those of management and power.

The survey data were further tested to reveal that the data were generally normally distributed, skewed and with kurtosis. Prior to preparing an exploratory factor analysis (EFA) on the survey data a number of relationship tests were performed that indicated the presence of interrelationships between the survey factors. Table 7.2 is a SPSS cross tab of management factor against the other surveyed factors.

Table 7.2 shows that management was associated with four of six other factors. Trust and stakeholder engagement were deemed to hold an unlikely association based on the *p*-values listed in the table. The subsequent EFA analysis showed that those two factors loaded into leadership rather than with management. A chi-squared test was performed as an alternate association test, considered

Table 7.1:   Survey Data Cronbach's Alpha – Post-optimisation (Donald, 2017).

Construct	Cronbach's Alpha	Cronbach's Alpha Based on Standardized Items	No. of Items
Leadership	0.814	0.815	5
Management	0.727	0.735	5
Workload	0.892	0.893	9
Politics	0.845	0.845	4
Power	0.757	0.762	4
Planning and analysis	0.798	0.799	5
Stakeholders	0.911	0.911	8

Table 7.2:   Independence Test – Management Association (Donald, 2017).

Construct 1	Construct 2	*p*-value	Conclusion
Management	Leadership	0.001	Likely associated
Management	Politics	–	Likely associated
Management	Stakeholders	0.064	Unlikely associated
Management	Trust	0.100	Unlikely associated
Management	Workload	–	Likely associated
Management	Planning/Analysis	–	Likely associated

preferable to alternative interrelationship tests (Hosmer, Hosmer, LeCessie, & Lemeshow, 1997), where again most of the factors were shown to be interrelated.

The final step in this research was to perform the EFA and review inter-relationships in the data (see Table 7.3).

The component matrix in Table 7.3 shows that management is highly related to the other seven factors. The demographic data of age, gender and industry appeared to have little significant interrelationships. The only significant relationship with demographic data occurred between experience and the leadership factor at a score of 0.828. The EFA model, created in SPSS® from the survey data where eight factors loaded into the model after missing data had been inferred, indicates strong reliability between the first four factors.

Table 7.3:   EFA Component Matrix (Donald, 2017).

	Component			
	1	**2**	**3**	**4**
mgt	0.763	0.72	0.226	0.233
leadership	0.884	0.038	0.025	−0.215
workload	0.812	−0.026	0.044	0.130
stakeholder	0.856	−0.093	−0.125	−0.010
trust	0.902	0.168	0.020	−0.127
politics	0.879	0.040	−0.019	−0.139
power	0.680	0.261	0.215	−0.180
planning_analysis	0.861	0.165	0.061	0.178
What is your sex?	−0.208	0.374	0.764	−0.053
What is your age?	0.077	0.699	−0.532	0.254
Which of the following best describes your occupation?	0.015	0.007	0.390	0.651
What Industry would you say that you currently work in?	0.236	−0.433	−0.183	0.652
Are you in a role that is designated as a Manager?	0.419	−0.586	−0.327	−0.141
How much experience would you say that you have in leading or supervising an element of organisational change	−0.147	0.828	−0.343	0.091

Component Matrix[a]

Extraction method: principal component analysis.

[a]Four components extracted.

A measure of the EFA model was performed with a KMO and Bartlett's test, based on individual questions; the result is shown in Table 7.4.

Table 7.4 shows that the KMO value was above 0.8, with a Bartlett's test of sphericity significance of 0.00, where the EFA model was considered to be containing useful information (Aldrich & Cunningham, 2015)

An alternate way to view the EFA data is that of a SPSS factor correlation matrix shown in Table 7.5.

To assist in analysing the matrix at Table 7.5, colour was placed into the matrix over the two highest absolute value correlations for each factor, where red represented the negatives and green the positives. The higher correlations occurred more in the first three factors, being those of leadership, workload and management. The right-hand column of Table 7.5 shows the names for each of the factors generated from the EFA model.

Table 7.4:   EFA KMO and Bartlett's Test (Donald, 2017).

KMO and Bartlett's Test		
Kaiser-Meyer-Olkin Measure of Sampling		0.848
Bartlett's Test of Sphericity	Approx.	2025.767
	df	703
	Sig.	0.000

Table 7.5:   Factor Correlation Matrix (Donald, 2017).

Factor Correlation Matrix								
Factor	1	2	3	4	5	6	7	8	
1	1.000	0.675	0.678	0.298	0.116	−0.035	0.439	−0.213	Leadership
2	0.675	1.000	0.605	0.117	0.030	−0.228	0.414	−0.174	Workload
3	0.678	0.605	1.000	0.270	−0.043	−0.156	0.261	−0.315	Management (control/ logic)
4	0.298	0.117	0.270	1.000	−0.008	0.217	0.197	0.071	Power
5	0.116	0.030	−0.043	−0.008	1.000	0.177	0.086	0.217	Workload (wellness)
6	−0.035	−0.228	−0.156	−0.217	0.177	1.000	0.051	0.148	Act and Monitor
7	0.439	0.414	0.261	0.197	0.086	0.051	1.000	0.100	Planning and Analysis
8	−0.213	−0.174	−0.315	0.071	0.217	0.148	0.100	1.000	Budget Adequacy

Extraction Method: Principal Axis Factoring.

Rotation Method: Promax with Kaiser Normalization.

The co-existence and interrelationships of RTC factors identified in this research is not unique, despite only limited multidimensional research on RTC previously. The factors identified in this research are broader than those of other multidimensional research involving dispositions (Oreg, 2003) and organisational operations (Hoag et al., 2002). Management was thought to be a factor in RTC since Lewin's (1945) first research, where this research has now detected that management may be interrelated to other factors.

Past group dynamics research included management as the owner of processes and the change programme, involving elements of freezing and unfreezing (Lewin, 1945). This research has identified RTC factors of act and monitor, planning and analysis, where those factors may be consistent with the previously reported freezing and unfreezing process (Lewin, 1945). This research found that there were highly interrelated factors of management, leadership and workload followed by less related factors of act and monitor, power, planning and analysis. A confirmatory factor analysis (CFA) was performed in the research but failed to calculate a scale due to the lack of participation size, although a number of CFA tests were passed. Previously, managers responsible for change had limited information about multiple forms of RTC and thus might have managed change one factor at a time or might have arbitrarily experimented between factors. The new research in a multidimensional framework improves knowledge on RTC, where factors of leadership, workload and management may be highly interrelated, where that knowledge may alter the way change itself is actioned.

The first phase of this research identified a number of RTC factors that were not included in the second phase. Further research into RTC and change factors may be influential in discovering additional factors. Culture is one factor that may in the future be shown to influence change as it was identified in the research interviews, only omitted from the survey phase for efficiency purposes. The prospect of culture being an additional change factor is discussed further towards the end of this chapter.

The senior managers and governance members, who commit the organisation to large change programmes, may in the future need to defend their change programmes. Ignorance of RTC or disruption and AI may be an inappropriate defence against stakeholder challenges, or incurred losses. Once there is appreciation that RTC is likely to be multidimensional, RTC itself may be an item appearing in risk registers and change plans of the future. Risk mitigation will likely change in a multidimensional RTC framework, where multiple risks may emerge and require simultaneous multiple mitigating actions. The survey of this research achieved good internal reliability and discriminant reliability, as well as forming valid EFA and CFA models. There is potential for the survey of this research to be re-used to form another RTC scale in the future, as was the case in previous multidimensional dispositional research (Oreg, 2003).

As the factors of management, leadership and workload were the most interrelated factors detected in this research, additional change steps to treat each factor may be required in the future. As examples from the data, it may be that where an organisation determines that there is a lack of trust, they may find it useful to implement leadership training. As leadership may be related to management, the implementation of new procedures may require a communication action. One of the strongest suggestions in the interview data was that management as a negative factor of organisational change may often be absent when required, or hold deficiency in skills, act at an inappropriate time or simply not make decisions.

Leadership emerged early in the interviews as a change factor, where it became the highest referenced factor once combined with the communication factor. Interview participants discussed leadership in terms of communication levels, type, regularity and language used. A number of participants indicated that change programmes success was linked to the amount and type of leadership, combined with the leader's level of involvement. Leadership also loaded into the EFA as being related to the politics factor. Leadership includes influence that is affecting, impelling or moving (Ammer, 2016). Politics can be defined as including activities that may influence the organisation (Kanter, 1977; Mintzberg, 1984; Russell, 1938), either informally or formally (McKendall, 1993). To gather effective influence in the organisation, leadership may require political skills, combined with elements of trust and communication.

Workload was the third most interrelated factor of this research and thus regular workload assessments may be beneficial during a change programme. Failure to address workload issues may also result in staff turnover, conflict and stress. Stress and related elements have the potential to affect organisational decision making, where poor decisions or delayed decisions may occur more regularly during stress.

This section of this chapter has discussed research conducted into organisational change factors by Donald (2017). The research lacked participation to derive a scale in the CFA, yet produced valid EFA and CFA models indicating change factor interrelationships. It is important for those responsible for change to recognise that the new age will be characterised by sudden, fast-paced regular change as there will likely be interrelationships between leadership, management and other factors to consider. Whilst many books and research reduce the factors that influence change to a handful of unrelated topics, this research strongly suggests that future change of the new age should be approached in a multidimensional way.

The rest of this chapter discusses potential ways change in the new age may be approached in light of the above recent research combined with discussions earlier in this book. As pointed out earlier, the following discussions are presented not as a predictor of the future but more as a guide to be considered by those responsible for change in their organisations of the future. It is encouraged that those reading this book apply critical thinking to the topics, extend and read more literature on the topics and be in a position to critique recommendations.

Disruption Register

Earlier in this book, it was noted that organisations may already hold risk registers in an attempt to control, rate and mitigate risk. Current risk registers may be mandated by senior management, governance bodies and broader stakeholders as they may be perceived as useful to review risk openly and check assumptions in order to promote openness and review of the organisations. Current risk registers may be based on probable risk and consequence estimates, where in the new age the current risk register process may be inadequate. Events that may have previously been considered as too remote or unlikely to occur and not included in risk registers of the past will likely need to reconsider those risks in the new age.

A methodological approach to identifying and assessing new age disruption and AI or robotics may be required in order to identify possible events, where some form of thought creativity may be required. Organisations today that assess risk may not be skilled and ready for the identification of risk and uncertainty that may lie ahead in the new age. Governance bodies that currently review risk registers may need further training in order to assess and confirm risks of the future. Risk register preparation that may have been completed and reviewed at regular intervals may be too inflexible and slow for the new age. Even when new age events are identified the data, information and consequence may be difficult to assess in the fast timeframes that the events may emerge, assisted by the globalisation and new forms of communication and social media.

As stakeholders will likely continue to require that risk be identified, assessed and mitigated, a change to the traditional risk register process is proposed to cater for the new age. In the new age, change is likely to be constant, where good risk assessment processes may be seen to be a key advantage for an organisation in the future. Various stakeholders may also insist that various forms of disruption and AI or robots be assessed for risk, irrespective of their low possibility. Organisations without new age risk assessment tools may be perceived as irresponsible or unworthy of support by stakeholders due to their unidentified or unassessed risks.

As the new age will be characterised by sudden and fast-paced change, disruption emergences should be tracked from the point of discovery. A concept that may appear improbable at the beginning may change its risk and uncertainty over time as more information or analysis arrives. Alternately concepts that may appear quite likely initially, may over time reduce in probability or magnitude once the analysis or verification process has taken place. Maintaining a disruption event monitoring table (DEMT) shown in Table 7.6 or otherwise named also the disruption register, may be one way of monitoring the emerging issues of the new age and available for use in briefings and updates to various stakeholders. Failure to hold and produce a DEMT for auditors, shareholders, banks and insurers may decrease their opinion of risk preparedness thus reducing key stakeholder trust in the organisational leadership and management.

The identification and monitoring of disruption for the small organisation may be difficult as they may not have resources and skills to identify and analyse. The larger organisation may have skills and resources for disruption monitoring, although the types that may affect it may be far wider due to international trade and other complexities in their trade. If organisations cannot resource and skill the disruption monitoring, they may choose to outsource some or all of that activity to specialists that may emerge over time including identification, or analysis or verification skills, or some combination. As the new age will involve almost constant change, the organisation may not be able to avoid investigating and monitoring disruption, where resource constraints may not be acceptable to the key stakeholders.

Unlike many past risk registers that may have been completed at set intervals, reviewed and approved internally, the new age will cause the DEMT to be completed regularly as items emerge and change. Formal internal review of the DEMT process may occur with insurers, banks and auditors to ensure that the table preparation is reasonable.

Table 7.6 is the disruption register, or DEMT, and has been populated with example data to show how it may be completed, where it should be monitored and updated at regular intervals, potentially weekly or daily depending upon how disruption is perceived to emerge. The DEMT is shown here as a table summary, where each item in the table may have vast amounts of reports and data behind each line item. It is possible that some disruptions may be identified and monitored for years, whilst others may be monitored for short periods and dismissed due to verification or analysis. The second column of the DEMT declares the source of information, where it can be very reliable or merely an idea as the table should include items that are less than probable.

In the new age, risk will be heightened due to the speed at which it transfers around the world based on the interconnectedness of organisations since the evolution of globalisation. Where a technology may take years to be introduced into another country or market it may take only a few days, where trade pressures and geopolitical changes may have taken years there will now occur almost instantly. Organisations can no longer just wait and watch world changes and adopt as they see fit. It may now be essential that the organisation move beyond the risk register that may be semi-static and lagging, only recognising risks that are reasonably foreseeable. In the traditional risk register, many modern day events as tabled in earlier chapters of this book may have been omitted. The inclusion of the risky, uncertain and improbable in the DEMT discussions, clarification and review with a wide range of stakeholders may occur.

The additional information provided from the DEMT may assist organisations in preparing for the new age of change or assist in the rating of risk. In the future, it may even be possible for organisations to share disruption risk through some form of insurance if DEMT, in a similar way to earthquakes and cyclones is insured. Organisations that do not actively seek out disruption and risk in an investigative style may be mere recipients of change. Items identified in a disruption register may have direct and indirect effects that should be listed against each item, where possible and probable opportunities or risks related should also be listed. It is important for management to remember that whilst risk and uncertainty may be heightened in the new age, the resulting events may not always be negative as opportunities are likely to arise as well.

The DEMT Part II, shown in Table 7.7, has been populated with an example based on a climate change disruption, for a hypothetical manufacturing organisation. As with Table 7.6, the Table 7.7 is at a summary level, where further detail, data and analysis may be held to support the actions and decisions shown in the summary. The purpose of Table 7.7 is to expand knowledge of a single disruption and set actions for the management and leadership to take in response.

Table 7.6: Disruption Event Monitoring Table or Disruption Register – Part I.

Disruption Identified	Data Source	Risk Likelihood Consequence	Opportunity Likelihood Consequence	Next Action	Date Updated	Next Update	Importance Rating
Brexit	Newspaper	Reduced supply 10% $1m pa.	Increased trade opportunity 20% $5m pa.	Monitor articles, journals and reports on Brexit	15/2/2019	15/6/2019	●
Trump	Articles and reports	Trade war 75% $6m pa.	Increased volume to China 40% $7m pa	Regular review of tweets, regulation changes in the United States	20/4/2019	20/5/2019	●
Robots	Competitor	Staff lost 50% $5m	Lower costs 50% $15m	Discuss with supplier	22/5/2019	30/6/2019	●

Table 7.7:   DEMT or Disruption Register – Part II.

Disruption Identified =	For example, climate change.
Potential direct effects	Flood, drought, increased temperatures.
Potential Indirect effects	Risk of war, supply restrictions, mobilisation of people, legal changes, community values.
Opportunities	Sales of green technology.
	Demolition of old coal fired power plants.
	New fuels and maintenance of new equipment.
Threats	Lost production.
	Lost sales.
	Lost customers.
Mitigating actions	
- Finance	Greenhouse taxes.
	New products to reduce emissions.
- Sales	Review market opportunities for increased sales.
	Discuss with customer their climate change effects.
- Development	Consider new products required if climate change occurs.
- People	Staff communication on the issue.
	Retraining of staff.
- Leadership	Communication to all stakeholders of this disruption and its potential effects. Discuss mitigation actions.
- Operations	Consider increasing power prices and operational costs. Review potential ways to minimise power costs and greenhouse emissions.
- Customer	Discuss the disruption with customer and build joint action strategy.
- Stakeholders	Build several detailed scenarios of what this disruption may do to the financial outcomes of the organisation and list other changes that may be required in the organisation should this disruption emerge.

The DEMT Part II may be expanded over time to include additional mitigation actions, where it may provide a checklist of appropriate review points for any particular disruption reviewed.

Question 7.1. Your organisation has recently been involved in a new age disruption, where a significant loss of market share resulted. The organisation designs and manufactures parts for the aviation security sector and has asked you to write a report about adopting DEMT Parts I and II, including a critique of the tool. Finally, the organisation has asked that you submit the report with a draft disruption register (i.e. being Part I and Part II of the DEMT). Please write the report requested explaining the DEMT and any benefits or risks that you foresee.

As you develop the organisation's DEMT, please consider and include the following disruptions on top of the new ideas that you formulate for the disruption register.

- Terrorist event that destroys the main workplace or main employees with intellectual knowledge of the organisation.
- Software invaded and data lost or key secrets exposed to competitors and market.
- Robotics improve rapidly and reduce your main competitor's workforce by 80%, leaving them with a significant cost advantage.
- Trade war ensues and input costs rise by 45%, significantly reducing profits, potentially placing your organisation into closure.

It is important to note that failure to derive sufficient disruptions for the DEMT may limit the organisation's ability to inform stakeholders and limit preparation for the new age. Management will likely need to build new processes and structures for the organisation to be able to identify disruption in a timely basis. Skills of innovation, politics, technology, economics, critical thought and broader brainstorming may be required in order to detect disruption early, where broad skill-based teams may be required to form. The new disruption identification processes will likely require staff that are able to work with shorter timeframes due to the pace of change. Staff that have abilities to work with information that is lacking completeness or veracity may be required as critical thinking and critiques of new ideas may be required in order to generate robust and defensible plans. Entrepreneurs, analysts and innovators with investigative resources may be required to identify the events of the new age.

The new age of change will likely require organisations to spend more time and effort identifying and analysing disruption, despite their uncertainty and risk. Globalisation has increased the speed of information, yet the information may be complete, inaccurate or fake news. Management of the future will no longer have the luxury of waiting for change to move from the impossible to the probable as the pace of change will be fast and the shocks sudden when disruption emerges. Creativity, analysis, verification and critical thought may be the key skills for management in the future to foster in order to gain advantage over competitors in respect of their disruption register preparation. Organisations will need to consider disruption in a formal way so as to reassure stakeholders and financiers that the risk of catastrophic failure is at last identified and mitigated. The benefits will be most realised where the registers are developed in an open way, identifying the less possible rather than merely the probable. Organisations with a robust and broad disruption register may, in the future, be most able to satisfy stakeholders and improve overall organisational value.

Corporate Social Responsibility (CSR)

CSR concept has existed for over 50 years, where stakeholders now expect an organisation to perform activities beyond those purely financial or profit in nature (Carroll, 2015). CSR activities may occur fully across the organisation or in partial ways (Rasche, Bakker, & Moon, 2013). Organisations that are innovators are more successful with CSR than those that are traditionally efficiency focussed (Yuan, Tian, & Yu, 2018). Investors may be attracted to organisations with CSR as they are focussed not only on financial measures (Benlemlih, 2017; Galema, Plantinga, & Scholtens, 2008). CSR is about including societal values in the organisation operations rather than merely being donations and the way the organisation spends its profits.

Organisations are increasingly investing in activities that generate societal value, this new direction is at variance to the traditional operations aimed at merely shareholder value (Wang, Tong, Takeuchi, & George, 2016). Employee engagement may increase with CSR activities by an organisation (Wang et al., 2016). Organisational reputation may improve when it conducts CSR activities (Cui, Jo, & Na, 2018). CSR intensities of action may vary according to the level of country development, where mature advanced economy organisations may deploy CSR in order to improve their external standing (Cuervo-Cazurra, 2018).

There may be considerable benefits for organisations to include CSR into their operations as customers, shareholders and staff may prefer those involved in CSR. The location and values of corporate head offices may affect the way that CSR influences financial results, where higher CSR valued countries yielded higher performances (Hoi, Wu, & Zhang, 2018). The efficiency of investment may also be enhanced in CSR-adopting organisations (Benlemlih & Bitar, 2018) and the adoption of CSR may improve the accuracy of financial forecasting (Lee, 2017).

The increased use of CSR may have many benefits for an organisation as shown above. In the new age, being connected to the community and society may be an excellent way to improve an organisation. The linkages to community and society may improve the organisational knowledge about impending change and may even be able to assist the organisation from introducing changes that are likely to be unfavourably accepted. Staff may also be attracted to organisations that have the reputation of being connected to society and sharing values, where the organisation may even gain advantage by attracting the most skilled staff this way. Investors and other stakeholders may prefer CSR-based organisations over those without, where already there are capital funds that will not invest in coal or cigarette activities based purely on appeal rather than financial return.

Management may likely be challenged in changing towards CSR as old habits and thinking may need to be altered in the transition. Processes and behaviours inside the organisation may need to adjust and be more openly externally focussed than ever before as they introduce CSR. Leadership positions will likely need to explain their organisations CSR position, justifying and attempting to build trust with the broader community, rather than merely staff and customers. Corporate image will likely need to align with CSR activities as stakeholders and society will monitor and judge when divergence occurs.

Governance and Ethics

As has been noted throughout this book the new age may be fast paced with sudden directional changes, where more information and data than ever may be available yet may be incomplete or unverifiable. A number of tools have been considered also in this book on how an organisation may need to alter its operations in such an unstable, uncertain and risky new age. This section extends thought on these matters by now considering how good governance and ethics may assist management and leadership move organisations through this challenging new age. A number of benefits of increasing governance and ethics in an organisation are discussed in this section.

Governance represents those activities, which manage risk that is linked to accountable individuals and organisational processes that respond to variances as they occur (Mcphee, 2014). Project governance may have evolved separately, where it is now envisaged it should conform with general organisational governance principles (Bekker, 2015). Other definitions describe governance as a broad process that manages resources between multiple stakeholder variable requirements (Daily, Dalton, & Cannella, 2003). The activities of decision making and strategy are not considered the part of governance, whereas controls, policies and procedures may be included and may assist organisational performances (McGrath & Whitty, 2015).

Technology organisations often require flexibility and compartmentalisation in order to foster more responsive, lower cost and faster-paced organisational responses (Luna, Kruchten, Pedrosa, Neto, & de Moura, 2014). Disruption effects may be reduced if governance is included as indicated after a post-global financial crisis (GFC) non-finance organisational review of investment decisions (Nguyen, Nguyen, & Yin, 2015). Organisations that are effective at governance may have superior financial returns above those without (Kral, Tripes, Pirozek, & Pudil, 2012).

Traditional governance structures and processes are often aimed at increasing control and review in an attempt to reduce risk and variation an organisation. Projects, as one sub-component of an organisation, may include governance from a selected senior management group or through dedicated project body called a Project Management Office. In larger organisations, governance may be specialised, performed by experts and professionals including reviews by external and internal audits of accounting, board reviews, safety, insurance, engineering and even environment amongst others. Often, these governance processes have been inflexible, set for certain times with set people to perform the reviews and make recommendations. The slower independent governance of the past has given stakeholders confidence in processes, authorities and decisions that cumulatively have increased the value of organisations and reduced risk.

In the new age, there may be increased potential for organisational governance bodies to assist and improve processes as the reviews will likely need to occur in shorter timeframes. The role of governance has historically been to independently provide review and mentorship, potentially identifying risk and uncertainty not identified by management. The need to independently review and provide mentoring is likely to be increase in the new age as management will be required to make fast decisions when information is missing. It is likely that the governance function of an organisation is likely to continue to exist and be more important, albeit in a different form. The slow inflexible governance review processes of the past may not be advantageous in the future, where delay and bureaucracy of governance may harm an organisation. In order to improve flexibility and response times, governance bodies may require to be involved in early briefings as new events emerge, prior to management direction or decision. The involvement of governance earlier in the disruption discovery process has potential to reduce its independence, yet faster response times and flexibility may assist the organisation achieve competitive advantage.

Linked closely with governance and CSR discussed above is the topic of ethics, where the subject is the responsibility of leadership. Ethics may be considered to be values that are legal as well as complying with societies' broad rules (Bommer, Gratto, Gravander, & Tuttle, 1987; Man-Fong Ho, 2011). The inclusion of leadership ethics may improve employee support during organisational change (Sharif & Scandura, 2014), thus may be an important skill for the organisation of the future to hold. Ethics may be derived from a combination of the organisations internal systems and the society laws or values (Belle, 2017; Robin, 2009). Critical thinking may be important to business ethics (Seele, 2018), where this book has promoted critical thinking as a key skill to be learned by management and leadership for the future. Business moral dilemmas are often thought to be resolved through human action, taking a detached position, or considered serious, or are issues that were not resolved by law or agreement (Morris, 2004).

The catastrophic system failures of the GFC, or the Asian crisis, should not discourage organisations into the future from using governance and ethical frameworks. Leadership and management of the future may find that it is prudent if they embrace and build governance and ethical principles into their staff, culture and systems. It has been argued that leadership is responsible for ethics, where the issues are involved beyond the mere financial outcomes of an organisation (Minkes, Small, & Chatterjee, 1999). Those that view the GFC-type systems failures as examples of why governance and ethics are not working and argue for heightened legislation might better spend their efforts in promoting a more ethical framework. The decline in behaviours is not limited to the private sector as some argue that the public sector is similarly affected (Năstase, 2014). Organisations are notoriously difficult to change and thus merely changing leaders may be insufficient in order to achieve a more ethical model (Donald, 2018).

Ethical frameworks may be more likely to prevent poor organisational behaviour than mere governance alone. Ethical issues are not isolated to the business sector as the public sector also has ethical matters to consider (Snellman, 2015). The public sector writes policies and procedures in an effort to guide and prevent individuals in pursuing their personal objectives over the public goals (Snellman, 2015). Governance may be useful in highlighting breaches of policies or past inefficiency or detection of fraud. The potential to prevent fraud or error with governance is merely due to an implicit the threat of discovery, publicity and law, where each could occur otherwise undetected. The training and adoption of an ethical model may be more preventative for unethical behaviour than governance.

In the new age, the fast pace of change may require processes and structures to be less defined and more flexible than in the past. Governance may still be required in order to detect errors or increase the critical review of decision making, yet the current governance systems may not be flexible or fast enough. Ethical learning and behaviour in the organisation may be one solution to improve flexibility and pace of change, whilst not diminishing standards. If staff are trained on ethics, there may be peer pressure to act ethically, or an improved risk of discovery, where both effects may influence decisions, processes and structures. Some argue that many top organisations already provide training on ethics and provide ethical vision statements, where the increased visibility assists decision making (Verschoor, 2000).

This section has argued that governance and ethics may improve organisational decision making as both may provide reference beyond the financial results. Society has values and rules that sit beyond the legal framework that organisations need to be cognisant of in the new age. Failure to act ethically, or in accordance with good governance may result in a lack of confidence by stakeholders that may eventuate in new laws or loss of value or even protests, so are worthy of consideration by management and leadership. The culture of an organisation may increasingly be placed under pressure in the new age and thus being another factor for consideration of organisations in the future.

Cultural Change

A new and developing area of research is involved in understanding the importance of organisational culture. Culture has been defined as those shared assumptions, beliefs and values that are held closely (Schein, 1985), including elements of power and structure, performance and risk (Koberg & Hood, 1991; Wallach, 1983). Culture is important in its influence over organisational performance as it can influence the type of staff, retention rates and knowledge (Cantanzaro, Moore, & Marshall, 2010). One should not assume that culture is homogenous, as even in a whistleblowing culture the wrongdoings of consultants have been found to be treated differently to wrong doings of employees (Ayers & Kaplan, 2005). A model to assess culture in a jail setting has indicated factors of commitment, turnover and satisfaction (Stohr et al., 2012) that has later been confirmed (Mei et al., 2017) and thus these factors may be indicators for other organisations to consider.

If an organisations culture lacks motivating resources, leadership may be effective at providing the gap (Hartnell, Kinicki, Lambert, Fugate, & Doyle Corner, 2016). Conversely, where leadership lack values for the organisation, culture may provide a satisfactory alternate (Hartnell et al., 2016). Culture can influence how satisfied staff are with their employment (Tsai, 2011) and thus indicating that culture should not be ignored in the future. If staff are likely to be stressed during the new age changes ahead, attention to culture and staff happiness may be significant issues for leadership to focus on. Leadership that is classified as exceptional, combined with a culture of support, has been shown to achieve higher levels of engagement and trust (Meng & Berger, 2018). The promotion of respect and other elements may improve organisational culture (Mallette & Rykert, 2018).

Organisational change may be linked to culture, despite culture not being the most common factor in that recent research (Donald, 2017). Whilst no relationship between performance and culture was found in another research set, charisma and culture were related (Wilderom, van Den Berg, & Wiersma, 2012). In the fast-paced new age, organisations may seek ways to reduce delays, where it is worth noting that delays in the construction industry have already been associated with organisational culture (Arditi, Nayak, & Damci, 2017).

Historically, overly controlled organisations with defined processes and structures may have, over time, inadvertently limited innovation and creativity. A transition from the current controlled organisation to the new age culture of speed, innovation, creativity and flexibility may provide significant challenges for leadership and management of the future. Staff and other stakeholders may not like the lack of structure required in the new age, or errors and confusion may result as processes are allowed to be more flexible. Change in the new age may require new approaches and additional factors to influence change in the transformation from control to flexibility.

Despite many forms of discrimination reducing in organisations through legislation and training, ageism has emerged in some organisational cultures. Some may argue that the old are resistant to change and not open to change, yet some research on resistance and change found no indication of this form of resistance amongst the many discovered (Donald, 2017). Ageism is a relatively under-researched topic despite the significant increase in aged people in many countries (Nelson, 2016), being a society issue (Levy & Macdonald, 2016) rather than merely a corporate one. A workplace that is not balanced and diverse, that exists without aged or more experienced staff, may be accused of a bias culture. A bias culture that lacks diversity may be less adaptive, creative and flexible than is required for the new age. Identifying and adapting to disruption is not a skill limited by age, or any other discriminatory factor and thus leadership might be expected to seek out and reduce or eliminate discrimination from a culture.

Culture is an area of research that is likely to continue to increase in focus as the new age will likely require an organisational culture that is dynamic and organic, one that can cope with fast-paced change and lack of complete or verified information. Organisational leadership is likely to increasingly be required to assess and change culture in order to gain advantage and as a means to address risk and governance issues. In the pursuit of new cultures, leadership will need to promote diversity and the hiring and retention of the most appropriate staff, discouraging discrimination and ageism. Organisations that cast out the old, are sexist or are discriminate on other demographic grounds may seriously limit their growth and ability to think creatively or critically. Leadership may need to employ new tactics in order to promote the hiring of the most qualified or best fit employee, no matter their demographic.

Question 7.2. You have just been appointed to run a long-established division of your organisation. Your predecessor has briefed you that the organisation is a high-performing division with little to worry about. You are aware that the staff turnover is higher than average and that there was an environmental incident at the site last year. Your new manager has asked you to change the culture in this division.

Write a detailed proposal for your manager as to how you will change the culture of this new division you will be heading. What will be your approach to assessing the organisational culture? What culture factors will you consider? How will you determine the culture? How will you critically assess the culture to ensure that you understand before introducing change?

Assessment tools for culture are yet to be widely accepted defined and confirmed in research, where the leadership and management will likely require assistance to adjust culture towards the new age. In France, research on ageism has indicated that there is a lack of data to research discrimination in workplaces (Challe, 2017) and thus data collection and analysis may be a starting point for improvement in future organisations. Young people may be less discriminatory when nostalgia is used as a communication path with the aged (Turner, Wildschut, & Sedikides, 2018), indicating that leadership may discover tools to change discriminatory or ageist cultures. Existing cultures may be difficult to change, where removing the no change option may be required (Mallette & Rykert, 2018).

Culture may be just one element of change required for the new age, where future research is likely to improve definition and understanding of the topics. Organisations are increasingly changing leaders in order to change, where merely changing the leader is insufficient in order to change organisational culture as expected (Donald, 2018). Assessment of culture may require an organisation to review its discrimination practices, staff engagement, stakeholder trust, skills and entrenched practices in order to adapt and transform ready for the new age. The final section of this chapter and this book is one that seeks to build upon the earlier writing in order to set out a direction for those involved in the leadership and management of the future.

Leadership and Management in the New Age

The new age is likely to emerge with increased disruption and AI or robotics, where Chapters 2 and 3 have discussed many of the current and likely new events. Further new age change events are likely to emerge suddenly, at a fast pace and be assisted by globalisation and new forms of communication. Consequently, organisations will need to be creative in identifying new forms of disruption and AI, flexible in their response to the change and innovative in their solutions. Whilst some organisations may already exist with some of the required characteristics, the new age will include ongoing change that may not be avoidable. The leadership and management within an organisation will likely be the positions responsible for organising and preparing the organisation to change in the future.

Disruption is a term that originated with technology change, where today it involves abrupt changes that reflect the dynamic environment created through globalisation from its interconnectivity and new forms of communication. Changes that once may have taken years to flow around the world and influence organisations far away in other industries, now can take minutes through social media and online news. Globalisation means that organisations can supply others around the world with ease, derived from trade interconnectivity, international travel, trade and commerce. Many disruption events are discussed in this book as a way of enlightening the reader without necessarily trying to be a predictor of the future. At the end of 2018, Brexit and trade wars are increasing risk and uncertainty, where the final direction of these two disruptions alone are still unknown, where investment and trade decisions are likely to be affected by the outcome.

AI and robots are also emerging with increased capabilities of technology in both speed, calculation complexity and reduced sizes. The dream of robots and AI improving service, reducing costs and emerging throughout society have been imagined for decades, where the dreams are likely to be reality within a few short years or the next decade. As AI emerges, it will change society and organisations forever as the technology eliminates or transforms whole industries in short time frames. The use of humans in the workplace will likely dramatically change and diminish in the new age, creating issues for workplace relations and society more generally. As was the case in the Industrial Revolution, some industries will be eliminated, whilst other industries will emerge and proliferate in the future.

Organisational leadership has the responsibility to prepare organisations for the new age of change ahead, where stakeholders each may have competing requirements. Despite involving overlapping themes, leadership is distinctly separate to management, where leaders are expected to explain the organisational direction to various stakeholders. Whilst simplicity and consistency has historically been used by leadership to build trust and engagement to move an organisation into the future, those skills may be less relevant in the new age. Leadership will likely be required to explain risk, multiple directions and uncertainty in the new age to gather stakeholder support, where neither simplicity nor consistency may be possible. Failure of leadership to communicate effectively, or a failure to choose appropriate directions may cause stakeholders to lose confidence and thus reducing organisational value or lower security of employment for leadership.

New leadership skills may be required in the new age, including those of assessing varying communication forms and regularity, skills to assess any stakeholder non-homogeneity, connection with societal values, governance and ethics. The likely organic style growth and flexibility of the future organisation may decrease leadership trust as directions will be less clear and controlled than in the past.

Openness may be a key strategy for the leadership of the future, where markets, stakeholders and cultures of the past may be unfamiliar with the sharing of information, uncertainty and risk required in the new age. Measures of change may be required to assist the organisation move forward so the leadership can monitor change factors, including trust and engagement (Donald, 2017).

Staff that will be retained in the new age will need to be able to work with lower human percentages and likely be of higher skills. Attracting and retaining the best staff will no longer easy, where leadership that can communicate the organisation well may achieve an advantage over those perceived as confusing or untrustworthy. Leadership can influence positive staff job satisfaction, where positive relationships between staff and leaders may be important (Tsai, 2011). Organisational ethics, governance and culture may be tools for leadership to use in attracting and retaining staff and other stakeholders in the future. Organisational values may also influence management competencies (Gorenak & Ferjan, 2015), where the promotion of values is a leadership responsibility.

It is quite possible for a person to hold excellent leadership skills and be a poor manager, or for a person to hold excellent management capability and be a poor leader. Many business people learn both skills through trial and error, practice and experience rather than learning either topic formally as an academic endeavour. The title of manager is overused in practice, often associated with higher pay grades than the skills required for management or leadership roles. The new age may soon require skills, rather than mere experience, where formal studies in both leadership and management may be required in order to improve organisational performance. Trust in leadership is unlikely to be advanced if manager roles continue to be employed as managers without formal knowledge of the topic. The trend towards higher tertiary education requirements already exist in this area, as leadership, management and critical thinking skills sought after by employers in Malaysia (Tay, 2001).

Senior management may be tempted to be in control and make all significant decisions within an organisation, yet the controlling style may inhibit creativity and responsibility. Critical thinking is considered important for those seeking leadership roles and for those in management, yet may still be deficient in those studying in the fields (Errington & Bubna-Litic, 2015). Optimisation may not always be possible in the new age, where the inclusion of critical thinking skills may assist when presented with difficult or conflicting decisions (Page & Mukherjee, 2007). It has been encouraged throughout this book that those seeking management roles in the future should consider critiquing and even disagreeing with positions presented, as the openness of varying positions may assist in the learning of management and leadership (Errington & Bubna-Litic, 2015).

Leadership and management roles may have traditionally preferred to set single organisational directions in order to create images of control and clear direction. To achieve a single organisational direction without options or critical thought, significant power struggles and internal competition may have ensued. A base case of doing nothing may be ignored when power and competition is involved in developing a single direction for the organisation, where the base case should be included and critically assessed. Openness may be required in the future, where leadership should assess options, recognise past errors or recognise past directions in order to maintain trust. Leaders that merely spin the positive, or ignore the past, or the future risks and uncertainty may harm their influence and trust in the organisation. Leaders may need to be less transactional in the future, rather being more creative and upholding integrity, including elements of ethics and credibility (Dumas & Beinecke, 2018).

Management will likely no longer be focussed merely on the operational or the day-to-day crisis as there are new requirements for the position in the new age. Flexibility, speed, creativity, innovation and critical thought may be characteristics of future management. The traditional slower approvals and controls processes used by management of the past may no longer be appropriate. Future management may require a broad set of skills in order to set the organisation ready for the new age, where formal qualifications may be required to hold a title of manager. Staff in roles of management without any formal qualifications in the topic may have traditionally led to trial and error, learning though experience. The fast-paced nature of change may no longer allow organisations to tolerate staff in management positions without some formal study into the topics.

The flexibility, creativity and speed of the new age will require changes in many of the management functions including, but not limited to, strategy, performance assessment, structures and processes. Organisations are likely to change the way that they operate, change the way they hire and retain staff as well as the way they manage services and products to market. In the new age, there will likely be a significant amount of incomplete and unverified information, where new decision-making skills may be required in order to cope with the associated higher risk and uncertainty. Senior management may need to support cohesion in order to cope in new age change, where the liberated kinetics may assist in a more graduated change (Spender & Grinyer, 1995).

Change in the new age is likely to be continuous and fast, where research has already commended into understanding the multifactored issues that may influence change in positive and negative ways (Donald, 2017). Positive perceptions of change and leadership may be achieved when there is employee participation and responsiveness, whereas management style and conflict resolution skills had less influence on those perceptions (Hearld & Alexander, 2014). A multifactored approach to change may be required in order to reduce resistance or improve change where factors of workload, engagement, power and politics may be required with that of leadership and management (Donald, 2017).

The new age ahead may be one of the most exciting and transformational times for leadership and management, where new skills and understanding may be required in order to reduce organisational failures or loss of value. Many of the strategies and skill required in the future organisation may be counter-intuitive to the traditional leadership and management practices of the past. Great risk and uncertainty will also provide opportunity for those that are creative and innovative. Balance will likely be required between the risk takers and good governance in order to timely address the lack of verified information available.

Summary

Whilst the change ahead in the new age will be fast, characterised with significant increased risk and uncertainty, the future is not necessarily bleak. Opportunities will arise for an organisation to take improved competitive positions, new products and new relationships, where governance may be a balance to reduce uncertainty and risk if it can modify appropriately. A traditional manager focussed on a market or an organisation without reference to international affairs, politics or emerging technology may not survive in the new age. The new leadership and management will be cognisant of the wider world, globalisation and emerging threats, be they in the form of disruption or AI. In order to attract good staff and lift performance, organisations will likely need to consider improvements in ethics, CSR as well as governance. Merging organisational goals with those for the broader society may assist in guiding the organisation past the less prescribed and controlled operating systems of the past.

One may consider that the new age will be an interesting and challenging time to be in leadership or management of an organisation. The range of topics and skills required in the future are likely to be broad, well beyond the traditional internally or externally focussed positions. Management roles may soon need to be qualified in the subject rather than the title merely being linked to pay grades and allowing people to learn through trial and error. Heightened risk and opportunity will associate with the new age where more formal knowledge of disruption, AI, leadership or management may assist organisations preparing for the constant change of the new age. Whilst staff numbers may diminish in the future, staff remaining in employment may be more important, requiring higher skills, where good staff relations and motivations will greatly assist an organisation adapt and grow in an organic way.

Critical thinking is required for both the leadership and management of the future, as the skill may assist in either identifying or assessing options in the new age. Information is likely to be more available in higher quantities than ever before, yet the information may be unverified or incomplete. Heightened analysis and decision-making skills may assist those in leadership and management roles cope with the risk and uncertainty as it emerges in this new age of disruption and AI. Whether you are likely to work in a small or large organisation, avoiding change may be impossible and thus it may be best to consider the new leadership and management skills you may require.

References

Abdollah Dehdashti, S. (2018). B2B unfair trade practices and EU competition law. *European Competition Journal*, 14(2–3), 305–341. doi:10.1080/17441056.2018.1520439

Akbar, H., Baruch, Y., & Tzokas, N. (2018). Feedback loops as dynamic processes of organizational knowledge creation in the context of the innovations' front-end. *British Journal of Management*, 29(3), 445–463.

Aldrich, J. O., & Cunningham, J. B. (2015). *Using IBM SPSS statistics: An interactive hands-on approach* (2nd ed.). Thousand Oaks, CA: Sage Publications.

Allen, D., & Faff, R. (2012). The global financial crisis: Some attributes and responses. *Accounting & Finance*, 52(1), 1–7.

Amcher, J. (2010). *A quantitative study on outsourcing help desk services*. Phoenix, AZ: University of Phoenix.

Ammer, C. (Ed.) (2016). *The American Heritage® dictionary of idioms*. Boston, MA: Houghton Mifflin Company.

Archick, K. (2014). *The European Union: Questions and answers*. Washington, DC: Congressional Research Service.

Arditi, D., Nayak, S., & Damci, A. (2017). Effect of organizational culture on delay in construction. *International Journal of Project Management*, 35(2), 136–147. doi:10.1016/j.ijproman.2016.10.018

Arlitsch, K., & Newell, B. (2017). Thriving in the age of accelerations: A brief look at the societal effects of artificial intelligence and the opportunities for libraries. *Journal of Library Administration*, 57(7), 789–798. doi:10.1080/01930826.2017.1362912

Atlas, T. (2018). Turkey signs missile deal with Russia. *Arms Control Today*, 48(1), 41.

Awojide, S., Arikhan, I., & Adeosun, J. (2018). The automation of restaurant business process towards food ordering in Nigeria Private University: The design perspective. A study of Samuel Adegboyega University Edo State Nigeria. *SAU Science-Tech Journal*, 3(1), 154–163.

Ayers, S., & Kaplan, S. E. (2005). Wrongdoing by consultants: An examination of employees' reporting intentions. *Journal of Business Ethics*, 57(2), 121–137.

Baker, S. (2018). Italy perceived as trouble: But not by all. *Pensions & Investments*, 46(12), 3.

Bals, L., & Turkulainen, V. (2017). Achieving efficiency and effectiveness in purchasing and supply management: Organization design and outsourcing. *Journal of Purchasing and Supply Management*, 23(4), 256–267. doi:10.1016/j.pursup.2017.06.003

Bandyopadhyay, T. (2012). Employing cost effective internet-based networking technologies to manage B2B relationship: The strategic impact on IT security risk. *International Journal of Risk and Contingency Management (IJRCM)*, 1(1), 12–28. doi:10.4018/ijrcm.2012010102

Bao, G. (2015). What theories are needed for strategic management? *Nankai Business Review International*, 6(4), 433–454. doi:10.1108/NBRI-05-2015-0012

Bass, B. M. (1985a). *Leadership and performance beyond expectations*. New York, NY: Macmillan.

Bass, B. M. (1985b). Leadership: Good, better, best. *Organizational Dynamics*, 13(3), 26–40.

Bawany, S. (2014). Leadership communication. *Leadership Excellence Essentials*, 31(9), 31.

Bedi, A., & Skowronski, M. (2014). Political skill at work: Good or bad? Understanding its predictors and consequences. *SAM Advanced Management Journal Spring*, 79(2), 39.

Beirne, J., & Fratzscher, M. (2013). The pricing of sovereign risk and contagion during the European sovereign debt crisis. *Journal of International Money and Finance*, 34(C), 60–82. doi:10.1016/j.jimonfin.2012.11.004

Bekker, M. C. (2015). Project governance: The definition and leadership dilemma. *Procedia Social and Behavioral Sciences, 194*(C), 33–43. doi:10.1016/j.sbspro.2015.06.117

Belias, D., & Koustelios, A. (2014). The impact of leadership and change management strategy on organizational culture. *European Scientific Journal, 10*(7), 451–470.

Belle, S. (2017). Knowledge stewardship as an ethos-driven approach to business ethics. *Journal of Business Ethics, 142*(1), 83–91. doi:10.1007/s10551-015-2710-5

Bellingkrodt, S., & Wallenburg, C. M. (2015). The role of customer relations for innovativeness and customer satisfaction: A comparison of service industries. *The International Journal of Logistics Management, 26*(2), 254–274. doi:10.1108/IJLM-06-2012-0038

Benlemlih, M. (2017). Corporate social responsibility and firm debt maturity. *Journal of Business Ethics, 144*(3), 491–517. doi:10.1007/s10551-015-2856-1

Benlemlih, M., & Bitar, M. (2018). Corporate social responsibility and investment efficiency. *Journal of Business Ethics, 148*(3), 647–671. doi:10.1007/s10551-016-3020-2

Benn, S., Dunphy, D., & Grffiths, A. (Eds.). (2014). *Organizational change for corporate sustainability* (2nd ed.). London: Routledge.

Bennett, H., & Durkin, M. (2000). The effects of organisational change on employee psychological attachment: An exploratory study. *Journal of Managerial Psychology, 15*(2), 126–146.

Benson, M. (2018). *Review – Kubrick's '2001' at 50 – The science-fiction classic saw far into the future, with flat-screen computers and artificial intelligence (but no, HAL was not a spoof of IBM)* (p. C.4). New York, NY: Dow Jones & Company Inc.

Bernardes, E. S., & Hanna, M. D. (2009). A theoretical review of flexibility, agility and responsiveness in the operations management literature: Toward a conceptual definition of customer. (Report). *International Journal of Operations & Production Management, 29*(1), 30–53. doi:10.1108/01443570910925352

Bisbe, J., & Malagueño, R. (2015). How control systems influence product innovation processes: Examining the role of entrepreneurial orientation. *Accounting and Business Research, 45*(3), 356–386. doi:10.1080/00014788.2015.1009870

Bizcommunity.com. (2017). Cryptocurrency, blockchain and ICOs: Funding digital decentralisation. Retrieved from https://www.bizcommunity.com/Article/196/516/166032.html

Blanchard, O. J., & Gali, J. (2007). *The macroeconomic effects of oil shocks: Why are the 2000s so different from the 1970s?* Retrieved from http://www.crei.cat/wp-content/uploads/users/pages/bgoil08wp.pdf

Blay, K. (2017). *Resilience in projects: Definition, dimensions, antecedents and consequences.* Ph.D. thesis, Loughborough University, Loughborough.

Bommer, M., Gratto, C., Gravander, J., & Tuttle, M. (1987). A behavioral model of ethical and unethical decision making. *Journal of Business Ethics, 6*(4), 265–280.

Bommer, W., Rich, G., & Rubin, R. (2005). Changing attitudes about change: Longitudinal effects of transformational leader behavior on employee cynicism about organizational change. *Journal of Organizational Behavior, 26*(7), 733–753.

Bono, J. E., & Ilies, R. (2006). Charisma, positive emotions and mood contagion. *The Leadership Quarterly, 17*(4), 317–334.

Bordia, P., Hunt, E., Paulsen, N., Tourish, D., & DiFonzo, N. (2004). Uncertainty during organizational change: Is it all about control? *European Journal of Work and Organizational Psychology, 13*(3), 345–365.

Bordley, R., & Pollock, S. (2012). Assigning resources and targets to an organization's activities. *European Journal of Operational Research, 220*(3), 752–761.

Bordo, M. (2018). An historical perspective on the quest for financial stability and the monetary policy regime. *The Journal of Economic History, 78*(2), 319–357. doi:10.1017/S0022050718000281

Bordo, M. D. (2017). *The second era of globalization is not yet over: An historical perspective.* Retrieved from https://www.hoover.org/sites/default/files/research/docs/17103-bordo.pdf

Boudette, N. E. (2018). *Toyota halts self-driving car tests after Uber accident. (Business/ Financial Desk)* (p. B4). New York, NY: The New York Times Company.

Boyd, R., & Holton, R. J. (2018). Technology, innovation, employment and power: Does robotics and artificial intelligence really mean social transformation? *Journal of Sociology, 54*(3), 331–345. doi:10.1177/1440783317726591

Bratasanu, V. (2018). Leadership decision-making processes in the context of data driven tools. *Calitatea, 19*(S3), 77–87.

Brauers, H., & Richter, P. M. (2016). *The Paris Climate agreement: Is it sufficient to limit climate change?* Retrieved from https://www.econstor.eu/handle/10419/127574

Bresnen, M., Hodgson, D., Bailey, S., Hyde, P., & Hassard, J. (2017). Mobilizing management knowledge in healthcare: Institutional imperatives and professional and organizational mediating effects. *Management Learning, 48*(5), 597–614. doi:10.1177/1350507617718257

Brooks, R. A. (1986). *Achieving artificial intelligence through building robots.* Retrieved from https://apps.dtic.mil/dtic/tr/fulltext/u2/a174364.pdf

Brown, H. S., & Vergragt, P. J. (2016). From consumerism to wellbeing: Toward a cultural transition? *Journal of Cleaner Production, 132*(C), 308–317. doi:10.1016/j.jclepro.2015.04.107

Bruckman, J. (2008). Overcoming resistance to change: Causal factors, interventions, and critical values. *The Psychologist-Manager Journal, 11*(2), 211–219. doi:10.1080/10887150802371708

Brumfiel, G. (2011). The collider that cried 'Higgs': Data leaks from particle hunters raise questions about scientific trust. *Nature, 473*(7346), 136. doi:10.1038/473136a

Brym, R., Godbout, M., Hoffbauer, A., Menard, G., & Zhang, T. H. (2014). Social media in the 2011 Egyptian uprising. *British Journal of Sociology, 65*(2), 266–292. doi:10.1111/1468-4446.12080

Buchanan, P. (2010). PIGS crash to earth. *American Conservative, 9*(7), 31.

Buckner, G. D., & Shah, V. (1993). Future vision: Impacts of artificial intelligence on organizational success. *Kybernetes, 22*(2), 40–50. doi:doi:10.1108/eb005962

Burnes, B. (2009). *Managing change* (5th ed.). London: FT/Prentice Hall.

Burnes, B. (2011). Introduction: Why does change fail, and what can we do about it? *Journal of Change Management, 11*(4), 445–450.

Burnes, B., & Jackson, P. (2011). Success and failure in organizational change: An exploration of the role of values. *Journal of Change Management, 11*(2), 133–162.

Burrows, A. (2018). Innovation and leadership in federal procurement organizations. *Contract Management, 58*(4), 26–36.

Buszynski, L. (2012). The South China Sea: Oil, maritime claims, and US–China strategic rivalry. *The Washington Quarterly, 35*(2), 139–156.

Candido, C., & Santos, S. (2015). *Strategy implementation: What is the failure rate?* CASEE Discussion Paper No. 18. Faculdae de Economia, Univeridado do Alvarve, Faro, Portugal.

Cantanzaro, D., Moore, H., & Marshall, T. (2010). The impact of organizational culture on attraction and recruitment of job applicants. *Journal of Business and Psychology, 25*(4), 649–662.

Carroll, A. B. (2015). Corporate social responsibility: The centerpiece of competing and complementary frameworks. *Organizational Dynamics, 44*(2), 87–96. doi:10.1016/j.orgdyn.2015.02.002

Caruso, L. (2018). Digital innovation and the fourth industrial revolution: Epochal social changes? *AI & Society, 33*(3), 379–392. doi:10.1007/s00146-017-0736-1

Cha, V. D., & Kang, D. C. (2018). *Nuclear North Korea: A debate on engagement strategies.* New York, NY: Columbia University Press.

Challe, L. (2017). Ageism and the business cycle: An exploratory approach. *The European Journal of Comparative Economics, 14*(2), 221–264. doi:10.25428/1824-2979/201702-221-264

Chapman, M. (2011). *Kodak* (pp. 20). London: Haymarket Business Publications Ltd.

Chemers, M. (2014). *An integrative theory of leadership*. New York, NY: Psychology Press.

Chen, J., Fei, Y., Lee, P. T.-W., & Tao, X. (2018). Overseas port investment policy for China's central and local governments in the belt and road initiative. *Journal of Contemporary China*, 28(116), 196–215.

Chen, W., Khalifa, A. S., Morgan, K. L., & Trotman, K. T. (2018). The effect of brainstorming guidelines on individual auditors' identification of potential frauds. *Australian Journal of Management*, 43(2), 225–240.

Chesbrough, H. (2006). *Open business models: How to thrive in the new innovation landscape*. Boston, MA: Harvard Business Press.

Choo, S., Halim, H., & Keng-Howe, I. (2010). The impact of globalisation on strategic human resources management: The mediating role of CEO in HR. *International Journal of Business Studies*, 18(1), 101–124.

Christensen, C. M., & Bower, J. L. (1996). Customer power, strategic investment, and the failure of leading firms. *Strategic Managerial Journal*, 17(3), 197–218.

Christensen, C. M., Raynor, M., & McDonald, R. (2015). Disruptive innovation? Twenty years after the introduction of the theory, we revisit what it does – and doesn't – explain. *Harvard Business Review*, 93(12), 44.

Ciuriak, D. (2018). The march into trade wars: US policy aims and the implications for reconciliation. Verbatum, August. Retrieved from https://www.cdhowe.org/sites/default/files/attachments/research_papers/mixed/Final%20for%20release%20Verbatim_Dan_2018%20July_WEB%20%%283%29.pdf

Clarke, M. R. (1987). ISM Interviews... Peter F Drucker. *Information System Management*, 4(1), 91–96.

Clayton, M. (2014). *Why you need the influence agenda*. London: Palgrave MacMillan.

Cohen, S. G., & Ledford, G. E., Jr. (1994). The effectiveness of self-managing teams: A quasi-experiment. *Human Relations*, 47(1), 13–43.

Cole, M., Walter, F., Bedeian, A., & O'Bolye, E. (2012). Job burnout and employee engagement: A meta-analytical examination of construct proliferation. *Journal of Management*, 38(5), 1550–1581.

Company, M. (2008). Creating organizational transformations. *The McKinsey Quarterly*, *July*, 1–7. Retrieved from http://static1.1.sqspcdn.com/static/f/151916/1862632/1219958417603/Organization+transformation+

Cools, M., Stouthuysen, K., & Van Den Abbeele, A. (2017). Management control for stimulating different types of creativity: The role of budgets. *Journal of Management Accounting Research*, 29(3), 1. doi:10.2308/jmar-51789

Cooper, B. (2013). *The lean entrepreneur how visionaries create products, innovate with new ventures, and disrupt markets*. Hoboken, NJ: Wiley.

Cosh, A., Fu, X., & Hughes, A. (2012). Organisation structure and innovation performance in different environments. *Small Business Economics*, 39(2), 301–317. doi:10.1007/s11187-010-9304-5

Coulson-Thomas, C. (2013). "New leadership" and creating the high performance organisation: Part 1. *Industrial and Commercial Training*, 45(1), 23–31.

Counts, G. E., Farmer, R. F., & Shepard, I. S. (1995). Leadership: Too elusive for definition? *Journal of Leadership & Organizational Studies*, 2(3), 30–41. doi:10.1177/107179199500200304

Cowden, B., & Alhorr, H. (2013). Disruptive innovation in multinational enterprises. *Multinational Business Review*, 21(4), 358–371. doi:10.1108/MBR-05-2013-0027

Cox, J. (1997). Manufacturing the past: Loss and absence in organizational change. *Organizational Studies*, 18(4), 623–654.

Cox, L.-V. (2016). *Understanding millennial, generation X, and baby boomer preferred leadership characteristics: Informing today's leaders and followers*. California, USA: Brandman University.

Cristiani, A., & Peiró, J. M. (2014). Human resource function strategic role and trade unions: Exploring their impact on human resource management practices in Uruguayan firms. *The International Journal of Human Resource Management, 26*(3), 1–20. doi:10.1080/09585192.2014.925946

Crombez, J., & Dahms, H. F. (2015). Artificial intelligence and the problem of digital ontotheology: Toward a critical rethinking of science fiction as theory. *Bulletin of Science, Technology & Society, 35*(3–4), 104–113. doi:10.1177/0270467616651192

Cuervo-Cazurra, A. (2018). The evolution of business groups' corporate social responsibility. *Journal of Business Ethics*, 1–20.

Cui, J., Jo, H., & Na, H. (2018). Does corporate social responsibility affect information asymmetry? *Journal of Business Ethics, 148*(3), 549–572. doi:10.1007/s10551-015-3003-8

Dahl, T. (2014). Robots in health and social care: A complementary technology to home care and telehealthcare? *Robotics, 3*(1), 1–21. doi:10.3390/robotics3010001

Dai, J., & Vasarhelyi, M. (2017). Toward blockchain-based accounting and assurance. *Journal of Information Systems, 31*(3), 5. doi:10.2308/isys-51804

Daily, C., Dalton, D., & Cannella, A. (2003). Corporate governance: Decades of dialogue and data. *Academy of Management. The Academy of Management Review, 28*(3), 371–382. doi:10.2307/30040727

Danisman, A. (2010). Good intentions and failed implementations: Understanding culture-based resistance to organizational change. *European Journal of Work and Organizational Psychology, 19*(2), 200–220. doi:10.1080/13594320902850541

Davenport, T., & Kirby, J. (2016). Just how smart are smart machines? *MIT Sloan Management Review, 57*(3), 21–25.

Davis, J. B. (2005). Neoclassicism, artificial intelligence, and the marginalization of ethics. *International Journal of Social Economics, 32*(7), 590–601. doi:doi:10.1108/03068290510601126

Davis, J. P., & Eisenhardt, K. M. (2011). Rotating leadership and collaborative innovation: Recombination processes in symbiotic relationships. *Administrative Science Quarterly, 56*(2), 159–201. doi:10.1177/0001839211428131

Daziano, R. A., Sarrias, M., & Leard, B. (2017). Are consumers willing to pay to let cars drive for them? Analyzing response to autonomous vehicles. *Transportation Research Part C: Emerging Technologies, 78*, 150–164.

de Graaf, M. M. A., Ben Allouch, S., & van Dijk, J. A. G. M. (2017). Why would I use this in my home? A model of domestic social robot acceptance. *Human–Computer Interaction, 34*(2), 115–173. doi:10.1080/07370024.2017.1312406

De la Porte, C., & Heins, E. (2016). A new era of European integration? Governance of labour market and social policy since the sovereign debt crisis. *Comparative European Politics, 13*(8). Retrieved from https://link.springer.com/article/10.1057/cep.2014.39#citeas.

Deardorff, A. V., & Stern, R. M. (2002). What you should know about globalization and the World Trade Organization. *Review of International Economics, 10*(3), 404–423.

Decker, P., Durand, R., Mayfield, C., McCormack, C., & Skinner, D. (2012). Predicting implementation failure in organizational change. *Journal of Organizational Culture, Communication and Conflict, 16*(2), 29–49.

Deichmann, D., & Jensen, M. (2018). I can do that alone...or not? How idea generators juggle between the pros and cons of teamwork. *Strategic Management Journal, 39*(2), 458–475. doi:10.1002/smj.2696

Della Torre, E., & Solari, L. (2013). High performance work systems and the change management process in medium-sized firms. *The International Journal of Human Resource Management, 24*(13), 2583–2607.

Denning, S. (2014). Riding the wave of "Big Bang Disruption". *Strategy & Leadership, 42*(3), 9–14.

Denning, S. (2016). Christensen updates disruption theory. *Strategy & Leadership*, *44*(2), 10–16. doi:10.1108/SL-01-2016-0005

Dhingra, S., Ottaviano, G. I., Sampson, T., & Reenen, J. V. (2016). The consequences of Brexit for UK trade and living standards. Retrieved from http://eprints.lse.ac.uk/66144/1/__lse.ac.uk_storage_LIBRARY_Secondary_libfile_shared_repository_Content_LSE%20BrexitVote%20blog_brexit02.pdf

Dionida, S. (2016). *Special agent manager perceptions of millennial generation characteristics and employee engagement strategies*. Omaha, USA: Creighton University. Retrieved from https://dspace2.creighton.edu/xmlui/bitstream/handle/10504/107875/Sdionida_dissertation_2DEC2016%20%28Final%29.pdf?sequence=1&isAllowed=y

Dionne, G. (2013). Risk management: History, definition, and critique. *Risk Management and Insurance Review*, *16*(2), 147–166. doi:10.1111/rmir.12016

Dixon, J. C., & Fullerton, A. S. (2014). For and against European Union expansion: Examining mixed opinion on enlargement and specific countries' entries. *International Journal of Comparative Sociology*, *55*(5), 357–378. doi:10.1177/0020715214557844

Dobrev, D. (2005). A definition of artificial intelligence. *Mathematica Balkanica*, *19*(1–2), 67–74.

Doh, J. P., Lawton, T. C., Rajwani, T., & Paroutis, S. (2014). Why your company may need a chief external officer: Upgrading external affairs can help align strategy and improve competitive advantage. *Organizational Dynamics*, *43*(2), 96–104. doi:10.1016/j.orgdyn.2014.03.003

Dombrowski, U., & Wagner, T. (2014). Mental strain as field of action in the 4th industrial revolution. *Procedia CIRP*, *17*, 100–105.

Donald, M. (2014). Project managers beware: The resistance to change you experience may be due to senior leadership rather than just your methods or employees. Paper presented at the AIPM National 2014 Conference Proceedings, Brisbane, Australia. Retrieved from http://www.aipm2014.com.au/images/files/papers/Donald-M.pdf and http://www.aipm2014.com.au/images/files/papers/AIPM_2014_Conference_Proceedings.pdf.

Donald, M. (2016). Organisational change factors: More than disgruntled employees or poor process. Paper presented at the AIPM 2016 Inaugural Regional Conference (Peer Reviewed Paper), Sydney, Australia. Retrieved from https://www.aipm.com.au/documents/aipm-key-documents/aipm_2016_national_conference_papers.aspx.

Donald, M. (2017). *Resistance to change forms and effects in Greater Western Sydney: A multidimensional approach*. Ph.D. thesis, Western Sydney University, Sydney, Australia.

Donald, M. (2018). Toppling bankers can be satisfying, but it's not enough to heal a sick culture. *The Conversation*. Retrieved from https://theconversation.com/toppling-bankers-can-be-satisfying-but-its-not-enough-to-heal-a-sick-culture-106242

Dong, Y., Bartol, K. M., Zhang, Z. X., & Li, C. (2017). Enhancing employee creativity via individual skill development and team knowledge sharing: Influences of dual-focused transformational leadership. *Journal of Organizational Behavior*, *38*(3), 439–458. doi:10.1002/job.2134

Doshi, H., Kumar, P., & Yerramilli, V. (2017). Uncertainty, capital investment, and risk management. *Management Science*. *64*(12), 5769–5786. Retrieved from https://pubsonline.informs.org/doi/abs/10.1287/mnsc.2017.2815 doi:10.1287/mnsc.2017.2815

Drori, I., & Ellis, S. (2011). Conflict and power games in a multinational corporation: Sensegiving as a strategy of preservation. *European Management Review*, *8*(1), 1–16. doi:10.1111/j.1740-4762.2010.01001.x

Drucker, P. (1963). Managing for business effectiveness. *Harvard Business Review*, *May–June*(3), 59–62.

Drucker, P. (2006). What executives should remember. *Harvard Business Review*, *84*(2), 144–153.

Drydakis, N. (2015). The effect of unemployment on self-reported health and mental health in Greece from 2008 to 2013: A longitudinal study before and during the financial crisis. *Social Science & Medicine*, *128*, 43–51.

Dumas, C., & Beinecke, R. H. (2018). Change leadership in the 21st century. *Journal of Organizational Change Management*, *31*(4), 867–876. doi:10.1108/JOCM-02-2017-0042

Durning, A. (1991). How much is enough. *Technology Review*, *94*(4), 1–7.

Dvir, D., Sadeh, A., & Malach-Pines, A. (2010). The fit between entrepreneurs' personalities and the profile of the ventures they manage and business success: An exploratory study. *Journal of High Technology Management Research*, *21*(1), 43–51. doi:10.1016/j.hitech.2010.02.006

Economist, T. (2018). Torn over Tehran; Charlemagne. (Iran nuclear deal split tests Europe's relation in U.S.). *The Economist*, *426*(9076), 47.

Eidam, E. (2015). Though less publicized, data leaks are more prevalent than data breaches. Government Technology. Retrieved from http://www.govtech.com/security/Though-Less-Publicized-Data-Leaks-Are-More-Prevalent-Than-Data-Breaches.html

Elder, S. (2014). Does the GFC as a change agent of financial regulatory models and approaches in Europe provide lessons for Asia? *Asia Europe Journal*, *12*(4), 419–430.

Engelbrecht, G. (2017). Disruptive innovation. *Accountancy SA*, October, 2.

Er, L. P. (2018). 12 Japan's rivalry with China in Southeast Asia. *Japan's Foreign Relations in Asia*, January(2), 158.

Ermasova, N., Nguyen, L., Clark, D., & Ermasov, S. (2018). The management skills of Russians: Do work, management, and government experiences matter? *Public Organization Review*, *18*(3), 299–312. doi:10.1007/s11115-017-0375-5

Errington, A., & Bubna-Litic, D. (2015). Management by textbook: The role of textbooks in developing critical thinking. *Journal of Management Education*, *39*(6), 774–800. doi:10.1177/1052562915594839

Etzioni, A. (1965). Dual leadership in complex organizations. *American Sociological Review*, *30*(5), 688–698.

Facada, M. (2018). *Li-ion batteries and the years ahead*. London: Euromoney Institutional Investor PLC.

Fahimnia, B., Jabbarzadeh, A., & Sabouhi, F. (2017). Sustainability analysis under disruption risks. ITLS working Paper. Retrieved from https://ses.library.usyd.edu.au/handle/2123/19109

Farkas, J., & Schou, J. (2018). Fake news as a floating signifier: Hegemony, antagonism and the politics of falsehood. *Javnost-The Public*, *25*(3), 298–314.

Faulkender, M., Kadyrzhanova, D., Prabhala, N., & Senbet, L. (2010). Executive compensation: An overview of research on corporate practices and proposed reforms. *Journal of Applied Corporate Finance*, *22*(1), 107–118.

Felsen, J. (1975). Automation of investment analysis. *ACM SIGART Bulletin*, *53*, 12–14. doi:10.1145/1216504.1216506

Fernandez, P. (2016). "Through the looking glass: Envisioning new library technologies" how artificial intelligence will impact libraries. *Library Hi Tech News*, *33*(5), 5–8. doi:doi:10.1108/LHTN-05-2016-0024

Fink, C. (2018). Dangeous speech, anti-Muslim violence, and Facebook in Myanmar. *Journal of International Affairs*, *71*(1.5), 43–52.

Flesher, D. L., & Martin, C. (1987). Artificial intelligence. (Impact of artificial intelligence on accounting and auditing professions). *Internal Auditor*, *44*(1), 32.

France24. (2018). Canada: Trump says does not endorse G7 communique, after 'weak' Trudeau comments. Retrieved from https://www.reuters.com/article/us-g7-summit-trump/trump-says-does-not-endorse-g7-communique-after-weak-trudeau-comments-idUSKCN1J510P

Friede, K. (2017). Five technology trends in B2B payments. *Las Vegas Business Press*, *34*(17), 13.

Fuchs, C., & Trottier, D. (2017). Internet surveillance after Snowden. *Journal of Information, Communication & Ethics in Society*, *15*(4), 412–444. doi:10.1108/JICES-01-2016-0004

Galema, R., Plantinga, A., & Scholtens, B. (2008). The stocks at stake: Return and risk in socially responsible investment. *Journal of Banking & Finance*, *32*(12), 2646–2654.

Gallie, D., Zhou, Y., Felstead, A., & Green, F. (2012). Teamwork, skill development and employee welfare. *British Journal of Industrial Relations*, *50*(1), 23–46. doi:10.1111/j.1467-8543.2010.00787.x

Gallus, J., & Frey, B. S. (2016). Awards: A strategic management perspective. *Strategic Management Journal*, *37*(8), 1699–1714. doi:10.1002/smj.2415

Galvin, P., & Arndt, F. (2014). Strategic management: Building depth as well as breadth. *Journal of Management and Organization*, *20*(2), 139–147. doi:10.1017/jmo.2014.35

Gans, J. (2016). The other disruption: When innovations threaten the organizational model. *Harvard Business Review*, *94*(3), 78.

Geis, G. S. (2010). An empirical examination of business outsourcing transactions. *Virginia Law Review*, *96*(2), 241–300. doi:10.2307/20700371

Gelfert, A. (2018). Fake news: A definition. *Informal Logic*, *38*(1), 84–117.

Georgalis, J., Samaratunge, R., Kimberley, N., & Lu, Y. (2015). Change process characteristics and resistance to organisational change: The role of employee perceptions of justice. *Australian Journal of Management*, *40*(1), 89–113.

Giangreco, A., & Peccei, R. (2005). The nature and antecedents of middle manager resistance to change: Evidence from an Italian context. *The International Journal of Human Resource Management*, *16*(10), 1812–1829. doi:10.1080/09585190500298404

Gibbons-Neff, T. (2015). This is the Russian plane that Turkey just shot down. (Sukhoi Su-24 attack aircraft). *The Washington Post*. November 24, 2015. Retrieved from https://www.washingtonpost.com/news/checkpoint/wp/2015/11/24/this-is-the-russian-plane-that-turkey-just-shot-down/?utm_term=.6f21dcb9ba88

Gibbs, E., & Deloach, J. (2006). Which comes first … managing risk or strategy-setting? Both! *Financial Executive*, *22*(1), 34–39.

Gibbs, S. (2017). Uber plans to buy 24,000 autonomous Volvo SUVs in race for driverless future. *The Guardian*, November 20, 2017. Retrieved from https://www.theguardian.com/technology/2017/nov/20/uber-volvo-suv-self-driving-future-business-ride-hailing-lyft-waymo

Gies, E. (2017). Businesses lead where US falters. *Nature Climate Change*, *7*(8), 543–546. doi:10.1038/nclimate3360

Gilley, A., McMillan, H., & Gilley, J. (2009). Organizational change and characteristics of leadership effectiveness. *Journal of Leadership and Organizational Studies*, *16*(1), 38–47.

Giurgiu, C., & Borza, A. (2015). Strategy from conceptualization to competitive advantage. *Annals of the University of Oradea: Economic Science*, *25*(1), 1109–1119.

Goeke, R. J., & Antonucci, Y. L. (2013). Differences in business process management leadership and deployment: Is there a connection to industry affiliation? *Information Resources Management Journal*, *26*(2), 43. doi:10.4018/irmj.2013040103

Gogolin, G., & Gogolin, E. (2017). The use of embedded mobile, RFID, location based services, and augmented reality in mobile applications. *International Journal of Handheld Computing Research*, *8*(1), 42–52. doi:10.4018/IJHCR.2017010104

Goh, E. (2016). *Rising China's influence in developing Asia*. Oxford: Oxford University Press.

Gold, D. (2012). *Stocks dive, tensions rise as EU's leaders hobnob* (p. B04). Los Angeles, CA: Investor's Business Daily, Inc.

Goldin, C., & Katz, L. F. (2018). The race between education and technology. Cambridge, Mass: Belknap Press of Harvard University Press.

Golightly, D., & Dadashi, N. (2017). The characteristics of railway service disruption: Implications for disruption management. *Ergonomics*, *60*(3), 307–320. doi:10.1080/00140139.2016.1173231

Gorenak, M., & Ferjan, M. (2015). The influence of organizational values on competencies of managers (business administration and management). *E+M Ekonomie a Management*, *18*(1), 67. doi:10.15240/tul/001/2015-1-006

Grawe, S. J., Chen, H., & Daugherty, P. J. (2009). The relationship between strategic orientation, service innovation, and performance. *International Journal of Physical Distribution & Logistics Management*, *39*(4), 282–300.

Griffin, R., & Van Fleet, D. (2013). *Management skills: Assessment and development.* Scarborough: Nelson Education.

Griffith, M. K., Steinberg, R. H., & Zysman, J. (2017). From great power politics to a strategic vacuum: Origins and consequences of the TPP and TTIP. *Business and Politics*, *19*(4), 573–592.

Gross, M. (2018). Watching two billion people. *Current Biology*, *28*(9), R527–R530. doi:10.1016/j.cub.2018.04.065

Grover, S. (2014). Unraveling respect in organization studies. *Human Relations*, *67*(1), 27. doi:10.1177/0018726713484944

Gurchiek, K. (2017). Artificial Intelligence Changes Skills Needs. HRNews, May 26, 2017. Retrieved from https://www.shrm.org/resourcesandtools/hr-topics/organizational-and-employee-development/pages/artificial-intelligence-changing-skills-needs.aspx.

Gustafsson, E., & Skohg, S. (2017). *Can attitudes towards globalization be explained by who perceive themselves to be losers from trade?* Lund, Sweden: Lund University School of Economics and Management. Retrieved from https://lup.lub.lu.se/student-papers/search/publication/8900654

Hacioglu, B., & Yarbay, P. (2014). A theoretical assessment on emotional intelligence as a competitive managerial skill. *International Journal of Research in Business and Social Science*, *3*(1), 170–187.

Hallemann, C. (2018). How a rumor about Prince Philip's death went viral. *Town and Country*, July.

Hambrick, D. C. (2004). The disintegration of strategic management: It's time to consolidate our gains. *Strategic Organization*, *2*(1), 91–98.

Handley, S. M. (2017). How governance misalignment and outsourcing capability impact performance. *Production and Operations Management*, *26*(1), 134–155. doi:10.1111/poms.12609

Hartnell, C. A., Kinicki, A. J., Lambert, L. S., Fugate, M., & Doyle Corner, P. (2016). Do similarities or differences between CEO leadership and organizational culture have a more positive effect on firm performance? A test of competing predictions. *Journal of Applied Psychology*, *101*(6), 846–861. doi:10.1037/apl0000083

Hauck, W. (2014). Fearless feedback boosts trust while replacing traditional performance appraisal at Independent Living, Inc. *Global Business and Organizational Excellence*, *33*(4), 50–62.

Hautz, J. (2017). Opening up the strategy process: A network perspective. *Management Decision*, *55*(9), 1956–1983. doi:10.1108/MD-07-2016-0510

Hearld, L. R., & Alexander, J. A. (2014). Governance processes and change within organizational participants of multi-sectoral community health care alliances: The mediating role of vision, mission, strategy agreement and perceived alliance value. *American Journal of Community Psychology*, *53*(1–2), 185–197. doi:10.1007/s10464-013-9618-y

Heisler, S. (2014). *The missing link: Teaching and learning critical success skills.* Lanham, MD: R&L Education.

Henderson, J., Appelbaum, R. P., Ho, S. Y., & Mohan, G. (2013). Beyond the enclave: Towards a critical political economy of China and Africa. (Report). *Development and Change, 44*(6), 1255. doi:10.1111/dech.12061

Henderson, N.-M., Pleitgen, F., & Demirjian, K. (2017, December 31). Watching for Human Rights Violations in Iran; At Least 2 Dead in Iran Anti-Government Protests; Trump Says "No Collusion"; DNC Struggling to Raise Money Ahead of 2018; Trump Eyes His Next Agenda Item: Infrastructure; Alabama Certifies Jones' Win Over Moore. Aired 8-9a ET/Interviewer: N. Hendersen. Inside Politics (CNN), CQ Roll Call, Atlanta.

Henriksen, A. (2018). Trump's missile strike on Syria and the legality of using force to deter chemical warfare. *Journal of Conflict and Security Law, 23*(1), 33–48.

Henry, M. (2001). Managing exceptionally. *Organization Science, 12*(6), 759–771. doi:10.1287/orsc.12.6.759.10081

Herrera, D. (2015). The record company as a learning structure: Identifying performance and learning inhibitors. *MEIEA Journal, 15*(1), 121–146. doi:10.25101/15.6

Hildebrandt, M. (2018). Law as computation in the era of artificial legal intelligence: Speaking law to the power of statistics. *University of Toronto Law Journal, 68*(1), 12–35. doi:10.3138/utlj.2017-0044

Hoag, B., Ritschard, H., & Cooper, C. (2002). Obstacles to effective organizational change: The underlying reasons. *Leadership & Organization Development Journal, 23*(1), 6–15.

Hobolt, S. B. (2016). The Brexit vote: A divided nation, a divided continent. *Journal of European Public Policy, 23*(9), 1259–1277. doi:10.1080/13501763.2016.1225785

Hoi, C., Wu, Q., & Zhang, H. (2018). Community social capital and corporate social responsibility. *Journal of Business Ethics, 152*(3), 647–665. doi:10.1007/s10551-016-3335-z

Hooi, J. (2014). Virtual currency not free from taxman. *The Business Times*. Retrieved from https://www.businesstimes.com.sg/top-stories/virtual-currency-not-free-from-taxman

Hosmer, D., Hosmer, T., LeCessie, S., & Lemeshow, S. (1997). A comparison of goodness-of-fit tests for the logistic regression model. *Statistics in Medicine, 16*(9), 965–980.

Hsieh, C.-C., & Wang, D.-S. (2015). Does supervisor-perceived authentic leadership influence employee work engagement through employee-perceived authentic leadership and employee trust? *The International Journal of Human Resource Management, 26*(18), 1–20. doi:10.1080/09585192.2015.1025234

Huarng, K.-H., Mas-Tur, A., & Calabuig Moreno, F. (2018). Innovation, knowledge, judgment, and decision-making as virtuous cycles. *Journal of Business Research, 88*, 278–281. doi:10.1016/j.jbusres.2018.02.031

Hughes, D. (2018a). Properties for sale: – Bitcoin accepted. *The Australian Financial Review, 24*.

Hughes, D. (2018b). Tax office team to tackle crypto cheats. *The Australian Financial Review, 6*.

Humphries, J. (2010). *Childhood and child labour in the British industrial revolution*. Cambridge: Cambridge University Press.

Iankova, S., Davies, I., Archer-Brown, C., Marder, B., & Yau, A. (2018). A comparison of social media marketing between B2B, B2C and mixed business models. *Industrial Marketing Management*. in press [in press], January. Retrieved from https://www.sciencedirect.com/science/article/abs/pii/S0019850117301116 doi:10.1016/j.indmarman.2018.01.001

Inglehart, R., & Norris, P. (2016). *Trump, Brexit, and the rise of populism: Economic have-nots and cultural backlash*. HKS Working Paper No. RWP16–026. Retrieved from https://www.hks.harvard.edu/publications/trump-brexit-and-rise-populism-economic-have-nots-and-cultural-backlash

Iqbal, M. (2017). Market testing procedures for B2C and B2B in perspective of radical innovation. *International Journal of Customer Relationship Marketing and Management,* *8*(1), 15–29. doi:10.4018/IJCRMM.2017010102

Jacobson, D. S. (1977). The political economy of industrial location: The Ford motor company at Cork 1912–26. *Irish Economic and Social History, 4*(1), 36–55. doi:10.1177/033248937700400103

Joo, S.-H., & Lee, Y. (2018). Putin and trilateral economic cooperation between Moscow, Seoul, and Pyongyang: Motivation, feasibility, and Korean peace process. *Asia Europe Journal, 16*(1), 81–99. doi:10.1007/s10308-017-0494-1

Joseph, R. A., & Degabriele, M. (2001). Electronic commerce in Australia: Changing reality or changing the way we think about reality? *Australian Journal of Communication, 28*(2), 77–90.

Kably, L. (2017). Bitcoin sale profit is taxable capital gains for investor [Tax]. *The Economic Times.* May 16, 2017. Retrieved from https://timesofindia.indiatimes.com/business/india-business/bitcoin-sale-profit-is-taxable-capital-gains-for-investor/articleshow/58691027.cms

Kaler, J. (2006). Evaluating stakeholder theory. *Journal of Business Ethics, 69*(3), 249–268.

Kallianos, Y. (2018). Infrastructural disorder: The politics of disruption, contingency, and normalcy in waste infrastructures in Athens. *Environment and Planning D: Society and Space, 36*(4), 758–775. doi:10.1177/0263775817740587

Kanter, R. (1977). *Men and women of the corporation.* New York, NY: Basic Books.

Kanter, R. (1995). Managing the human side of change. In D. A. Kolb, I. M. Rubin, & J. S. Osland (Eds.), *The organizational behavior reader* (5th ed.). Englewood Cliffs, NJ: Prentice-Hall.

Kanter, R. (2008). Transforming giants. *Harvard Business Review, 86*(1), 43–52.

Kanungo, R., & Misra, S. (1992). Managerial resourcefulness: A reconceptualization of management skills. *Human Relations, 45*(12), 1311–1332. doi:10.1177/001872679204501204

Kaplan, R. D. (2010). The geography of Chinese power: How far can Beijing reach on land and at sea? *Foreign Affairs, 89*(3), 22–41.

Kass, M. J. (2018). The end of the road for gas-powered automobiles? *Natural Resources & Environment, 32*(4), 53–54.

Katz, D., & Kahn, R. L. (1978). *The psychology of organizations* (2nd ed.). New York, NY: John Wiley & Sons.

Kazuaki, N. (2015). *Laundry-folding robot unveiled at Tokyo trade fair.* The Japan Times. Retrieved from https://www.japantimes.co.jp/news/2015/10/09/business/tech/laundry-folding-robot-unveiled-tokyo-trade-fair/#.XIspHygzbIU.

Kelleher, B. (2009). Employee engagement carries ENSR through organizational challenges and economic turmoil. *Global Business and Organizational Excellence, 28*(3), 6–19.

Kelley, C. (2018). Debating the US decision to pull out of the Iran deal. *The Washington Report on Middle East Affairs June-July,* 53–54.

Ketter, P. (2014). Critical competencies. *The Public Manager, 43*(3), 5.

Khandelwal, P., & Taneja, A. (2010). Intuitive decision making in management. *Indian Journal of Industrial Relations, 46*(1), 150–156.

Kim, J. S., & Chung, G. H. (2017). Implementing innovations within organizations: A systematic review and research agenda. *Innovation, 19*(3), 372–399. doi:10.1080/14479338.2017.1335943

Klein, D. (1970). *Some notes on the dynamics of resistance to change: The defender role* (2nd ed.). Boston, MA: Boston University, Human Relations Center.

Koberg, C., & Hood, J. (1991). Cultures and creativity within hierarchical organizations. *Journal of Business and Psychology, 6*(2), 265–271.

Kobie, N. (2017). Cash is king. Long live the king? *PC Pro*(269), 124–125.

Kocher, M., Pogrebna, G., & Sutter, M. (2013). Other-regarding preferences and management styles. *Journal of Economic Behavior & Organization, 88*(C), 109. doi:10.1016/j.jebo.2013.01.004

Kofman, M., & Rojansky, M. (2018). What kind of victory for Russia in Syria? *Military Review, 24*, 384.

Kostas, M., Kostas, E., Emannuel, S., & John, P. (2003). Decision support through knowledge management: The role of the artificial intelligence. *Information Management & Computer Security, 11*(5), 216–221. doi:doi:10.1108/09685220310500126

Kotschwar, B. (2014). China's economic influence in Latin America. (Report). *9*(2), 202. doi:10.1111/aepr.12062

Kotter, J. P. (1995). Leading change: Why transformational efforts fail. *Harvard Business Review, 73*(2), 59–67.

Kotter, J. P. (1996). *Leading change*. Boston, MA: Harvard Business School Press.

Krafcik, J. F. (1988). Triumph of the lean production system. *MIT Sloan Management Review, 30*(1), 41.

Kral, P., Tripes, S., Pirozek, P., & Pudil, P. (2012). *Two-dimensional governance matrix: A framework to evaluate organizational governance* (pp. 272–XIV). Kidmore End: Academic Conferences International Limited.

Kraus, J.-L. (2018). Is artificial intelligence associated with chemist's creativity represents a threat to humanity? *AI & SOCIETY*, 1–3. doi:10.1007/s00146-018-0832-x

Krug, B., & Reinmoeller, P. (2003). The hidden cost of ubiquity: Globalisation and terrorism. (No. ERS-2003-062-ORG). Retrieved from http://hdl.handle.net/1765/993

Krush, M. T., Agnihotri, R., & Trainor, K. J. (2016). A contingency model of marketing dashboards and their influence on marketing strategy implementation speed and market information management capability. *European Journal of Marketing, 50*(12), 2077–2102. doi:10.1108/EJM-06-2015-0317

Kuchler, H. (2017). Start-ups see opportunity in tackling fake news; technology. Brand reputation fighting misinformation on social media has proved lucrative for tech groups. (Business.) *The Financial Times*, p. 16.

Kumle, J., & Kelly, N. (2006). leadership vs. management. *Supervision, 67*(8), 11–13.

Kuzmina, D. (2016). Efficienct assessment of outsourcing transactions. *Journal of Economics and Economic Education Research, 17*, 54–62.

Kwak, K.-C. (2009). Face recognition with the use of tensor representation in home robot environments. *IEICE Electronics Express, 6*(4), 187. doi:10.1587/elex.6.187

Lane, P. R. (2012). The European sovereign debt crisis. *Journal of Economic Perspectives, 26*(3), 49–68.

Larkin, J. (2017). HR digital disruption: The biggest wave of transformation in decades. *Strategic HR Review, 16*(2), 55–59. doi:10.1108/SHR-01-2017-0006

Laursen, F., & Roederer-Rynning, C. (2017). Introduction: The new EU FTAs as contentious market regulation. *Journal of European Integration, 39*(7), 763–779.

Law, J. (2016). *Management development*. Oxford: Oxford University Press.

Lawrence, P. R. (1954, Reprint 1969). How to overcome resistance to change. *Harvard Business Review, 32*(3), 49–57.

Lazcano, A., Avedillo, A., & Del Real, F. (2018). Artificial intelligence, privacy, and gaming: An equation with almost no regulation. *Gaming Law Review, 22*(6), 295–301.

Leake, J. (2015). The great diesel car deception speeding us to a toxic death: Drivers and pedestrians have been misled by EU tests aimed at cutting lethal air pollution, writes Jonathan Leake. (Features). *Sunday Times*, p. 4. Retrieved from https://primo.csu.edu.au/discovery/fulldisplay?docid=gale_ofa414757411&context=PC&vid=61CSU_INST:61CSU&lang=en&search_scope=MyInst_and_CI&adaptor=Primo%20Central&tab=Everything&query=any,contains,diesel%20car%20scandal%20deception&sortby=rank&offset=0

Leavy, B. (2017). Two strategies for innovating in the face of market disruption. *Strategy & Leadership, 45*(4), 9–18. doi:10.1108/SL-05-2017-0051

Lee, D. (2017). Corporate social responsibility and management forecast accuracy. *Journal of Business Ethics, 140*(2), 353–367. doi:10.1007/s10551-015-2713-2

Lee, J.-Y., Kozlenkova, I., & Palmatier, R. (2015). Structural marketing: Using organizational structure to achieve marketing objectives. *Journal of the Academy of Marketing Science, 43*(1), 73–99. doi:10.1007/s11747-014-0402-9

Lees, C. (2018). Fake news: The global silencer: The term has become a useful weapon in the dictator's toolkit against the media. Just look at the Philippines. *Index on Censorship, 47*(1), 88–91.

Lehman-Wilzig, S. (1981). Frankenstein unbound: Towards a legal definition of artificial intelligence. *Futures, 13*(6), 442.

Lemaignan, S., Warnier, M., Sisbot, E., Clodic, A., & Alami, R. (2017). Artificial cognition for social human-robot interaction: An implementation. *Artificial Intelligence, 247*, 45.

Levy, S. R., & Macdonald, J. L. (2016). Progress on understanding ageism. *The Journal of Social Issues, 72*(1), 5–25. doi:10.1111/josi.12153

Lewin, K. (1945). The research center for group dynamics at Massachusetts Institute of Technology. *Sociometry, 8*(2), 126–136.

Li, M., Zhang, W., & Hart, C. (2018). What have we learned from China's past trade retaliation strategies? *Choices, 33*(2), 1–8.

Likert, R. (1967). *The human organization: Its management and value.* New York, NY: McGraw-Hill.

Lourdes, P., Victor, D. S. P., & Jesus, C.-F. (2017). Taking advantage of disruptive innovation through changes in value networks: Insights from the space industry. *Supply Chain Management: An International Journal, 22*(2), 97–106. doi:doi:10.1108/SCM-01-2017-0017

Lu, W., & Wang, J. (2017). The influence of conflict management styles on relationship quality: The moderating effect of the level of task conflict. *International Journal of Project Management, 35*(8), 1483–1494. doi:10.1016/j.ijproman.2017.08.012

Lucas, H. C., Jr., & Goh, J. M. (2009). Disruptive technology: How Kodak missed the digital photography revolution. *The Journal of Strategic Information Systems, 18*(1), 46–55.

Luna, A. J. d. O., Kruchten, P., Pedrosa, M. L. d. E., Neto, H. R., & de Moura, H. P. (2014). State of the art of agile governance: A systematic review. *International Journal of Computer Science & Informaiton, 6*(5), 121–141.

Lusby, R. M., Larsen, J., & Bull, S. (2018). A survey on robustness in railway planning. *European Journal of Operational Research, 266*(1), 1–15. doi:https://doi.org/10.1016/j.ejor.2017.07.044

Lyrintzis, C. (2011). Greek politics in the era of economic crisis: Reassessing causes and effects. Hellenic Observatory papers on Greece and Southeast Europe (GreeSE paper no. 45). Retrieved from http://eprints.lse.ac.uk/33826/

Notarantonio, E. M., & Quigley., C. J., Jr (2013). Extending technology for market disruption: A case study. *Journal of Product & Brand Management, 22*(4), 309–313. doi:10.1108/JPBM-10-2012-0200

Macdonald-Smith, A. (2018). Caltex CEO backs fuel security via strong supply chains. *The Australian Financial Review*, p. 11.

Macho, A. (2018). Eastern Europe's appetite for dirty old diesels. *WirtschaftsWoche*. Retrieved from https://global.handelsblatt.com/companies/eastern-europe-romania-germany-diesel-vehicles-904576

Madhani, A. (2018). U.S. steel: Trump tariff means we'll reopen plant. (MONEY). *USA Today*, March 7, 2018. Retrieved from https://www.usatoday.com/story/money/2018/03/07/u-s-steel-says-reopen-illinois-steel-plant-trump-tariffs/403064002/

Maillet, J. (2018). *The evolution of malware in America's adversaries: A study of evolving cyber threats*. (Degree of Master of Science in Cybersecurity), Utica College, New York, USA. Retrieved from https://search.proquest.com/openview/14dc1bbc46e1c5 167daeb8ea72a4562d/1?pq-origsite=gscholar&cbl=18750&diss=y

Mainardes, E. W., Ferreira, J., & Raposo, M. (2014). Strategy and strategic management concepts: Are they recognised by management students? *Ekonomie a management, 17*(1), 43–61. doi:10.15240/tul/001/2014-1-004

Makridakis, S. (2017). The forthcoming artificial intelligence (AI) revolution: Its impact on society and firms. *Futures, 90*, 46–60.

Mallette, C., & Rykert, L. (2018). Promoting positive culture change in nursing faculties: Getting to maybe through liberating structures. *Journal of Professional Nursing, 34*(3), 161–166. doi:10.1016/j.profnurs.2017.08.001

Man-Fong Ho, C. (2011). Ethics management for the construction industry. *Engineering, Construction and Architectural Management, 18*(5), 516–537. doi:10.1108/ 09699981111165194

Marchiondo, L., Gonzales, E., & Ran, S. (2016). Development and validation of the workplace age discrimination scale. *Journal of Business and Psychology, 31*(4), 493–513. doi:10.1007/s10869-015-9425-6

Mark, K. C. (2018). Russia-United Kingdom diplomatic crisis over salisbury nerve agent attack: An analysis. *International Journal of Law and Public Administration, 1*(1), 58–67.

Marshall, D. (1998). Understanding the Asian crisis: Systemic risk as coordination failure. *Economic Perspectives-Federal Reserve Bank of Chicago, 22*, 13–28.

Martin, T., Eun-Young, J., & Russolillo, S. (2017). *World News: North Korea suspected in bitcoin theft — Pyongyang's hackers accused of turning to cryptocurrency, banks as regime seeks funds* (p. A.18). New York, NY: Dow Jones & Company Inc.

Maslach, C., Jackson, S. E., & Leiter, M. P. (1996). *Maslach burnout inventory manual*. Mountain View, CA: Consulting Psychologists Press.

Maslow, A. H. (1970). *Motivation and personality*. New York, USA: Harper & Row.

Mason, C., Griffin, M., & Parker, S. (2014). Transformational leadership development. *Leadership & Organization Development Journal, 35*(3), 174–194. doi:10.1108/ LODJ-05-2012-0063

Mason, D. L. (2012). The rise and fall of the cooperative spirit: The evolution of organisational structures in American thrifts, 1831–1939. *Business History, 54*(3), 381–398. doi:10.1080/00076791.2011.638488

Maurer, T. J., Lippstreu, M., & Judge, T. A. (2008). Structural model of employee involvement in skill development activity: The role of individual differences. *Journal of Vocational Behavior, 72*(3), 336–350. doi:10.1016/j.jvb.2007.10.010

Mayfield, J., & Mayfield, M. (2017). Leadership communication: Reflecting, engaging, and innovating. *International Journal of Business Communication, 54*(1), 3–11. doi:10.1177/2329488416675446

Mazzetti, M., & Schmidt, M. S. (2013). Officials say U.S. may never know extent of Snowden's Leaks. (National Desk) (Edward J. Snowden). *The New York Times*, p. A1.

McCarthy, A. M., & Garavan, T. N. (2001). 360° feedback process: Performance, improvement and employee career development. *Journal of European Industrial Training, 25*(1), 5–32. doi:10.1108/03090590110380614

McGrath, S. K., & Whitty, S. J. (2015). Redefining governance: From confusion to certainty and clarity. *International Journal of Managing Projects in Business, 8*(4), 755–787. doi:10.1108/IJMPB-10-2014-0071

McKendall, M. (1993). The tyranny of change: Organizational development revisited. *Journal of Business Ethics, 12*(2), 93–104.

McNair, B., Bruns, A., & Schapals, A. K. (2018). Fake news and democratic culture. In *Digitizing Democracy* (pp. 19–29).

Mcphee, J. E. (2014). *Mastering strategic risk: A framework for leading and transforming organizations*. NJ, USA: John Wiley & Sons Inc.

Mearsheimer, J. (2014). Why the Ukraine crisis is the West's fault: The liberal delusions that provoked Putin. *Foreign Affairs.*, *93*, 77.

Measuring innovation: A new perspective. (2010). Paris: OECD.

Mei, X., Iannacchione, B., Stohr, M. K., Hemmens, C., Hudson, M., & Collins, P. A. (2017). Confirmatory analysis of an organizational culture instrument for corrections. *The Prison Journal*, *97*(2), 247–269. doi:10.1177/0032885517692831

Melander, A., Löfving, M., Andersson, D., Elgh, F., & Thulin, M. (2016). Introducing the Hoshin Kanri strategic management system in manufacturing SMEs. *Management Decision*, *54*(10), 2507–2523. doi:10.1108/MD-03-2016-0148

Meltzer, A. (2011). *Leave the Euro to the PIGS* (p. A.17). New York, NY: Dow Jones & Company Inc.

Meng, J., & Berger, B. K. (2018). The impact of organizational culture and leadership performance on PR professionals' job satisfaction: Testing the joint mediating effects of engagement and trust. *Public Relations Review.* *45*(1), 64–75. doi:https://doi.org/10.1016/j.pubrev.2018.11.002

Menon, B. (2011). Duality strategy of customer centricity and employee focus in software services management. *Drishtikon: A Management Journal*, *2*(2), 124–167.

Minkes, A. L., Small, M. W., & Chatterjee, S. (1999). Leadership and business ethics: Does it matter? Implications for management. *Journal of Business Ethics*, *20*(4), 327–335.

Mintzberg, H. (1971). Managerial work: Analysis from observation. *Management Science*, *18*(2), B97–B110. doi:10.1287/mnsc.18.2.B97

Mintzberg, H. (1980). Structure in 5's: A synthesis of the research on organization design. *Management Science*, *26*(3), 322–341. doi:10.1287/mnsc.26.3.322

Mintzberg, H. (1984). Power and organization life cycles. *The Academy of Management Review*, *9*(2), 207–224.

Mintzberg, H. (1987). The Strategy Concept I: Five Ps for Strategy. *California Management Review*, *30*(1), 11. doi:10.2307/41165263

Miro Xavier, A., Kuhn, R., & Brayda, L. (2008). Interactive personalized robot for home use. Retrieved from https://patents.google.com/patent/US20050137747

Montano, D., Reeske, A., Franke, F., & Hüffmeier, J. (2017). Leadership, followers' mental health and job performance in organizations: A comprehensive meta-analysis from an occupational health perspective. *Journal of Organizational Behavior*, *38*(3), 327–350. doi:10.1002/job.2124

Moore, C., Mayer, D. M., Chiang, F. F. T., Crossley, C., Karlesky, M. J., & Birtch, T. A. (2018). Leaders matter morally: The role of ethical leadership in shaping employee moral cognition and misconduct. *Journal of Applied Psychology.* *104*(1), 123–145. doi:10.1037/apl0000341

Morris, D. (2004). Defining a moral problem in business ethics. *Journal of Business Ethics*, *49*(4), 347–357.

Morris, M. (2018). Crypto critics: Fact or fiction? *Investment Week*, p. 16.

Moss, T. (2017). China now has a rail link into the heart of Europe. (One Belt, One Road initiative) (World/Asia/China News.) *The Wall Steet Journal Eastern Edition,* May 11, 2017. Retrieved from https://www.wsj.com/articles/china-now-has-a-rail-link-into-the-heart-of-europe-1494519829.

Motevalli, G., & Talev, M. (2018). Iran protests accelerate Trump's weighing of new sanctions. *Bloomberg Wire Service*. Retrieved from https://www.bloomberg.com/news/articles/2018-01-02/white-house-threatens-new-sanctions-on-iran-over-protest-rights

Mousavi, S., & Gigerenzer, G. (2014). Risk, uncertainty, and heuristics. *Journal of Business Research*, *67*(8), 1671. doi:10.1016/j.jbusres.2014.02.013

Muincu, C., & Comanescu, R. (2015). Lean and JIT operations for effective flexible packaging industry. *Calitatea, 16*, 49–61.

Mullen, T. (2014). The Scottish independence referendum 2014. *Journal of Law and Society, 41*(4), 627–640.

Nag, R., Hambrick, D. C., & Chen, M. J. (2007). What is strategic management, really? Inductive derivation of a consensus definition of the field. *Strategic Management Journal, 28*(9), 935–955. doi:10.1002/smj.615

Nagy, D., Schuessler, J., & Dubinsky, A. (2016). Defining and identifying disruptive innovations. *Industrial Marketing Management, 57*(C), 119–126. doi:10.1016/j.indmarman.2015.11.017

Nascimento, A. M., & Silveira, D. S. D. (2017). A systematic mapping study on using social media for business process improvement. *Computers in Human Behavior, 73*, 670–675. doi:10.1016/j.chb.2016.10.016

Năstase, A. (2014). Catering to organizational needs in ethics management: The case of the European commission. *International Journal of Public Administration, 37*(2), 93–105.

Nathan, B., & Smith, P. (2016). Cybersecurity: Watch out for data leaks! (TECH PRACTICES). *Strategic Finance, 97*(7), 62.

Needleman, S. (2017). IBM chief says AI won't be job killer. *Wall Street Journal, January, 2017*, B.4.

Nelson, A., Earle, A., Howard-Grenville, J., Haack, J., & Young, D. (2014). Do innovation measures actually measure innovation? Obliteration, symbolic adoption, and other finicky challenges in tracking innovation diffusion. *Research Policy, 43*(6), 927–940. doi:10.1016/j.respol.2014.01.010

Nelson, T. D. (2016). The age of ageism. *Journal of Social Issues, 72*(1), 191–198. doi:10.1111/josi.12162

Nesheim, T., & Smith, J. (2015). Knowledge sharing in projects: Does employment arrangement matter? *Personnel Review, 44*(2), 255–269. doi:10.1108/PR-11-2013-0203

Nguyen, T., Nguyen, H. G. L., & Yin, X. (2015). Corporate governance and corporate financing and investment during the 2007–2008 financial crisis. *Financial Management, 44*(1), 115. doi:10.1111/fima.12071

Niessen, C., Mäder, I., Stride, C., & Jimmieson, N. L. (2017). Thriving when exhausted: The role of perceived transformational leadership. *Journal of Vocational Behavior, 103*, 41–51. doi:10.1016/j.jvb.2017.07.012

Nizzero, A., Cote, P., & Cramm, H. (2017). Occupational disruption: A scoping review. *Journal of Occupational Science, 24*(2), 114–127. doi:10.1080/14427591.2017.1306791

Noack, R. (2018). Cryptocurrency mining in Iceland is using so much energy, the electricity may run out. The Washington Post, February 14, 2018. Retrieved from https://nationalpost.com/news/world/cryptocurrency-mining-in-iceland-is-using-so-much-energy-the-electricity-may-run-out

Nonet, G., Kassel, K., & Meijs, L. (2016). Understanding responsible management: Emerging themes and variations from European business school programs. *Journal of Business Ethics, 139*(4), 717–736. doi:10.1007/s10551-016-3149-z

Oldenkamp, R., van Zelm, R., & Huijbregts, M. A. (2016). Valuing the human health damage caused by the fraud of Volkswagen. *Environmental pollution, 212*, 121–127.

Olson, E. L. (2017). Will songs be written about autonomous cars? The implications of self-driving vehicle technology on consumer brand equity and relationships. *International Journal of Technology Marketing, 12*(1), 23–41.

Oreg, S. (2003). Resistance to change: Developing and individual differences measure. *Journal of Applied Psychology, 88*(4), 680–693.

Oreg, S. (2006). Personality, context, and resistance to organizational change. *European Journal of Work and Organizational Psychology, 15*(1), 73–101. doi:10.1080/13594320500451247

Ozturk, S., & Sozdemir, A. (2015). Effects of global financial crisis on greece economy. *Procedia Economics and Finance, 23*, 568–575.

Pace, M., & Cavatorta, F. (2012). The Arab uprisings in theoretical perspective: An introduction. *Mediterranean Politics, 17*(2), 125–138.

Paetz, P. (2014). *Disruption by design: How to create products that disrupt and then dominate markets.* New York, NY: Apress.

Page, D., & Mukherjee, A. (2007). Promoting critical-thinking skills by using negotiation exercises. *Journal of Education for Business, 82*(5), 251–257. doi:10.3200/JOEB.82.5.251-257

Paluch, S., & Wünderlich, N. V. (2016). Contrasting risk perceptions of technology-based service innovations in inter-organizational settings. *Journal of Business Research, 69*(7), 2424–2431. doi:10.1016/j.jbusres.2016.01.012

Park, B. (2018). The EU and Turkey: Bridge or barrier? In D. Brown & A. Shepherd (Eds.), *The security dimensions of EU enlargement: Wider Europe, Weaker Europe?* (pp. 157–173). Manchester, UK: Manchester University Press.

Park, H. (2018). Trust but verify: Donald Trump, Kim Jong Un and a denuclearising North Korea after the Singapore Summit. *East Asian Policy, 10*(03), 5–18.

Parnas, D. (2017). The real risks of artificial intelligence. *Communications of the ACM, 60*(10), 27–31. doi:10.1145/3132724

Passariello, C. (2017). *WSJ D.Live (A Special Report) – In defense of an Ad Model: Jonah Peretti of BuzzFeed talks about social media, algorithms and fake news.* (pp. R.9). New York, NY: Dow Jones & Company Inc.

Patel, K. (2018). Australia's petroleum supply and its implications for the ADF. *Australian Defence Force Journal, 204*, 71.

Patrício, D. I., & Rieder, R. (2018). Computer vision and artificial intelligence in precision agriculture for grain crops: A systematic review. *Computers and Electronics in Agriculture, 153*, 69–81.

Peters, B. (2018). Cryptocurrency theft feared after Japan exchange halts altcoin trades. *Investor's Business Daily*, January 26, 2018. Retrieved from https://www.investors.com/news/cryptocurrency-theft-feared-after-japan-exchange-halts-altcoin-trades/

Phillips, R. (2018). Crash to paywall: Canadian newspapers and the great disruption. *Canadian Journal of Communication, 43*(1). Retrieved from https://cjc-online.ca/index.php/journal/article/view/3239/3488

Piazza, A., & Castellucco, F. (2014). Status in organization and management theory. *Journal of Management, 40*(1), 287–315. doi:10.1177/0149206313498904

Pickett, L. (2013). Evolving talent strategy to match the millennial workforce reality. *Training & Development, 40*(4), 14–15.

Pipper, J., Inoue, M., Ng, L. F., Neuzil, P., Zhang, Y., & Novak, L. (2007). Catching bird flu in a droplet. *Nature Medicine, 13*(10), 1259.

Porter, M. E. (1980). *Compeitive strategy.* New York, NY: The Free Press.

Porter, M. E. (1985). *Competitive advantage: Creating and sustaining superior performance.* New Yor, NY: The Free Press.

Power, M. (2004). *The risk management of everything: Rethinking the politics of uncertainty.* London: Demos.

Proff, H., & Fojcik, T. M. (2015). Information acceleration to improve strategic management decisions. *Management Decision, 53*(7), 1560–1580. doi:10.1108/MD-01-2015-0005

Project Management Institute, P. (2004). *A guide to the project management body of knowledge (PMBOK® Guide)* (Vol. 3, 3rd ed.). Boulevard, PA: Project Management Institute.

Pugh, D. (1993). Understanding and managing organizational change. In C. Mabey, B. Mayon-White, & W. M. Mayon-White (Eds.), *Managing change* (pp. 108–112). London: Paul Chapman Publishing Ltd in association with The Open University.

Quinn, J. B., Mintzberg, H., & James, R. M. (1988). *The strategy process: Concepts, contexts, and cases.* New Jersey, USA: Prentice-Hall.

Rahman, W., & Nas, Z. (2013). Employee development and turnover intention: Theory validation. *European Journal of Training and Development, 37*(6), 564–579. doi:10.1108/EJTD-May-2012-0015

Ramana, A. (2013). Applying Moore's law to business processes. *Industrial Engineer, 45*(11), 33.

Ramos, P., Mota, C., & Corrêa, L. (2016). Exploring the management style of Brazilian project managers. *International Journal of Project Management, 34*(6), 902–913. doi:10.1016/j.ijproman.2016.03.002

Rank, J., Unger, B. N., & Gemünden, H. G. (2015). Preparedness for the future in project portfolio management: The roles of proactiveness, riskiness and willingness to cannibalize. *International Journal of Project Management, 33*(8), 1730–1743. doi:10.1016/j.ijproman.2015.08.002

Rasche, A., Bakker, F., & Moon, J. (2013). Complete and partial organizing for corporate social responsibility. *Journal of Business Ethics, 115*(4), 651–663. doi:10.1007/s10551-013-1824-x

Rice, C. (2012). *The engagement equation leadership strategies for an inspired workforce.* Hoboken, NJ: Wiley.

Ris, C., Trannoy, A., & Wasmer, É. (2017). The new caledonian economy beyond nickel. *Notes du Conseil D'analyse Économique, 3*, 1–12.

Risse, T., Engelmann-Martin, D., Knope, H., & Roscher, K. (1999). To Euro or not to Euro?: The EMU and identity politics in the European Union. *European Journal of International Relations, 5*(2), 147–187. doi:10.1177/1354066199005002001

Robin, D. (2009). Toward an applied meaning for ethics in business. *Journal of Business Ethics, 89*(1), 139–150.

Robinson, C. (2015). *An exploration of external environmental scanning and the strategy process.* Ph.D. thesis, Heriot-Watt University, Edinburgh.

Rosenberg, S., & Mosca, J. (2011). Breaking down the barriers to organizational change. *International Journal of Management and Information Systems, 15*(3), 139–146.

Rosenstand, C., Gertsen, F., & Vesti, H. (2018). A definition and a conceptual framework of digital disruption. Paper presented at the ISPIM Innovation Symposium, Manchester, UK..

Roundy, P. T., Harrison, D. A., Khavul, S., Pérez-Nordtvedt, L., & McGee, J. E. (2018). Entrepreneurial alertness as a pathway to strategic decisions and organizational performance. *Strategic Organization, 16*(2), 192–226. doi:10.1177/1476127017693970

Rowell, J. (2018). Do organisations have a mission for mapping processes? *Business Process Management Journal, 24*(1), 2–22. doi:10.1108/BPMJ-10-2016-0196

Russell, B. (1938). *Power: A new social analysis.* London: George Allen and Unwin.

Rutland, P. (2017). Trump, Putin, and the future of US-Russian relations. *Slavic Review, 76*(S1), S41–S56. doi:10.1017/slr.2017.157

Ryan, C. (2012). The new Arab cold war and the struggle for Syria. *Middle East Report, 262*, 28–31.

Sackmann, S., Eggenhofer-Rehart, P., & Friesl, M. (2009). Sustainable change: Long-term efforts toward developing a learning organization. *The Journal of Applied Behavioral Science, 45*(4), 521–549.

Sadler-Smith, E. (2008). The role of intuition in collective learning and the development of shared meaning. *Advances in Developing Human Resources, 10*(4), 494–508.

Marí Saéz, A., Weiss, S., Nowak, K., Lapeyre, V., Zimmermann, F., Düx, A., …, Leendertz, F. H. (2015). Investigating the zoonotic origin of the West African Ebola epidemic. *EMBO molecular medicine, 7*(1), 17–23.

Salisbury, P. (2015). Yemen and the Saudi–Iranian 'Cold War'. *Research Paper, Middle East and North Africa Programme, Chatham House, the Royal Institute of International Affairs*, p. 11.

Schapals, A. K., Bruns, A., & McNair, B. (2018). *Digitizing democracy*. New York, NY: Routledge.

Schein, E. (1985). *Organisational culture and leadership: A dynamic view*. San Francisco, CA: Jossey-Bass.

Schemeil, Y. (2013). Bringing international organization: Global institutions as adaptive hybrids. *Organization Studies, 34*(2), 219. doi:10.1177/0170840612473551

Schendel, D., & Hofer, C. W. (1979). *Strategic management: A new view of business policy and planning*. Boston, MA: Little, Brown.

Schneider, G., & Weber, P. M. (2018). *Punishing Putin: EU sanctions are more than paper tigers*. Stars: for the leaders of the next generation. Retrieved from http://www.the-stars.ch/media/399276/gerald-schneider_punishing-putin-eu-sanctions-are-more-than-paper-tigers.pdf

Schuelke-Leech, B. (2017). A model for understanding the orders of magnitude of disruptive technologies. *Technological Forecasting and Social Change. 129*, 261–274. doi:10.1016/j.techfore.2017.09.033

Schultz, J. (2013). The elements of leadership. *Global Business & Organizational Excellence, 32*(6), 47–54.

Schwartz, F. (2018). North Korea has not yet confirmed a Kim-Trump meeting, Tillerson says. *Wall Street Journal*, March 2018. Retrieved from https://www.wsj.com/articles/tillerson-cuts-short-africa-trip-amid-pressing-demands-in-the-u-s-1520858216.

Scott, P. (2000). Globalisation and higher education: Challenges for the 21st century. *Journal of Studies in International Education, 4*(1), 3–10. doi:10.1177/102831530000400102

Seele, P. (2018). What makes a business ethicist? A reflection on the transition from applied philosophy to critical thinking. *Journal of Business Ethics, 150*(3), 647–656. doi:10.1007/s10551-016-3177-8

Segal, S. (2011). A Heideggerian perspective on the relationship between Mintzberg's distinction between engaged and disconnected management: The role of uncertainty in management. *Journal of Business Ethics, 103*(3), 469–483. doi:10.1007/s10551-011-0874-1

Seilby, J. (2014). Be ready for the challenge. *Talent Development, 68*, 58.

Selznick, P. (1957). *Leadership in administration: A sociological interpretation*. New York, NY: Harper & Row.

Senturia, T., Flees, L., & Maceda, M. (2008). *Leading change management requires sticking to the PLOT*. London: Bain & Company.

Seo, Y., Kim, S., Kisi, O., & Singh, V. P. (2015). Daily water level forecasting using wavelet decomposition and artificial intelligence techniques. *Journal of Hydrology, 520*, 224–243.

Service, T. R. N. (2017). Russia: Exports of Russia's S-400 missile systems [Press release]. Retrieved from http://tass.com/defense/969682

Shah, N. (2010). A study of the relationship between organisational justice and employee readiness for change. *Journal of Enterprise Information Management, 24*(3), 224–236.

Sharif, M., & Scandura, T. (2014). Do perceptions of ethical conduct matter during organizational change? Ethical leadership and employee involvement. *Journal of Business Ethics, 124*(2), 185–196. doi:10.1007/s10551-013-1869-x

Sharma, A. (2007). The shift in sales organizations in business-to-business services markets. *Journal of Services Marketing, 21*(5), 326–333. doi:10.1108/08876040710773633

Shaughnessy, K. M., Quinn Griffin, T. M., Bhattacharya, J. A., & Fitzpatrick, J. J. (2018). Transformational leadership practices and work engagement among nurse leaders. JONA: *The Journal of Nursing Administration. 48*(11), 574–579. doi:10.1097/NNA.0000000000000682

Sheldon, N. (2018). Leadership expert puts emphasis on trust within organization. *Rochester Business Journal, 34*(3), 2–2.

Sheth, J., & Sinha, M. (2015). B2B branding in emerging markets: A sustainability perspective. *Industrial Marketing Management, 51*, 79–79.

Shrivastava, S. (2017). Digital disruption is redefining the customer experience: The digital transformation approach of the communications service providers. *Telecom Business Review, 10*(1), 41–52.

Sier, J. (2016). *Bitcoin surges 17pc in a week* (p. 3). Melbourne: Fairfax Media Publications Pty Limited.

Sierra, C. (2004). Agent-mediated electronic commerce. *Autonomous Agents and Multi-Agent Systems, 9*(3), 285–301. doi:10.1023/B:AGNT.0000038029.82331.c0

Singh, A., & Shoura, M. (2006). A life cycle evaluation of change in an engineering organization: A case study. *International Journal of Project Management, 24*(4), 337–349.

Singh, D., & Jain, A. (2018). A look into the artificial intelligence and its application in various fields of life. Paper presented at the International Conference on Advances in Computer Technology and Management (ICACTM), Pune, Maharashtra.

Skubinn, R., & Herzog, L. (2016). Internalized moral identity in ethical leadership. *Journal of Business Ethics, 133*(2), 249–260. doi:10.1007/s10551-014-2369-3

Skvoretz, J., & Fararo, T. (1996). Status and participation in task groups: A dynamic model network model. *American Journal of Sociology, 101*(5), 1366–1414.

Sloan, P., & Oliver, D. (2013). Building trust in multi-stakeholder partnerships: Critical emotional incidents and practices of engagement. *Organization Studies, 34*(12), 1835–1868.

Smith, G. J., Vijaykrishna, D., Bahl, J., Lycett, S. J., Worobey, M., Pybus, O. G., …, Rambaut, A. (2009). Origins and evolutionary genomics of the 2009 swine-origin H1N1 influenza A epidemic. *Nature, 459*(7250), 1122.

Smith, P., & Sharma, M. (2002). Developing personal responsibility and leadership traits in all your employees: Part 1 – Shaping and harmonizing the high-performance drivers. *Management Decision, 40*(7/8), 764–774.

Smith, P. G. (2008). Change: Embrace it, don't deny it: Tools and techniques inspired by software development can introduce the flexibility needed to make changes during product development with minimal disruption. *Research-Technology Management, 51*(4), 34. doi:10.1504/IJEH.2004.004659

Snellman, C. L. (2015). Ethics management: How to achieve ethical organizations and management? *Business, Management and Education, 13*(2), 336–357.

Sony, U. S. Univ. to develop home-use food preparation robot. (2018). Tokyo, Japan: JIJI Press America, Ltd.

Sousa, M. J., & Rocha, Á. (2019). Skills for disruptive digital business. *Journal of Business Research, 94*, 257–263. doi:10.1016/j.jbusres.2017.12.051

Sousa, R. (2003). Linking quality management to manufacturing strategy: An empirical investigation of customer focus practices. *Journal of Operations Management, 21*(1), 1–18. doi:10.1016/S0272-6963(02)00055-4

Spector, M. (2017). California steers agenda on cleaner cars: State has power to set its own mandate for zero-emission vehicles, separate from Washington's rules. *Wall Street Journal, February 2017*, B.1.

Spender, J. C., & Grinyer, P. H. (1995). Organizational renewal: Top management's role in a loosely coupled system. (Special Issue: Corporate Governance and Control). *Human Relations, 48*(8), 909. doi:10.1177/001872679504800805

Stanislavov, I., & Ivanov, S. (2014). The role of leadership for shaping organizational culture and building employee engagement in the Bulgarian gaming industry. *Turizam: Znanstveno-stručni Časopis, 62*(1), 19–40.

Steiger, J. (2013). *An examination of the influence of organizational structure types and management levels on knowledge management practices in organizations.* Ph.D. thesis, Alliant International University, San Diego, CA.

Stewart, R. (1991). Classifying different types of managerial jobs. *Personnel Review, 20*(3), 20–26. doi:10.1108/EUM0000000000790

Stohr, M. K., Hemmens, C., Collins, P. A., Iannacchione, B., Hudson, M., & Johnson, H. (2012). Assessing the organizational culture in a jail setting. *The Prison Journal, 92*(3), 358–387.

Stone, R. (2017). Cryptocurrency adoption growing, but not immediate threat to payment servicers. Retrieved from https://www.spglobal.com/marketintelligence/en/news-insights/trending/aag6spioimzavrhjf0-mcw2

Strandvik, T., Holmlund, M., & Lähteenmäki, I. (2018). "One of these days, things are going to change!" How do you make sense of market disruption? *Business Horizons, 61*(3), 477–486. doi:10.1016/j.bushor.2018.01.014

Strasser, M., Weiner, N., & Albayrak, S. (2015). The potential of interconnected service marketplaces for future mobility. *Computers and Electrical Engineering, 45*(C), 169–181. doi:10.1016/j.compeleceng.2015.06.008

Strickland, E. (2017). Special report : Can we copy the brain? – From animal intelligence to artificial intelligence. *Spectrum, IEEE, 54*(6), 40–45. doi:10.1109/MSPEC.2017.7934230

Subramanian, S. (2017). India warily eyes AI: Technology outsourcing has been India's only reliable job creator in the past 30 years. Now artificial intelligence threatens to wipe out those gains. *MIT Technology Review, 120*(6), 38.

Sutherland, N. (2018). Investigating leadership ethnographically: Opportunities and potentialities. *Leadership, 14*(3), 263–290. doi:10.1177/1742715016676446

Synnelius, S. (1974). Industrial robots in foundries. *Industrial Robot: An International Journal, 1*(5), 210–212. doi:10.1108/eb004727

Talley, K. (2018). Is artificial intelligence the great job eliminator or creator? *FierceCEO.* Retrieved from https://www.fierceceo.com/technology/still-too-soon-to-definitively-assess-ai-s-job-impact

Tay, A. (2001). Management's perception of MBA graduates in Malaysia. *Journal of Management Development, 20*(3), 258–274. doi:10.1108/02621710110386499

Taylor, H., & Cooper, C. (1988). Organisational change-threat of challenge? The role of individual differences in the management of stress. *Journal of Organizational Change Management, 1*(1), 68–80.

Teece, D. J. (2017). A capability theory of the firm: An economics and (strategic) management perspective. *New Zealand Economic Papers, 53*(1), 1–43. doi:10.1080/00779954.2017.1371208

Tether, B. S. (2002). Who co-operates for innovation, and why: An empirical analysis. *Research Policy, 31*(6), 947–967.

Thomas, K. (1992). Conflict and conflict management: Reflections and update. *Journal of Organizational Behavior, 13*(3), 265–274.

Thomas, M., & Rowland, C. (2014). Leadership, pragmatism and grace: A review. *Journal of Business Ethics, 123*(1), 99–111. doi:10.1007/s10551-013-1802-3

Todnem, R. (2005). Organisational change management : A critical review. *Journal of Change Management, 5*(4), 369–380.

Toffler, A. (1970). *Future shock.* New York, NY: Random House.

Tolbert, P., & Hall, R. (2009). *Organizations: Structures, processes, and outcomes.* London: Pearson Education Inc.

Tollefson, J. (2017). Trump pulls United States out of Paris climate agreement. (Donald Trump and United Nations Framework Convention on Climate Change). *Nature, 546*(7657). Retrieved from https://www.nature.com/news/trump-pulls-united-states-out-of-paris-climate-agreement-1.22096 doi:10.1038/nature.2017.22096

Tomasz, J. (2014). Organisational structures as an expression of the maturity of project management in the enterprise. *Torun Business Review*, *13*(13), 193–208.

Trappey, C. V., Trappey, A. J. C., Chang, A.-C., & Huang, A. Y. L. (2010). Clustering analysis prioritization of automobile logistics services. *Industrial Management & Data Systems*, *110*(5), 731–743. doi:10.1108/02635571011044759

Trebilcock, B. (2013). Giant Eagle makes the case for mobile robots. (system report). *Modern Materials Handling*, *68*(6), 18.

Tsai, Y. (2011). Relationship between organizational culture, leadership behavior and job satisfaction. *BMC Health Services Research*, *11*(1), 98–98. doi:10.1186/1472-6963-11-98

Turner, R. N., Wildschut, T., & Sedikides, C. (2018). Fighting ageism through nostalgia. *European Journal of Social Psychology*, *48*(2), 196–208. doi:10.1002/ejsp.2317

Twenge, J. M. (2010). A review of the empirical evidence on generational differences in work attitudes. (Author abstract) (Report). *Journal of Business and Psychology*, *25*(2), 201. doi:10.1007/s10869-010-9165-6

Vahlne, J.-E., Hamberg, M., & Schweizer, R. (2017). Management under uncertainty: The unavoidable risk-taking. *Multinational Business Review*, *25*(2), 91–109. doi:10.1108/MBR-03-2017-0015

Van Dam, K., Oreg, S., & Schyns, B. (2008). Daily work contexts and resistance to organisational change: The role of leader–member exchange, development climate, and change process characteristics. *Applied Psychology*, *57*(2), 313–334.

Van Knippenberg, B., Martin, L., & Tyler, T. (2006). Process-orientation versus outcome-orientation during organizational change: The role of organizational identification. *Journal of Organizational Behavior*, *27*(6), 685–704. doi:10.1002/job.391

Vanzeebroeck, N., & Bughin, J. (2017). The best response to digital disruption. *MIT Sloan Management Review*, *58*(4), 86.

Vasconcelos, A. F. (2015). Older workers: Some critical societal and organizational challenges. *The Journal of Management Development*, *34*(3), 352–372. doi:10.1108/JMD-02-2013-0034

Vasilopoulou, S. (2016). UK Euroscepticism and the Brexit referendum. *The Political Quarterly*, *87*(2), 219–227.

Veloutsou, C., & Taylor, C. S. (2012). The role of the brand as a person in business to business brands. *Industrial Marketing Management*, *41*(6), 898–907. doi:10.1016/j.indmarman.2012.02.004

Verbeke, A., & Tung, V. (2013). The future of stakeholder management theory: A temporal perspective. *Journal of Business Ethics*, *112*(3), 529–543. doi:10.1007/s10551-012-1276-8

Verma, A., & Fang, T. (2002, November). Do workplace practices contribute to union/non-union wage differentials? Paper presented at the Conference on Workplace and Employee Survey, Statistics Canada, Ottawa, Canada.

Verschoor, C. C. (2000). To talk about ethics, we must train on ethics. *Strategic Finance*, *81*(10), 24.

Vinnari, E., & Skærbæk, P. (2014). The uncertainties of risk management. *Accounting, Auditing & Accountability Journal*, *27*(3), 489–526. doi:10.1108/AAAJ-09-2012-1106

Viola, A. (2018). Blockchain's role in health IT. *Journal of AHIMA*, *89*(9), 34–54.

Walker, D., Bourne, L., & Shelley, A. (2008). Influence, stakeholder mapping and visualization. *Construction Management & Economics*, *26*(6), 645–658.

Wallach, E. (1983). Individuals and organizations: The cultural match. *Training and Development Journal, February*, 29–36.

Wang, H., Tong, L., Takeuchi, R., & George, G. (2016). Corporate social responsibility: An overview and new research directions. *Academy of Management Journal*, *59*(2), 534. doi:10.5465/amj.2016.5001

Watson, G. (1970). Resistance to change. In W. G. Bennis, K. D. Benne, & R. Chin (Eds.), *The planning of change* (2nd ed.). London: Holt, Rinehart & Winston.

Weinberg, S. B., Smotroff, L. J., & Pecka, J. C. (1978). Communication factors of group leadership. *Journal of Applied Communication Research, 6*(2), 85–91. doi:10.1080/00909887809360261

West, M. A., & Farr, J. L. (1989). Innovation at work: Psychological perspectives. *Social behaviour. 4*(1), 15–30.

West, M. A., Hirst, G., Richter, A., & Shipton, H. (2004). Twelve steps to heaven: Successfully managing change through developing innovative teams. *European Journal of Work and Organizational Psychology, 13*(2), 269–299. doi:10.1080/13594320444000092

Wieteska, G. (2016). Building resilient relationships with suppliers in the B2B market. *Management, 20*(2), 307–321. doi:10.1515/manment-2015-0067

Wilderom, C. P. M., van Den Berg, P. T., & Wiersma, U. J. (2012). A longitudinal study of the effects of charismatic leadership and organizational culture on objective and perceived corporate performance. *The Leadership Quarterly, 23*(5), 835–848. doi:10.1016/j.leaqua.2012.04.002

Williams, C., McWilliams, A., & Lawrence, R. (2016). *MGMT3* (3rd ed.). Australia: Cengage Learning Australia.

Williams, J. (2012). The value of mobile apps in health care: Learn how mobile applications and technologies are improving quality of care, patient satisfaction, safety, and convenience--and reducing costs. (Feature Story). *Healthcare Financial Management, 66*(6), 96.

Wilson, H., Daugherty, P., & Bianzino, N. (2017). The jobs that artificial intelligence will create. *MIT Sloan Management Review, 58*(4), 14–17.

Winning, N. (2016). *World News: Oxford English Dictionary makes a place for 'Brexit'* (p. A.11). New York, NY: Dow Jones & Company Inc.

Wise, R., & Morrison, D. (2000). Beyond the exchange: The future of B2B. *Harvard Business Review, 78*(6), 86–96.

Wong, C. H., & Hutzler, C. (2017). Killing of Kim Jong Un's brother intrigues North Korea's estranged ally China. (Kim Jong Nam). *Wall Street Journal (online), 0*. Retrieved from https://www.wsj.com/articles/in-china-intrigue-swirls-around-north-koreans-killing-1487148374

Wright, L. (2017). The causes of new threats. In *People, risk, and security: How to prevent your greatest asset from becoming your greatest liability* (pp. 25–38). London: Palgrave Macmillan.

Wu, B., & Knott, A. (2006). Entrepreneurial risk and market entry. *Management Science, 52*(9), 1315–1330. doi:10.1287/mnsc.1050.0543

Wyman, M. (1989). *Hard rock epic: Western miners and the industrial revolution, 1860–1910*. Berkeley, CA: University of California Press.

Xiong, K., Lin, W., Li, J. C., & Wang, L. (2016). Employee trust in supervisors and affective commitment: The moderating role of authentic leadership. *Psychological Reports, 118*(3), 829–848. doi:10.1177/0033294116644370

Yonemoto, K., & Shiino, K. (1977). Present stale and future outlook for industrial robots in Japan. *Industrial Robot: An International Journal, 4*(4), 171–179. doi:10.1108/eb004484

Yu, H.-C., & Miller, P. (2005). Leadership style: The X generation and baby boomers compared in different cultural contexts. *Leadership & Organization Development Journal, 26*(1), 35–50.

Yuan, Y., Tian, G., & Yu, Y. (2018). Business strategy and corporate social responsibility. *Journal of Business Ethics*, 1–19. doi:10.1007/s10551-018-3952-9

Zaltman, G., & Duncan, R. (1977). *Strategies for planned change*. New York, NY: John Wiley & Sons.

Zeng, J., Phan, C., & Matsui, Y. (2013). Shop-floor communication and process management for quality performance. *Management Research Review*, *36*(5), 454–477. doi:10.1108/01409171311327235

Zhang, W., Wang, P., Li, X., & Shen, D. (2018). Some stylized facts of the cryptocurrency market. *Applied Economics*, *50*(55), 5950–5965. doi:10.1080/00036846.2018.1488076

Zhao, C.-L., & Tang, H.-Y. (2010). Scheduling deteriorating jobs under disruption. *International Journal of Production Economics*, *125*(2), 291. doi:10.1016/j.ijpe.2010.02.009

Zhao, M., Park, S., & Zhou, N. (2014). MNC strategy and social adaptation in emerging markets. *Journal of International Business Studies*, *45*(7), 842–861. doi:10.1057/jibs.2014.8

Zhou, Y., Baylis, K., Coppess, J., & Xie, Q. (Producer). (2018). Dispatches from the trade wars. *Farmdoc Daily*. Retrieved from https://farmdocdaily.illinois.edu/wp-content/uploads/2018/08/fdd290818-1.pdf

Ziegler, C. E. (2017). International dimensions of electoral processes: Russia, the USA, and the 2016 elections. *International Politics*, *55*(5). doi:10.1057/s41311-017-0113-1

Zopiatis, A., & Constanti, P. (2012). Extraversion, openness and conscientiousness. *Leadership & Organization Development Journal*, *33*(1), 86–104. doi:10.1108/01437731211193133

Index